DECISION AT LEYTE

By the same author

BATAAN: THE MARCH OF DEATH

DECISION
AT LEYTE

Stanley L. Falk

NEW YORK

W · W · NORTON & COMPANY · INC ·

Library of Congress Catalog Card No. 65-13035.
All rights reserved. Published simultaneously in
Canada by George J. McLeod, Toronto, Canada.
Printed in the United States of America for the
publishers by the Vail-Ballou Press, Inc.

1 2 3 4 5 6 7 8 9 0

To my parents

Contents

Illustrations

Photographs (between pages 160 and 161)

Admiral William F. Halsey, Third Fleet

Vice Admiral Jesse B. Oldendorf, Battleship Squadron One

Major General Verne D. Mudge, General Douglas MacArthur, Lieutenant General R. K. Sutherland, General Walter Krueger, and Lieutenant General G. C. Kenney on Leyte, October 22

U.S.S. *Princeton* afire, as seen from U.S.S. *Birmingham*

Part of landing fleet at Dulag Bay

A-Day at Dulag

Landing ships at Tacloban Airstrip

77th Division heavy machine guns north of Ormoc

1st Cavalry Division Patrol in Tacloban

7th Cavalry Regiment motor pool

Engineers trying to repair White Beach access road

A forward aid station

Filipino porters supporting 1st Cavalry Division near Carigara

155-millimeter long toms near Carigara

Elements of the 24th Division at Pawing Hill

Japanese ships under air attack in Ormoc Bay

All photographs courtesy of Department of Defense and maps by B. C. Mossman

Preface

WHEN Japanese forces invaded the Philippines in early 1942, General Douglas MacArthur, the American commander in the islands, was ordered to escape to Australia. He left unwillingly, and swore that he would return. By the time he did, two and one half years later at the head of a powerful armada, the Japanese had determined to defend the Philippines to the death. They planned to fight a major air, sea, and land battle for the island of Leyte that would prove decisive in the struggle for the mastery of the Pacific.

This book is the story of that battle. It is a story that, in all its aspects, has not been told before in a single volume. Here I have tried to blend into one narrative an account of the fighting in the air, at sea, and on the ground—for the struggle for Leyte was carried on simultaneously in all three settings. To portray it simply as a slugging match between armies, a naval battle, or a series of aerial dogfights is to ignore the relationship of these contests and the important effect each had on the others. By the same token, I have woven into this account as much as possible of the Japanese side of the story, for an understanding of Japanese actions and intentions is necessary to appreciate the full meaning of the great battle for Leyte.

Yet to cover in one narrative all the intricate and tedious details of the Leyte campaign would require a far longer and more complex exposition than this one—less meaningful, perhaps, than comprehensive. What I have sought to do, then, is to present an over-all impression of what happened, from the highest levels of policy and strategy to the actions of a few individuals in one corner of a battlefield. I have tried to portray the significant, the meaningful, the unusual, and, within reasonable limits, the ordinary events of those bloody months in late 1944 when the fate of the Japanese Empire was sealed.

It would have been far more difficult to write this book without the published American official histories—Army, Navy, Air Force, and Marine—each of which presents in copious detail the record of its service's participation in the battle. I have supplemented these accounts with the official records and reports of the Leyte campaign, including unpublished narratives and histories prepared on the scene. I have also drawn on the various memoirs of commanders and reminiscences of other participants, on unit histories, and on secondary accounts of the campaign. I have purposely refrained from interviewing participants at this late date. Anything important or controversial that might be said is already in the record and in most cases has been published. Besides, memories fade after twenty years.

On the Japanese side there is a great deal of valuable material available, despite the completeness of the Japanese defeat. Documents captured during the campaign and prisoner of war interviews are of course present in the official American records. Then, immediately after the war, American military and naval officials conducted extensive interrogations of Japanese survivors and took steps to preserve whatever documentary material could be discovered. At the direction of American military historians serving in the occupation of Japan, Japanese veterans prepared detailed accounts of the Leyte campaign, based on their memories and on whatever official documents were available. These accounts were then supplemented by further interrogations and interviews. I was fortunate to be able to participate in much of this activity and worked personally with many of the Japanese involved. A final source of Japanese material is the transcript of the war crimes trial of General Tomoyuki Yamashita, which, except for two short interrogations, is the only place where the Japanese army commander in the Philippines was able to speak for himself.

For assistance in locating some of my source material and for making it more readily available, I am indebted to Miss Hannah M. Zeidlik of the Office of the Chief of Military History, Department of the Army, and Mrs. Lois Aldrich and Mr. Wilbur J. Nigh of the World War II Records Divisions of the National Archives.

STANLEY L. FALK

DECISION AT LEYTE

Part One

I SHALL RETURN

‹‹‹

›››

i The Escape

THERE WERE FOUR of them. Low, squat, narrow boats called PT's, rushing south in the growing darkness. As they picked up speed their bows lifted clear of the sea and the small craft planed across the water. They shuddered almost lurching, each time their bottoms pounded against the incredibly hard surface of the Pacific. A rooster tail of white froth chased the stern of each boat and a great wave rolled out on either side. The strong easterly wind threw sheets of water across the raised bows, drenching the helmsmen.

On the deck of the first boat, unable to keep his feet in the heavy seas, sat a sixty-two-year-old general named Douglas Mac-Arthur. His plain leather jacket bore four shiny silver stars. Tarnished gold braid adorned the visor of his cap. Between his teeth he clenched, almost incongruously, the stem of a simple corncob pipe. His wife, young son, the boy's nurse, and four members of the general's staff were clustered around him. Other staff members rode in the PT's to the rear. The date was March 11, 1942. The American commander in the Philippines was escaping from the Japanese.

Behind him lay the besieged fortress of Corregidor, the doomed peninsula called Bataan, and the island of Luzon, with its capital, Manila, the Pearl of the Orient, under the heel of the Japanese. Behind him, also, lay nearly half a century of service, of keeping "the soldier's faith," as he liked to put it. His first post as a young lieutenant had been the Philippines, not long after Amer-

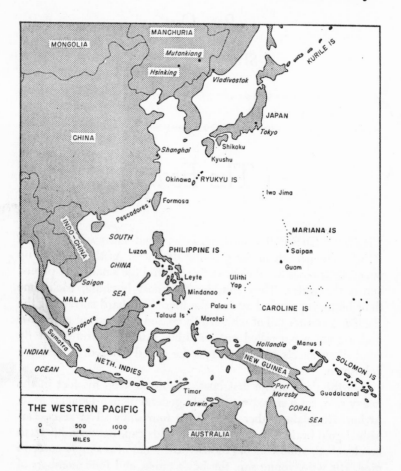

THE WESTERN PACIFIC

0   500   1000
          MILES

ican troops, some of them led by his father, had conquered the islands. Fifteen years later, at the end of World War I, he himself was commanding a division as a major general. In 1930, he became army chief of staff, the highest post possible for an American soldier. Then, after his retirement, he took on the job of military adviser to the Commonwealth of the Philippines, with the exalted and unprecedented rank of field marshal.

A brave and brilliant officer, devoted to his duty and gifted with an imagination, ability, and will such as few men possess, MacArthur was the perfect field marshal. He combined an aloofness and hauteur with a sincerity and cordial wit that could not impair his dignity but only softened it and somehow made it seem just right. A tall, slim, erect figure, with dark piercing eyes, straight black hair, and a prominent nose, he had that quality that in a younger officer would have been called dashing and in a middle-aged man was overwhelmingly impressive. To this appearance he added a firm stride, strong grip, and deep, persuasive voice. He was, in a word, a commander.

Beneath his cool exterior MacArthur concealed a spirit both vain and emotional. His pride and sense of destiny could fill him with incredible—and often justifiable—optimism. At other times he could fall into a deep pessimism, the result, it appeared, of a dramatic flair for tragedy. His nature was theatrical, his staging so carefully planned that it appeared nonchalant, his timing perfect. He had a tendency to speak in Shakespearean cadences, an ability to be flamboyant yet not ridiculous. He gave the appearance of always being right. More often than not he was.

It was in the Philippines that the threatening war clouds of 1941 found MacArthur. It was there that President Roosevelt recalled him to active duty and placed him in command of all American and Filipino troops in the islands. And it was from this post, after three months of bitter and hopeless defense against impossible odds, that he was ordered by Roosevelt to escape to Australia.

Behind him lay defeat. Ahead, a new command. But first he must slip from blockaded Corregidor and travel through 500 miles of Japanese-patrolled waters to the southern Philippine island of Mindanao. Then, if all went well, he would fly the long, hazardous route to Australia, another 1,500 miles away. A submarine would be best for the trip, at least as far as Mindanao, but the Japanese navy was making obvious preparations to intercept, and there was no time to wait for the sub. So the American commander in the Philippines, the most important Allied officer in the Far East, would have to take his chances on the surface, in a little motor torpedo boat that was just about ready for overhaul.

What manner of craft was this PT boat that would brave the dangers of the Japanese blockade? Seventy-seven feet of plywood on a hull of mahogany planking, four torpedo tubes and as many machine guns, and not an inch of armor—it hardly seemed a match for anything larger than a gunboat. But it had three rugged Packard engines, designed to send it skimming the wavetops at better than forty knots. The only drawback was that twelve weeks of combat had just about worn out the engines on American PT's in the Philippines. Several of the motors on the boats carrying MacArthur and his staff were clogged with carbon and ready for replacement. Compounding the difficulties were twenty heavy steel drums of high octane gasoline, lashed to the deck of each PT. They provided additional fuel but meant extra weight for the tired engines to push.

The ten or twelve young sailors who manned each boat and their almost equally youthful skippers had no hopes of even approaching forty knots. "Oh, some PT's do seventy-five," went the song, "and some do sixty-nine. When we get ours to run at all, we think we're doing fine. . . ." And if any of the four boats failed to outdistance a Japanese pursuer, a single hit on the drums of highly volatile gasoline would be enough to blow the craft and its passengers into oblivion.

MacArthur's boat was PT 41, with Lieutenant John D. Bulkley the skipper and squadron commander. As the night deepened and the sea became rougher, the other boats began to fall astern. On PT 34 the engine crew had to disconnect the throttle and push the carburetors up by hand to give the boat enough power. PT 35 couldn't maintain the pace by any means and soon was well behind. PT 32 was reduced to two straining engines after a few hours. All four boats had to stop occasionally to clean their gasoline filters, and before too long the formation was widely scattered up and down Mindoro Strait.

Just before dawn Lieutenant Vincent E. Schumacker, commanding PT 32, saw what he thought was a Japanese destroyer bearing down on him. Enemy warships had given all the PT's a scare earlier in the night, so now Schumacker jettisoned his deckload of gasoline drums in hopes of making another escape. But still his pursuer gained. The young skipper ordered his craft turned around and readied to make a desperate torpedo attack. It was either that or let the destroyer's 3-inch guns blow him out of the water. Suddenly someone recognized the warship as Bulkley's PT 41, which had somehow fallen behind and was now strangely magnified in the semilightness of dawn. Soon the sharp figure of

MacArthur could be clearly seen on deck.

Bulkley had hoped to spend the daylight hours of March 12 with his small flotilla in a secluded cove on an island about half-way to Mindanao. But it was late afternoon before PT's 41 and 32 limped into the planned hideaway. PT 34 had been there since morning, but PT 35 was nowhere in sight. By now, also, Schumacker's 32 was unable to continue. He transferred his passengers to the other two boats and sat down to await the arrival of PT 35. Bulkley took the remaining craft south again into the night.

With PT 41 again in the lead, the two crowded boats started the last leg of the journey. An hour later they changed course to avoid a Japanese cruiser and then pressed swiftly on again through increasingly heavy seas. As the wind grew more intense, great foaming waves crashed across the decks, shaking the light boats, drenching the crews, and stinging their eyes with the heavy saltiness. MacArthur was lying down below deck. Partially shielded from the elements, he was tossed about in his berth as if, he said later, he were "in a cocktail shaker."

But the darkness, high seas, and frequent rain squalls had hidden the small craft from Japanese patrols, and by daylight of the 13th the worst was over. An hour later the two boats reached their destination, the small harbor of Cagayan on the north coast of Mindanao. As the drenched and exhausted passengers and crews debarked, MacArthur turned to Bulkley and thanked him. "You've taken me out of the jaws of death," he said, "and I won't forget it." The squadron commander and all his men would be awarded the Silver Star.

PT 35, with the remainder of the passengers, showed up that afternoon. PT 32 never completed the trip. Altogether unserviceable, it was destroyed by its crew, who were then picked up by submarine.

On Mindanao, MacArthur and his party reached Del Monte airfield, atop a plateau a few hours' drive inland. Here four B-17's were supposed to be waiting. Instead, only one sat on the airstrip, a beat-up old veteran with brakes and superchargers not working properly, the only one of a flight of four that had been able to make it up from Australia. MacArthur was infuriated. He had specifically radioed Lieutenant General George H. Brett, the American army commander in Australia, for "the best available planes in top condition." The worn-out bomber that confronted him hardly approached that description. MacArthur ordered it to return to Australia without him and sent off a sharp repeat of his first request. "This trip is most important and desperate and must be set up with the greatest of care lest it end in disaster," he explained.

General Brett had actually done his utmost to comply with MacArthur's original radio, and had sent him the best planes he had. Now he managed to borrow three others, in better condition, from the navy. Two of these reached Mindanao late on the 16th. They landed by the light of hastily lit flares, refueled quickly, and shortly after midnight took off for Darwin with their distinguished cargo.

The flight was uneventful, although once, east of Timor in the Indies, Japanese fighters rose to intercept but missed the bombers in the darkness. Shortly before nine the next morning, the two planes approached the Australian coast. To the dismay of those aboard, they discovered that Darwin was in the midst of an air raid. Fortunately, the B-17's managed to slip into Batchelor Field unmolested.

The long, hazardous journey from Corregidor was over, a trip, according to MacArthur, "unique in military annals." Now the general and his party flew quickly to Alice Springs, the terminus of the rail line leading south to Melbourne. In that great city MacArthur would receive a tumultuous reception from the enthusiastic Australians, cheering him for his stout defense of the Philippines and welcoming him as Australia's bulwark against the Japanese.

As is often the case on such occasions, however, the press could not wait for the official reception. Several reporters had come north to Alice Springs, and as MacArthur stepped off his plane they clustered around him, greeting him warmly, and calling for a statement. It was an important moment, too dramatic, MacArthur realized, for just an offhand oral remark. It required the kind of utterance that would be remembered by posterity. He sat down and, on the back of a used envelope that someone handed him, he started to write very carefully.

"The President of the United States," he began, "ordered me to break through the Japanese lines and proceed from Corregidor to Australia for the purpose, as I understand it, of organizing the American offensive against Japan, a primary object of which is the relief of the Philippines."

He paused a moment, and then added this line:

"I came through and I shall return."

ii The Road Back

ACCORDING TO General MacArthur, he had come to Australia to organize the American offensive against Japan. This was something of an overstatement, although certainly an understandable one. Clearly the best way to begin this offensive was to choose an officer to organize it, put everything in the Pacific under his command, and give him his head. So far so good. But was MacArthur the man for the job?

Obviously, he thought so. As did the rest of the army. Yet the navy would certainly play a major role in the war against Japan. And the navy was not going to turn the fleet over to MacArthur under any circumstances.

The naval candidate was Admiral Chester W. Nimitz, commander of the Pacific Fleet. An experienced and extremely able officer, Nimitz could hardly hope to match MacArthur in either prestige or popularity. He was, moreover, quite junior to MacArthur—as was anyone else, for that matter. Not that it made any difference. The army would consider no one but MacArthur to head a joint Pacific command.

The only way out of this impasse was to split the drive on Japan in two: one army command, one navy command; one MacArthur, one Nimitz. Nimitz's command included most of the vast reaches of the Pacific, from Alaska, through Hawaii and the Japanese mandates of the Central Pacific, to the islands of the South Pacific and New Zealand. It was called the Pacific Ocean Areas, or simply POA, and considerably dwarfed the zone assigned to MacArthur. It even included Japan itself. MacArthur's command was designated the Southwest Pacific Area, usually referred to as SWPA. It included Australia, New Guinea, the Philippines, the Bismarck Archipelago and the Solomons, and all of the Netherlands Indies east of Sumatra.

With British and Australian approval, all Allied forces in the SWPA were placed under MacArthur, who was given the grandiose title of supreme commander. It must have been a little too much even for him, for he quickly changed it to commander in chief. During the remainder of the war he would be known as CINCSWPA, a combination of letters that when read aloud sounded like the name of an Indian chieftain: "sink-swa-pa."

The arrangements for Pacific command were concluded within two weeks of MacArthur's departure from the Philippines. They were to remain substantially the same for the rest of the war. From time to time, however, the idea of establishing a single American command in the Pacific arose again, simply because logic continued to cry out for the acceptance of this ideal solution. But on each occasion the difficulty of the course seemed to outweigh its advantages. One high-ranking staff officer in Washington felt that the only real problem was General MacArthur himself. With MacArthur out of the way, this officer argued, a single command organization might be established by giving the top post to whichever of the armed services appeared to be playing the major role in the Pacific war. As for MacArthur, the proposed solution was to send him to Moscow as American ambassador, an idea which would probably have astounded the Russians as much as it would have astonished MacArthur. Fortunately or unfortunately, depending on the point of view, nothing ever came of the proposal, and command in the Pacific remained a dual responsibility.

Despite MacArthur's hopes of leading an immediate Allied offensive back to the Philippines, the first directive he received as CINCSWPA was essentially an order to defend Australia. But he was to defend it as a base "for future offensive action" and he himself was to "prepare to take the offensive." These two key phrases MacArthur interpreted as a directive to mount an offensive. He immediately began preparing to do so. A major target of his drive would be the Philippine Islands, where, early in May, 1942, the American defenses finally collapsed.

By now the Japanese controlled most of the Southwest Pacific. They held an area from Singapore through the Indies to the Solomons. And they continued to press forward. A repulse in the

naval and air battle of the Coral Sea in May and a punishing defeat at Midway a month later failed to halt them. By summer
they were preparing air bases in the lower Solomons and simultaneously driving across the New Guinea mountains toward Port
Moresby, an Allied base on the southern coast of Papua, little
more than 300 miles across the Coral Sea from Australia. To Mac-
Arthur his course was clear. He would not wait for the enemy to
attack Australia. He would move forward to New Guinea to stop
him there.

His first problem was to halt the Japanese drive on Port
Moresby. For this he had only limited forces, since the American
buildup in Australia was just getting under way. In early August,
however, Marines from Admiral Nimitz's command invaded
Guadalcanal, in the Solomons. This move not only succeeded in
turning Japanese attention away from New Guinea but, more
important, it diverted Japanese troops and supplies from Papua.
In mid-September the Japanese advance ground to a halt, just
twenty miles from Port Moresby. Exhausted by their long drive
across the mountains and—thanks to relentless American air attacks on their supply line—almost completely out of food and
ammunition, the Japanese could go no farther. A week later Australian and American forces under MacArthur went over to the
offensive.

Now the long drive back to the Philippines began in earnest.
And for the next two years, as American air, ground, and sea
units pressed ever forward, the thought of returning to the Philippines was always in MacArthur's mind. This was the target. This
was the goal. MacArthur had pledged his honor and that of his
country that his beloved Philippines would not be forgotten.

By the beginning of 1943 the Japanese had been driven out of
southeastern New Guinea and Guadalcanal. A year of hard fighting later, American troops had secured critical portions of the
central and northern Solomons, landed on the vital Bismarck
Archipelago, and made large gains in their push along the northern coast of New Guinea. In the process they had wiped out or
bypassed and cut off large numbers of enemy troops and, more
important, destroyed a considerable part of Japanese airpower in
the Southwest Pacific. The seizure of the Gilbert Islands by
Marines and soldiers under Admiral Nimitz's general command

marked the successful beginning, also, of an American offensive across the Central Pacific.

A two-pronged assault was thus under way, aimed at the heart of the Japanese Empire. One wing of the attack, Mac-Arthur's, would press forward along the north coast of New Guinea to the Philippines. The other, under Nimitz, would strike across the broad reaches of the Pacific through the Marshall Islands to the Marianas and Palaus, and then on to Iwo Jima and Okinawa. Capture of these objectives would enable American forces to cut Japan's supply lines to the south and to strike directly at the enemy home islands.

MacArthur's strategy was built on moving land-based airpower forward in successive bounds to seize local air superiority, give safe cover to the advancing troops, and isolate each successive Japanese base before beginning the final air, ground, and naval assault to capture it. First airfields—or areas where they could be built—would be seized, then planes moved in to defend the area while it was being developed into a major base, and finally forces built up there for the next jump forward. The idea was to strike where the Japanese were weakest, bypassing their strong points, and leaving the garrisons to die on the vine, isolated from supply and reinforcement. Each successive advance was meticulously planned, each target carefully chosen within aircover range of the area just seized. By this method of warfare, MacArthur brought to bear his strongest weapons against the weakest Japanese defenses, a technique that implied and ultimately brought success.

In Admiral Nimitz's area, the vast reaches of the Pacific dictated another form of strategy. This was an offensive based on fast carrier task forces operating in support of hard-hitting amphibious groups to seize vital islands as steppingstones across the ocean. Once a target had been picked, carrier planes would knock out Japanese air defenses and bombard the island objective, heavy fleets would move in close to blast shore defenses, and then Marines and soldiers would make an assault landing to overwhelm the last bitter enemy resistance. Ingenious new techniques of amphibious warfare, developed through careful planning and bloody experience, helped guarantee success. Once an island had been secured, airfields would be established to project

American land-based airpower forward and ensure domination of Japanese bases that had been bypassed. The navy would quickly build up harboring and repair facilities and the whole island would be developed into a forward supply base. Then the carriers and amphibious forces would move on to the next objective.

Both the Southwest and Central Pacific methods were hard and grueling, with much difficult and dangerous fighting against an enemy who preferred death to surrender. But they both worked. And they pushed American power relentlessly closer to the core of Japanese resistance.

By the spring of 1944 American operations in the Pacific were proceeding at a rapid pace, outdistancing even the most optimistic of earlier hopes. Faced with this most pleasant surprise, and encouraged even more by enthusiastic reports from MacArthur and Nimitz, the Joint Chiefs of Staff in Washington directed their two Pacific commanders to accelerate operations even more. Key Japanese positions, whose capture had earlier been believed essential to the success of the American offensive, were now to be bypassed. The assault on other Japanese bases would be speeded. And on November 15 MacArthur's forces would land on Mindanao. The invasion of this huge island at the southern base of the Philippine archipelago would mark the redemption of his dramatic pledge made in Australia two years earlier.

But Mindanao was only one island, and its recapture would still leave the greater part of the Philippines in Japanese hands. To MacArthur this was a situation which could not be long tolerated. Yet even as he readied his plans to strike from Mindanao to Leyte, an island in the central Philippines, and then on to Luzon, the Joint Chiefs were raising the question of whether invading any part of the Philippines was really necessary. Wouldn't it be better, they wondered, to bypass the archipelago altogether in favor of a direct attack on Formosa, or even the main islands of Japan itself? Wouldn't such a strategy accelerate the pace of the advance even more and bring the war to an earlier end?

Both MacArthur and Nimitz took a dim view of this proposal, especially MacArthur. While Nimitz was willing to at least consider bypassing Luzon, assuming that major air and naval bases could be established in the central and southern Philippines, MacArthur was adamant in his insistence that no major part of the

Philippines could be left in Japanese hands. Not only, he declared, was this essential in military terms—to cut completely the Japanese supply line to the south and to provide adequate air and logistical support for an invasion of Formosa or Japan—but there were also other, even more pressing considerations.

"The Philippines," MacArthur radioed to the army chief of staff, General George C. Marshall, "is American territory where our unsupported forces were destroyed by the enemy." Almost all of the Filipinos, he insisted, had remained loyal to the United States and were "undergoing the greatest privation and suffering because we have not been able to support or succor them." Their liberation was "a great national obligation." To abandon the Filipinos would be to "admit the truth of Japanese propaganda" that the United States was unwilling to "shed American blood to redeem them." To deliberately bypass any part of the Philippines had "sinister" implications and would compromise American honor and prestige in the Far East, with adverse effects "for many years to come." If the Joint Chiefs were seriously considering this course of action, MacArthur concluded, he wished to be allowed to come to Washington to present his views in full.

This strong expression elicited a somewhat cool response from General Marshall. If the issue arose, the chief of staff replied, he would "speak to the President" about MacArthur's coming to Washington. But he cautioned his subordinate against letting "our personal feeling and Philippine political considerations" transcend the primary objective of the Pacific war, the defeat of Japan. "Bypassing," he informed MacArthur, was not "synonymous with abandonment," and the United States did not intend to abandon the Filipinos.

Whatever MacArthur's reaction to this view, he was soon to have his day in court. The navy member of the Joint Chiefs of Staff, Admiral Ernest J. King, had an equally strong view about the Philippines. His opinion was that they should be bypassed, and he expressed it frequently and forcefully. Most navy planners agreed with him. Army planners in Washington were divided three ways. Some agreed with MacArthur, some with King, and some, like Nimitz, were in the middle, willing at least to bypass Luzon. As a result, the Joint Chiefs could reach no decision to change plans already agreed upon. But they still sought some way of accelerating Pacific operations.

These problems were of course no secret to President Roosevelt, who had been kept informed of the tenor of the strategic discussion. Roosevelt had planned a Pacific inspection tour for July 1944, and he now decided that this would be a good opportunity to get some firsthand views. Accordingly, he ordered MacArthur and Nimitz to meet him at Pearl Harbor. Marshall and King would not be present, and the President would get a chance to hear the unadorned arguments of his Pacific commanders.

The celebrated "Pearl Harbor Conference" of Roosevelt, MacArthur, and Nimitz has been the subject of several conflicting descriptions. According to some, it was a triumph for MacArthur, who with dramatic skill, keen logic, and undeniable eloquence convinced the President that the Philippines could not be bypassed. Others claim that F.D.R. had already decided not to drop the proposed Mindanao landing and that, pointing to that island on a map of the Pacific, he asked MacArthur, "Well, Douglas, where do we go from here?" "Leyte, Mr. President," supposedly replied MacArthur, "and then Luzon." Whereupon, according to this version, the decision to liberate all of the Philippines was made.

What actually appears to have happened was this: Both MacArthur and Nimitz supported an invasion of the southern and central Philippines. With this accomplished, Nimitz would then have bypassed Luzon to strike directly at Formosa. MacArthur argued impressively in favor of Luzon, however, including in his talk a dramatic plea for the plight of the Filipinos. The President listened carefully to both views, but made no commitment. Plans for landings on Mindanao and Leyte remained in effect and no decision was reached on the question of Luzon vs. Formosa. A final solution of this controversial problem would not, in fact, come until little more than two weeks before the invasion of Leyte, several months off, by which time strong military reasons had arisen to force a decision for Luzon.

During the summer of 1944 MacArthur's staff was busy developing plans for the return to the Philippines. These called for the seizure, in September and October, of Morotai and the Talaud Islands, northwest of New Guinea, to provide air bases to cover the move to Mindanao. The landing there would come, as scheduled,

on November 15. Additional air bases would then be constructed
to support the Leyte invasion, projected for December 20. And
Leyte would become a major air and supply base from which to
invade the rest of the Philippines or Formosa and, indeed, to
dominate the entire South China Sea area. The whole operation
was carefully planned in the SWPA tradition of successive advances always made under effective cover of land-based airpower.

The code name for the Mindanao operation was King-I, for
Leyte, King-II. And, since the expression "D day" had already
been established in the public mind as referring to the Normandy
invasion of the previous June, MacArthur picked other designations for the target dates in the Philippines. The Mindanao landing would come on W-day, a name almost no one recalls. The
date of the Leyte invasion was designated A-day.

The Joint Chiefs of Staff approved these plans early in September with a directive to MacArthur to carry them out and one
to Nimitz telling him to support them with the Pacific Fleet.

During the preliminary operations some of Nimitz's land and
sea forces, under Admiral William F. Halsey, would also seize the
Palau Islands, east of Mindanao, as well as Yap, northeast of the
Palaus, both as a continuation of the Central Pacific drive and to
provide additional bases for support of operations in the Philippines. In accordance with this scheme, during the first part of
September fast carrier task forces of Admiral Halsey's Third
Fleet struck at Japanese airfields and shipping in the Palaus, at
Yap, and in the central and southern Philippines. The results
were astonishingly good and the Japanese opposition surprisingly
weak. Few enemy planes rose to meet the American flyers and no
Japanese warships sortied against Halsey's fleet. The Americans
quickly destroyed any planes and ships they did discover and
severely damaged Japanese ground installations.

This pattern was especially true in the Philippines, where
Third Fleet units at times sailed with impunity within sight of
land. The whole situation was "staggering," according to Halsey's
War Diary, "and the lack of resistance amazing and fantastic."
Indeed, Filipino guerrillas told one American carrier pilot who
was forced down on Leyte that there were no Japanese at all on
the island. This information, combined with the lack of effective

opposition anywhere else, convinced Halsey that the Philippines were "wide open" and ripe for plucking. A bold, imaginative, and aggressive officer, he was never one to let slip an opportunity. On September 13, then, he sent off a radio to Nimitz that brought a dramatic advance in the schedule for the liberation of Leyte.

Halsey's message to Nimitz recommended that all preliminary operations be dropped in favor of an immediate start on King-II, the invasion of Leyte. The Palau, Yap, Talaud, and Mindanao operations were no longer necessary, he felt. The Third Fleet could provide the air support that would have come from Mindanao to cover the Leyte landing and three army divisions scheduled for Yap could be used to beef up MacArthur's invasion forces. This concept was acceptable to Admiral Nimitz and, after removing the proposal to skip the Palau operation which he still believed necessary, he passed Halsey's idea on to the Joint Chiefs with his approval.

The plan reached the Chiefs in Quebec, where they had gone with President Roosevelt for a conference with Winston Churchill and his military advisers. They at once radioed MacArthur for his opinion. MacArthur, however, was at this time on board a cruiser in the Morotai invasion force, maintaining radio silence and out of touch with the rest of the world. His chief of staff, Lieutenant General Richard K. Sutherland, was therefore faced with an immediate decision. Sutherland knew from SWPA intelligence sources that Japanese strength in the Philippines was greater than Halsey had estimated, and especially that the report of no Japanese troops on Leyte was in error. He was also aware that a direct invasion of Leyte would violate MacArthur's principle of always providing land-based air cover for amphibious assaults.

Yet Sutherland had not served six years under the imaginative and audacious MacArthur for nothing. He well understood how effective carrier aircraft could be in protecting a landing: operations in the Central Pacific had amply demonstrated this. And he welcomed the addition of the three divisions diverted from Yap. Above all, he appreciated the value of advancing the Pacific schedule and keeping the Japanese off balance. He therefore radioed the Joint Chiefs, over MacArthur's name, that he concurred in the proposed new plan.

The American Chiefs were in the midst of a formal dinner

with Canadian officers when Sutherland's message arrived. Excusing themselves from their hosts, they withdrew to reach a rapid decision. "Having the utmost confidence in General MacArthur, Admiral Nimitz, and Admiral Halsey," recalled Marshall after the war, "it was not a difficult decision to make." Less than ninety minutes after Sutherland's radio reached Quebec, the Joint Chiefs sent orders to MacArthur and Nimitz to forget Yap, the Talauds, and Mindanao, and to land on Leyte on October 20. An acknowledgment from MacArthur's headquarters was in Marshall's hands a few minutes after the chief of staff had finished his dinner.

Thus it was that on the afternoon of October 18, 1944, General MacArthur stood on the bridge of the light cruiser *Nashville* as it joined the main convoy of Vice Admiral Thomas C. Kinkaid's Seventh Fleet approaching Leyte Gulf. Across the horizon stretched a mighty flotilla of hundreds of warships and transports, extending as far as he could see, while overhead fighter aircraft maintained a constant vigil. It was a proud and auspicious meeting for the general. "Welcome to our city," flashed a blinker message from Kinkaid. "Thanks," replied MacArthur. "As Ripley says, believe it or not we are almost there."

Part Two

PROLOGUE TO DECISIVE BATTLE

‹‹‹

››

iii The Tiger of Malaya

ALMOST EXACTLY three years before General Douglas Mac-Arthur returned to the Philippines, another general began a journey that would bring him to the islands at almost the same time. That general was Tomoyuki Yamashita (pronounced Ya-MASH-ta) and his journey began in Hsinking, Manchuria, where in the fall of 1941 he maintained his headquarters as commander of the Kwantung Defense Army. Recalled at that time suddenly to Imperial General Headquarters in Tokyo, he was given command of the Japanese Twenty-fifth Army and assigned the important mission of capturing the great British fortress of Singapore.

Singapore was widely regarded as impregnable. Ten years in the building, it stood at the tip of the Malay Peninsula, staunch guardian of the passage from South China Sea to Indian Ocean. Its great guns and the mighty British fleet protected it from assault by sea. A land attack on the fortress would have to overcome difficult jungle terrain and defeat a large British army. Yet Singapore's capture was critical to the success of Japanese plans for the conquest of Southeast Asia. The Twenty-fifth Army staff had therefore drawn up careful plans and coordinated them closely with the Japanese navy. These plans called for initial overwhelming air attacks, sudden landings on the northeast coast of the Malay Peninsula, and then a drive south to subdue the Singapore garrison. The forces allotted to the campaign were not large—since Japan's military resources were spread thin to meet the demands of the great Pacific offensive. But they were well supported by aircraft and tanks, and Imperial General Headquarters believed they would be sufficient. They would have to be.

After a week of military staff conferences in Tokyo, General Yamashita flew to Saigon, French Indo-China, headquarters of Field Marshal Count Hisaichi Terauchi's Southern Army, the overall command for Japan's campaign in the south. There, in late November, Yamashita completed and approved plans for the Malayan campaign. "I know I shall be able to carry out the landing plan," he confided to his diary. "I also believe we shall win."

Just after midnight on the night of December 7–8, 1941, Yamashita's forces began landing along the Malayan coast. With close and effective air support—which two days later sank the *Repulse* and *Prince of Wales*, the heart of the British Far East Fleet—the Twenty-fifth Army then began a remarkable drive on Singapore. In an extraordinary campaign, in which he effectively used his overwhelming superiority in planes and tanks to more than counter the two-to-one British edge in troops, Yamashita pushed rapidly ahead. Striking by sea again and again at the defenders' rear, he combined aggressive tactics, brilliant improvisation, and steady pressure. Two months after he first set foot on Malayan soil Yamashita landed on Singapore Island.

Now the Malayan campaign had reached its climax. The British, their morale visibly shaken by eight weeks of successive defeats and by the continued ferocity of the Japanese attack, were low on food, water, and ammunition. They were completely without air cover and exposed to massive artillery and tank attacks. As the hopeless fight continued, Lieutenant General Sir Arthur E. Percival the British commander, knew the end was in sight. "There comes a stage," he reported, "when in the interests of the troops and civil population further bloodshed will serve no useful purpose."

But Yamashita also had his problems. Outnumbered three to one on the island, and with his own troops low on supplies and ammunition, he feared a long fight for Singapore City. An extended struggle would expose his weaknesses and might even bring his defeat. So he pushed his troops as hard as he could.

By February 11 the Japanese held half of Singapore Island. The day was *Kigensetsu*, a great national holiday commemorating the ascension to the throne, 660 years before the birth of

Christ, of Jimmu, the first Japanese emperor. As if to mark the occasion, great clouds of black smoke arose from huge fires burning in and around the beleaguered city of Singapore. From the sky, Japanese planes swooped low to drop a message from Yamashita to Percival. "In a spirit of chivalry," it began, "we have the honour of advising your surrender."

For the next three days Yamashita awaited Percival's reply with growing apprehension. How much longer could his own supplies last? He was already dangerously short of small-arms ammunition. Were the British expecting reinforcements? Could they hold out long enough to mount a counterattack and throw him back into Johore Strait? Then, on the afternoon of the 15th, the end came. Three British officers waving a white flag approached the Japanese lines with an offer to surrender.

Percival's decision to give up had come when his food, ammunition, and gasoline were all but exhausted. Even more important, he had enough water to last but one more day. Continued fighting would put the great city of Singapore and its huge civilian population completely at the mercy of the attacking Japanese. By surrendering, he hoped to avoid a massacre.

But Yamashita suspected a trick, a ruse to gain time or to achieve some other cunning objective. He sent word of his terms for surrender and directed Percival to meet him at 6 P.M. At the same time he ordered a battalion of Japanese troops to be on hand for the meeting and he directed Japanese air units to be especially vigilant against the possibility of any British reinforcements attempting to sneak in during the relaxation in the fighting.

The meeting took place at a Ford automobile factory northeast of Singapore City. Percival was half an hour late, which only served to increase Yamashita's apprehension and his desire to secure an immediate capitulation. While reporters and cameramen crowded closely around them, the two generals shook hands across a long table and sat down to begin their formal conversation.

Yamashita hoped to conclude matters swiftly. Yet a barely competent interpreter and a nervous and exhausted Percival threatened to drag matters on interminably. After some preliminary questions about prisoners and other matters, Yamashita asked the British general if he was ready to surrender immedi-

ately. Percival asked if he could delay his reply until 10:30 that
night. Yamashita demanded an immediate answer. Otherwise, he
warned, the Japanese troops would resume their attack. Percival
then agreed to surrender, but asked if the actual cease-fire could
not wait until the next morning.

The conversation up to this point had been somewhat confused. Yamashita's interpreter kept stumbling over words, and
the efforts of British and Japanese staff officers to help him only
impeded matters further. By now nearly half an hour had passed.
Yamashita was growing more and more concerned about the
delay, especially since Percival's request to postpone the final surrender until morning seemed to reinforce the Japanese commander's previous fears of a British trick. Irritated, tired, and
thoroughly impatient, Yamashita turned to his interpreter. He
wanted no more equivocating by Percival, he said angrily, and no
more lengthy translations of involved sentences. He desired only
a simple answer to his demand for an immediate capitulation and
cease-fire. "I want to hear nothing from him," he told the flus-
tered interpreter in a loud voice, "except yes or no!"

The interpreter passed this on to the British commander,
emphasizing, as had Yamashita, the words "yes or no." To
Percival, the meaning of this was clear, and he wearily agreed to
surrender immediately and unconditionally. To the assembled
reporters, however, it seemed more than just a demand for a
straight answer to end a long and tiresome conversation. It
appeared, instead, that a harsh and haughty victor was laying
down fierce terms to a humbled and defeated adversary. Yes or
no. Surrender or death. This was not just a victorious general.
This was a fierce beast, a veritable tiger. This was, as one reporter
put it, the "Tiger of Malaya."

And the name stuck. From this time on, until his death and
even after, Yamashita would be known as the Tiger of Malaya, a
ferocious and cunning animal, with sharp claws, terrible fangs,
and a cruel, voracious appetite.

What manner of man was this Tiger of Malaya? A large individual of imposing physique, he had big hands, a full face, and a
black mustache (which he later removed when it began to turn
gray). His hair, cropped close in the Japanese military style, also
was black, although graying at the temples, and his dark eyes

were full and alert. His appearance of formidability was somewhat marred, however, by more than a hint of a potbelly. Also, as
some of his staff were aware, he was not averse, on occasion, to
using a bit of hair dye on that gray at the temples. For the surrender ceremony he wore his simple gray-brown officer's field
uniform, the two stars of a Japanese lieutenant general on his
lapel, and a chest full of ribbons that he had apparently donned
for the occasion. He was, in fact, more of a man than a tiger. But
he was, nonetheless, a man to be reckoned with.

Fifty-six years old at the time of his great victory, Yamashita
had been born in a tiny village on Shikoku, the smallest of Japan's
four main islands. His father was a country doctor, and young
Yamashita grew up in the quiet hills and fields around his home,
isolated from crowded, noisy city life. Perhaps because the boy
was big for his age and quite muscular, his father encouraged him
to take the entrance examination for Japan's military academy.
Yamashita passed this test, and many others, with honors, and in
1906, a year after the end of the Russo-Japanese War, he was
commissioned a second lieutenant of infantry.

Industrious and imaginative, Yamashita proved an excellent
officer. His early career included study and attaché service in Europe and the usual assignments of a young officer. Generally these
alternated between command and staff. In the latter capacity,
while serving with the War Ministry, he drew up a plan for extensive disarmament, which earned him both praise and criticism.
His highest post was that of inspector general of army aviation,
one of the three most important positions in the Japanese army.
Another top assignment came after the signing of the Tripartite
Pact in late 1940, when, for six months, he headed a military mission to Japan's Axis partners in Europe.

There was nothing flamboyant or dramatic about Yamashita.
He was poised and dignified, simple and sincere. He had a keen
sense of duty and a quiet awareness of the responsibilities it im-
posed upon him. Nor was he aloof or insensitive. Friendly and
personable, innately courteous, he was popular with both superior and subordinate. A former war minister described him as "a
strong character, clean and honest and of a kindly and gentle
disposition." He had a perceptive and active mind and a pleasant
sense of humor.

As a troop commander he was always considerate of his men. He encouraged initiative, paying close heed to what his subordinates did, but leaving them free wherever possible to solve their problems themselves. This attitude and his commanding physical appearance inspired confidence and high morale. It also created long-lasting loyalties. He was, as one staff officer put it very simply, "a commander of outstanding qualities."

For his victory at Singapore, such a commander would be expected to be rewarded with bigger and more important assignments. But, after an attack of dengue fever in the spring, Yamashita was ordered not south, where the fighting was, but north, back to Manchuria. Imperial General Headquarters, fearful of a Russian attack on Japan's exposed northern flank, was rushing troops and equipment to meet this threat. The entire military command in Manchuria was being reorganized from top to bottom and divided into two new major subordinate commands. The larger, more important of these was the First Area Army, charged with the defense of eastern Manchuria and, if war came, the capture of the vital Siberian port of Vladivostok. Its new commander was Yamashita, who shortly received his third star as a full general.

Thus Yamashita was holding down what might become the most important field command in the Japanese army. Many Japanese, however, including perhaps Yamashita himself, have attributed this assignment to Premier Hideki Tojo's jealousy. According to this theory, General Tojo had long feared Yamashita as a dangerous rival and, wherever possible, had tried to keep him in remote assignments and out of the public eye. By sending him to Manchuria in 1942, Tojo was supposedly attempting to bury his rival.

But why, if this view is correct, did Tojo allow Yamashita to be given command of the vital Malayan operation in the first place? And why did Field Marshal Terauchi, extremely influential in his own right and an old friend of Yamashita's, acquiesce without a battle in the transfer of his prize subordinate to Manchuria —if he had not felt the transfer was necessary? Terauchi had requested Yamashita for the Singapore campaign in the first place, and he could have made good use of him elsewhere after it was over. There is also some doubt that Tojo was powerful enough to control major army assignments. Nor is it clear just how he could predict that there would not be a war with the Russians.

Be that as it may, there was no war. And Yamashita remained in Manchuria, training troops for the most part, for the next two years. While bitter fighting went on in the Pacific, the conqueror of Singapore was kept in his northern exile. Perhaps it was Tojo's influence, perhaps just the fortunes of war. But during these years Yamashita was a forgotten hero—frustrated, disappointed, but apparently not embittered.

From his headquarters in Mutankiang, Yamashita watched Japan's fortunes ebb. Slowly the fruits of victory so brilliantly won by the Japanese were wrested from their grip. Step by step they were pushed back across the Pacific, each month bringing another defeat, another "strategic withdrawal." By June, 1944, MacArthur's forces had occupied most of the strategic north coast of New Guinea and were beginning their final approach to the Philippines. At the same time, in the Central Pacific, Marines and soldiers stormed ashore on Saipan, within bomber range of Japan itself, while Japanese fleet and naval air units suffered a punishing defeat in the crucial battle of the Philippine Sea.

The sacred home islands of Japan now stood uncovered to the ravages of American long-range bombers. The Philippines and Formosa were open to invasion. For another nation, less dedicated and determined, such reverses might have meant surrender. But to the Japanese surrender was unthinkable. Surely another great effort could turn the tide. Surely courage, perseverance, and sacrifice would throw back the enemy and save the Empire. While the cabinet of Premier Tojo came down in ruins about its now discredited leader, a new government, under General Kuniaki Koiso, committed itself irrevocably to fighting the war to the bitter end.

What Yamashita thought of Tojo's fall is not evident. If he blamed the former premier for his Manchurian exile, he must have anticipated a new assignment. He did not have long to wait. Late in September, 1944, less than ten weeks after Tojo resigned, Yamashita received sudden orders placing him in command of Japanese forces in the Philippines. Stopping off in Tokyo for briefings and conferences about his new assignment, he learned that he had been considered earlier for the post of war minister and then for that of commander of the armies defending the Japanese home islands. But political considerations had barred him from the first position and the overriding need for a first-class commander in Manila had ruled out the second.

Yamashita knew almost nothing about the situation in the Philippines, about his troops or state of supplies, or about the enemy soon to invade. And what he learned in Tokyo was not calculated to make him very happy. He faced a difficult assignment, all the more so because of the immediacy of the American threat.

Early in October he boarded a plane for Manila. His wife believed she would never see him again—and he appears to have shared her feeling.

iv Prelude to Victory

WHEN General Yamashita landed at the Philippine capital he was unaware that MacArthur's return was barely two weeks away. But he fully realized that an American invasion could be expected at any time. So he immediately set about familiarizing himself with his new command and with the plans already made to meet the American attack.

It did not take him long to discover that Japanese defenses in the Philippines were, as he later put it, "in an unsatisfactory condition." For two years after the Japanese seized the islands, they had done nothing about defending them. During this time they regarded the Philippines as a rear area supply depot and staging area. The great Japanese victories of the first six months of the war had provided an outer defense perimeter within which the islands lay snug and secure. Protected thus from American attack by distance and by the Japanese forward defenses, the relatively few occupation troops left in the Philippines had little to do but grow fat and chase guerrillas. Lieutenant General Shigenori Kuroda, the commander during most of this period, was a rather quiet gentleman who spoke English with a British accent and nourished pleasant memories of assignments in London and India. He spent much of his time on the Manila golf links or, reportedly, engaged in certain less ambulatory indoor sports. He seems to have felt that the Philippines were indefensible anyway and gave little thought to attempting a prolonged defense. Until the spring of 1944, then, Japanese plans to defend the islands were all but nonexistent.

By April of that year, however, MacArthur's forces were pushing rapidly along the north coast of New Guinea, pressing ever closer toward the Philippines. To Field Marshal Terauchi, commander of the Southern Army, the threat was clear even if his subordinate, General Kuroda, seemed oblivious to it. He immediately began preparations to defend the islands against a major invasion.

Terauchi's fears soon spread to his superiors in Tokyo. Forced now to take a closer look at the threat to the Philippines, the army staff of Imperial General Headquarters was quick to share the Southern Army commander's opinion. It directed him to accelerate and enlarge on his plans to build up Philippine defenses. Airfields and supply bases would be greatly expanded and troop and aircraft reinforcements brought in. Also, despite Terauchi's objections about his responsibilities elsewhere, Imperial General Headquarters ordered him to move his own headquarters to Manila to supervise these preparations. Rumors concerning General Kuroda had reached Tokyo and the general staff wanted to be sure its orders would be carried out properly.

This was only the beginning. In July, following the loss of Saipan and of further territory in New Guinea, Japanese strategists took a broad look at the progress of the Pacific war. What they saw led to major changes in their plans, especially those concerning the Philippines, where defensive preparations were still less than half completed.

On July 24 Imperial General Headquarters issued a new and comprehensive "Plan for the Conduct of Future Operations." These operations, optimistically dubbed *Sho*, or "Victory," were aimed at holding a major defensive front embracing the Philippines, Formosa, the Ryukyus, the four main Japanese islands, and the Kuriles. American attempts to pierce this front would be met with overwhelming air, sea, and land attacks in a climactic "decisive battle" to determine the outcome of the war. The planners in Tokyo felt that the first American assault would probably come against the Philippines. Nevertheless, to meet all possibilities, they developed four alternative plans. The first, *Sho*-1, covered the expected attack on the Philippines. *Sho*-2 provided for the defense of Formosa and the Ryukyus. *Sho*-3 included southern and central Japan. *Sho*-4 applied to northern Japan and the Kuriles. Japanese army, navy, and air forces would be husbanded to meet a major offensive against any one of these four areas. Then the target area would be designated a "decisive battle theater" and all available strength would be concentrated against the attacking enemy.

First to be committed would be the Japanese air forces. Previous attempts by Japanese land- and carrier-based planes to destroy American invasion fleets approaching a target area had all too often resulted in the destruction of the Japanese aircraft without any appreciable effect on the invaders. Consequently, there were rarely enough Japanese planes left to oppose the actual landing. Staff officers in Imperial General Headquarters therefore decided on a change in tactics. Japanese aircraft would be held back until the actual landing was about to take place. Then they would strike simultaneously at the American transports and aircraft carriers covering the assault in an all-out attempt to destroy the invaders at the last possible moment.

A change in naval tactics also was prescribed. By this stage of the war the Japanese navy had lost so many aircraft carriers, planes, and trained pilots that it was no longer capable of fighting the type of carrier-based air-sea conflict that it had waged so brilliantly in the early months of the war. Indeed, the Combined Fleet, which had once boasted the most powerful carrier forces in the world, was now reduced to one first-class carrier, five small carriers, and two partially converted battleships capable of launching aircraft by catapult. It did, however, still possess considerable surface firepower, including the world's largest battleships, the 64,000-ton *Musashi* and *Yamato*. When the *Sho* operations began, then, the major elements of the Japanese surface fleet would launch an attack against the enemy landing force just as it was being struck by Japanese land-based airpower. The remaining Japanese carriers and a few other naval units would constitute a decoy element and attempt to draw off major American carrier forces from the scene of action, inflicting, in the process, as much damage as possible on the enemy. The combination of Japanese land-based air attacks and the guns of the Japanese warships, it was hoped, would destroy the invasion forces before the American carriers could return.

What would happen when they did return was not considered —for even if their planes then wiped out the Japanese battle fleet, the destruction of the transports and landing force would already have been accomplished. The Japanese navy might be sunk, but it would have died a glorious death in successful defense of the Empire.

The final action in the *Sho* operation was the responsibility of the Japanese army, charged with the defeat of whatever American troops managed to get ashore. Here, too, a change in tactics was called for. Hitherto Japanese doctrine had called for the defense against enemy landing operations to be concentrated at the "water's edge." The primary tactical principle had involved constructing strong beach positions, with little or no emphasis on secondary defenses, and attempting to destroy the attacking troops from the forward positions as they came ashore. Experience, however, had shown that these tactics would not work in the face of the overwhelming and devastating pre-assault bombardment of which the American fleet was capable. After considerable study, Japanese army planners in Tokyo decided on new tactics to be employed in the *Sho* operations. These called for the organization of defensive positions in considerable depth, with the main line established far enough inland to escape heavy punishment by the preparatory enemy bombardment. Only minor attempts would be made to halt the assault troops on the beaches, where they would enjoy strong cover from naval support units, but any attempt to advance inland would meet stout resistance. Japanese troops would contest every inch of ground from deep defenses made as nearly impregnable as possible, while substantial forces would be held in reserve to launch a counterattack at the right moment. The American troops would then be cut off and destroyed.

The *Sho* plans, it is clear, required a considerable shift in Japanese tactical thinking. They involved a change from positive to negative tactics, brought about by the desperate circumstances to which the Empire had been reduced by July, 1944. Despite the optimistic designation, *Sho,* the new plans were not those of a nation sure of victory. They were, rather, the children of desperation. On their success or failure rested the fate of Japan. And if they proved inadequate, this fate could no longer be doubted.

The *Sho* plans would have to be implemented at the proper time and place. To act on them too early would be to expend irreplaceable resources recklessly. To hold off too long would be to miss an opportunity presented only once and would dissipate

Japanese strength piecemeal. All actions would also have to be closely coordinated and centrally controlled, for no local commander could be permitted to jump the gun, delay unnecessarily, or pursue his own objectives. The decision, therefore, on when and where to activate the *Sho* operation would be made at the very highest level, Imperial General Headquarters.

While preparations for *Sho* began immediately, it was not until August 19 that the plans received formal imperial sanction at a meeting of the Supreme Council for the Direction of the War. The Council, consisting of the Japanese premier, foreign minister, and army and navy ministers and chiefs of staffs, was a sort of an inner war cabinet where representatives of the civil government and Imperial General Headquarters formulated the highest national policy. The meeting on the 19th was a special one, held before the Emperor. While His Imperial Highness listened in silence on his throne atop a raised dais, the participants sat facing each other across a long table. Premier Koiso presided, and each Council member rose in turn, bowed to the Emperor, and stood stiff in front of his chair to speak. In accordance with custom, the participants made set speeches, previously written and rehearsed, explaining the various aspects of the *Sho* plan with which they were all concerned. Normally that would have been all. But on this occasion Koiso, according to his postwar testimony, raised an unexpected question. How determined, he asked, were the military and naval high commands to win a major victory at the decisive battle envisioned in the *Sho* plan?

When Koiso took office a month earlier, he had publicly announced his determination to fight on to victory. This, however, was primarily to satisfy the country's military leaders, for he himself had felt that Japan was actually defeated when Saipan fell. But he also realized that a surrender offer after Saipan would have brought "merciless terms," as he put it. This, in turn, might have caused a revolution, for the Japanese people had been told repeatedly that Japan was winning the war. Yet Koiso believed that if the nation now threw all its energies into winning the planned decisive battle Japan could sue for peace while riding "the wave of victory," and thereby obtain lighter and less odious terms. So he urged the army and navy to seek more than just an exchange of blows with the enemy, a sacrifice of Japanese "hide"

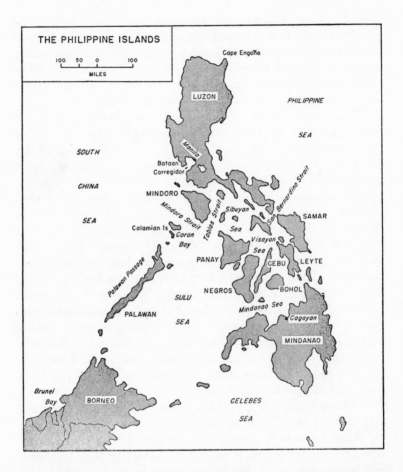

for American "flesh." This would accomplish nothing. What he wanted was a definite promise by Imperial General Headquarters to throw the entire national strength into the decisive battle in an all-out effort for victory.

This was the commitment Koiso pressed for on August 19. And, while the Emperor followed the discussion attentively, this was the commitment he got. The high command would fight the decisive battle "with the firm conviction of victory"—a promise that Koiso would bitterly recall in the waning days of the struggle for Leyte.

Meanwhile, at the end of July, on the same day that Imperial General Headquarters issued the basic *Sho* orders, the army staff in Tokyo held a meeting with officers from the Southern Army and its major subordinate commands. The conference covered all aspects of the *Sho* plans, with special emphasis on the Philippines, *Sho*-1. Under *Sho*-1, Japanese naval and air forces would attack the Americans wherever they first struck, and would wage a "decisive battle" against the invaders. If these efforts were unsuccessful, then a second "decisive battle" would be fought by the ground forces. The problem here was to determine in advance which island or islands of the Philippines would be the site of the "decisive" land battle. If this could be established, it would be that much easier to prepare for the fight.

Colonel Yozo Miyama, the Southern Army operations officer, argued that the decisive ground battle, like the air and naval contest, should be fought wherever and whenever the Americans landed. For if the invaders were permitted to secure bases in any one part of the Philippines they could dominate the air and sea throughout the islands and overwhelm Japanese land defenses anywhere—including whatever particular site had been previously chosen for the decisive ground battle. Obviously, said Miyama, army forces would have to make an all-out attempt to defeat any American landing regardless of where or when it came.

The Tokyo planners regarded this course as completely impracticable. For one thing, they told Colonel Miyama, there was no way of knowing just where the Americans would land. And there were simply not enough Japanese troops available to station major forces on every Philippine island that might be invaded. Once the landings began, also, American air- and seapower would be able to prevent any large shift of Japanese forces from one part of the Philippines to another.

It seemed clear that Luzon was the most important of the Philippine Islands, both strategically and politically. Sooner or later it would be invaded. Despite the probability that the first American landings might come in the central or southern Philippines, there was no guarantee that these areas and any Japanese troops stationed in them might not be bypassed in favor of a direct assault on Luzon. Luzon, moreover, seemed to offer the

strongest possibility of successful defense. Its road net, the best in
the islands, provided the defenders with mobility and flexibility
to meet any attack. The Japanese supply system on Luzon was
far better than anywhere else in the Philippines. And, finally,
Luzon, unlike many of the other Philippine islands, was big
enough to permit large-scale tactical maneuvering. As General
Yamashita often observed, it was "impossible to execute any real
ground operations on islands as small as *geta*"—*geta* being the
wooden clogs the Japanese wear. All things considered, the safest
course seemed to be to mass troops on Luzon and await the invasion there. Only small covering forces should be left to defend the
islands to the south.

The argument at the Tokyo strategy conference did not last
long. Colonel Miyama, as might have been expected, was overruled. The decisive Philippine land battle would be waged on Luzon. Only holding or delaying actions would be fought anywhere
else in the islands.

In accordance with this concept, Tokyo now ordered a reorganization of Japanese army forces in the Philippines. The islands
themselves remained under the general control of Field Marshal
Terauchi's Southern Army. General Kuroda's command was designated the Fourteenth Area Army. Charged with the over-all
ground defense of the Philippines, it had direct responsibility for
the decisive operations on Luzon. To defend the central and
southern Philippines, a new command was established as a subordinate unit of the Fourteenth Area Army. This was the Thirty-
fifth Army, with headquarters on Cebu. Lieutenant General So-
saku Suzuki, a talented officer who had been chief of staff to
Yamashita during the Singapore campaign, was the new army's
commander. Army air operations in the Philippines were under
the Fourth Air Army of Lieutenant General Kyoji Tominaga who,
like Kuroda, reported to Terauchi.

On August 5 the Southern Army chief assembled his major
subordinate commanders and their top staff officers in his Manila
headquarters. Here he explained the essentials of the *Sho* plan
and, in particular, the scheme for the defense of the Philippines.
Under his watchful eye, also, the group joined with top naval
officers to hold war games—or "tabletop maneuvers," as they
were called—to test the *Sho* defenses. The primary assumption in

these games was that the American landing would be made on the shores of Leyte Gulf. In accordance with Tokyo directives, however, Luzon remained the appointed site for the decisive ground battle.

During August, Terauchi and Kuroda and their respective staffs and subordinate commanders continued to plan and prepare for the coming invasion. Estimates were updated, necessary orders issued, and airfield and ground defense construction pushed to meet the changed tactical concepts included in the *Sho* plans. At the same time troops and aircraft reinforcements began to pour into the Philippines from rear areas of the Japanese Empire. From Manchuria came the 2nd Armored and 8th Divisions, from Mongolia the 26th Division, from Japan itself four brigades, as well as a variety of smaller units and individual replacements from many sources.

But the condition of these reinforcements left much to be desired. All had sustained serious losses in transit, in both men and equipment, thanks to the efficient operations of American submarines. Many of the survivors, also, turned out to be recent recruits, poorly trained and disciplined. Even the officers, often as high as regimental level, proved to be inadequately trained or experienced, and, as General Kuroda put it succinctly, "incompetent." Kuroda was particularly disturbed by the condition of the 26th Division, a unit he had formerly commanded. Extended garrison duty had turned this once crack division into a soft, easygoing outfit, weakened still further by the transfer of many of its veterans to combat units. To make matters worse, well over a battalion had been lost at sea.

While major units of the Japanese army were thus preparing for the defense of the Philippines under the *Sho* plan, the Japanese navy also was readying for decisive battle. Admiral Soemu Toyoda, commander in chief of the Combined Fleet, had received his *Sho* directive from the Navy Section of Imperial General Headquarters in late July, at about the same time that similar instructions were going to the army. An experienced, perceptive, and well-informed officer, Toyoda had been in his present post barely two months. A realistic, if not conservative strategist, he had not only opposed Japan's decision for war but had also urged caution in seeking objectives beyond the nation's capabilities. He distrusted the Japanese army—a feeling not uncommon among naval officers—and complained that it failed to cooperate with the navy. Presumably he was skeptical about working closely with the army under the *Sho* plans, but he was enough of a fatalist not to be unduly concerned by his doubts.

In accordance with the Navy Section orders, Toyoda placed almost all of his surface combat forces in what he called the First Mobile Fleet, under Vice Admiral Jisaburo Ozawa. And this he broke down into three tactical groups. The first, under Ozawa himself and composed primarily of the aircraft carriers, was called the Main Body. The next, the 1st Striking Force of Vice Admiral Takeo Kurita, was a heavy force of battleships, cruisers, and destroyers. The third consisted of cruisers and destroyers organized under Vice Admiral Kiyohide Shima as the 2nd Striking Force.

Ideally, the entire Mobile Fleet should have been stationed in home waters, ready to strike as a unit in any direction. Yet American submarines had done such an excellent job of cutting Japan's supply lines to the south that there was not enough oil available in home ports to support the entire fleet. Admiral Kurita's heavy units were therefore based at Lingga Roads, a hot, sandy anchorage across the strait from Singapore, where fuel, at least, was not a major problem. Ozawa's Main Body remained in the quiet waters of the Inland Sea, awaiting replacement aircraft and training new pilots. Here too was based Shima's small force. Toyoda himself maintained his flag ashore at Tokyo.

By mid-November, it was hoped, the fleet might be reunited at Lingga, with sufficient fuel, planes, and flyers to constitute a powerful armada. Until then, however, it would have to carry out the *Sho* plans in its divided condition—a complicating factor in an already difficult situation. In case of an American offensive that set off the *Sho* operation, Kurita's force would make the main attack on the enemy. Ozawa and Shima would undertake diversionary maneuvers from the north, with Shima, if the opportunity presented itself, launching a blow against the flank of the American task force. Land-based naval air units with attached army aircraft—the Fifth Base Air Force in the Philippines and the much larger Sixth Base Air Force stationed from Formosa to Kyushu—would assist in Kurita's attack.

During the late summer of 1944, then, Japanese land, sea, and air preparations to defend the Philippines continued at a rapid pace, spurred by the almost certain knowledge of a coming invasion. Imperial General Headquarters placed particular emphasis on airfield construction and the buildup of air strength in the islands—since airpower would be the first to oppose an American thrust at the Philippines. By late September roughly sixty all-weather airfields were in operation throughout the islands, and army and naval air units and replacement aircraft were steadily moving in. Many of the reinforcing units, however, were still short of both planes and trained flyers and Japanese air strength was well below what was necessary. To meet these deficiencies, air units underwent constant reorganization and staff officers of the Fourth Air Army conferred closely with their naval opposite numbers to develop plans for coordinated air action.

In the midst of all these preparations came the carrier-based air blows of Halsey's Third Fleet—the astonishing results of which would advance the date of the invasion of Leyte. On September 9 and 10 Halsey's planes made heavy strikes against Mindanao. The Japanese, conserving their short supply of aircraft, failed to have enough patrols in the skies to intercept the attackers, and the Americans achieved complete surprise. Furthermore, since the Japanese had decided not to commit the bulk of their aircraft until the actual invasion, when the *Sho* plan would be implemented, the attacking planes were all but unopposed. They inflicted widespread and severe damage on ground installations, airfields, and other targets, and sent back jubilant reports on the lack of Japanese resistance.

On the ground, many of the Japanese were near panic. Commanders alerted their troops against the possibility of invasion and an air of tense expectancy settled over the southern Philippines. In the midst of the tension and confusion someone set off a false alarm. At 9:30 on the morning of the 10th, a naval lookout post in southern Mindanao reported the approach of American landing craft. This report was hastily sent out to all major commands, which immediately took steps to meet an invasion. Admiral Toyoda, the Combined Fleet commander, alerted all naval forces for the execution of *Sho*-1. General Suzuki issued an alert order to the Thirty-fifth Army. The Fourth Air Army began moving aircraft from forward positions back to the Philippines. All went into readiness to begin the *Sho* operation.

It was midafternoon before Japanese aircraft, searching in vain for an American invasion fleet, could report that none was to be seen. And it was 4:30 before all major commands could be informed that the original alarm had been an error. All alert orders were quickly canceled, but the false start had a vital effect on later developments. For one thing, the hasty recall of army aircraft to the Philippines—already carried out before it could be rescinded—stripped Japanese forward defenses and eased the American invasion of Morotai a few days later. More important, however, was the fact that almost all Japanese army and navy commanders had been fooled by someone crying wolf. Acutely embarrassed, they would be extremely wary of accepting any other invasion reports without careful checking. This would definitely influence their ability to react promptly to the American invasion when it actually came.

Two days later Halsey's raiders struck again—this time at the Visayas, or central Philippines. Again the attackers had amazing success and again Japanese nerves were severely jangled. The effect of both series of raids was to badly weaken Japanese air strength in the Philippines: the few Japanese planes that rose to meet the Americans were knocked down, and many of those held in reserve on the ground were destroyed where they sat. Installations were wrecked, supplies burned, training disrupted, and the morale of the defenders severely bruised.

In his Manila headquarters it seemed clear to Field Marshal Terauchi that the invasion of the Philippines was about to begin. He therefore urged Imperial General Headquarters to implement *Sho*-1—that is, to designate the Philippines as the area of decisive battle and concentrate all efforts there. Terauchi had also expressed doubts earlier about the wisdom of holding back air strength until the last possible moment before an American landing, and he now urged his superiors to reconsider this policy. Far better, he argued, to carry out air attacks on American carriers at sea than to let planes from those carriers destroy on the ground Japanese aircraft that were being hoarded for strikes against the anticipated landing.

To add force to these recommendations, Terauchi once again sent Colonel Miyama, with two other staff officers, to present the Southern Army viewpoint to Imperial General Headquarters. The Tokyo staff officers, Miyama recalls, listened to him politely, but were not persuaded. Everything possible was being done to prepare for *Sho*-1, they said, and furthermore there was grave doubt that air attacks on American carriers would be successful. There would be no change in existing policy, they told Miyama. So once again that unhappy officer had to inform Terauchi that the Southern Army arguments had been overruled.

But Marshal Terauchi, if it was any consolation to him, could have assured himself that he was more nearly correct than his superiors in Tokyo. Even before Colonel Miyama had reached Imperial General Headquarters, American troops, supported by powerful air and naval gunfire attacks, had stormed ashore on Morotai and in the Palaus. Within a few days strong forces quickly secured important points in both areas. All of Mindanao, as well as the southern Visayas, now lay within easy range of American land-based bombers. The door was wide open for the direct invasion of the Philippines.

Just how wide stood the door became clear on September 21 and 22, when Halsey's carriers returned for still another devastating visit. This time the target was Luzon, in the first carrier attack of the war on that island. The Third Fleet planes swooped down on Manila, nearby airfields, and the great harbor of the Philippine capital. Again the Japanese were caught by surprise—some even mistook the first wave of attackers for Japanese aircraft— and again Halsey's men took a heavy toll. Many Japanese planes were destroyed on the ground, many more when they tardily rose to meet their attackers. Ground installations and shipping also suffered heavy damage and large stocks of vitally needed supplies went up in flames. As he hastily sought shelter from these attacks, Marshal Terauchi had good reason to wish that Colonel Miyama had been more persuasive on his visit to Tokyo.

By now, however, even the most dubious officers at Imperial General Headquarters were just about convinced. Still unwilling to actually implement the *Sho* plan, the high command was ready to concede formally that the Philippines would be the decisive

battle area and that operational preparations for *Sho*-1 would
have to be pushed as never before. On September 21 Navy Section of Imperial General Headquarters issued this order:

> Execution of the *Sho* Operation in the Philippine
> area . . . in or after the last part of October is an-
> ticipated. Naval forces will prepare for the *Sho*-1
> Operation with the highest priority.

A day later Imperial General Headquarters Army Section put out
its version:

> 1. Imperial General Headquarters generally des-
> ignates the Philippine Islands as the area of decisive
> battle and estimates that the time of this battle will
> be sometime during or after the last ten days of
> October.
>
> 2. The Commander-in-Chief of the Southern
> Army and [other commanders] will generally com-
> plete operational preparations by the last part of
> October for the accomplishment of their respective
> missions.

To support these orders Tokyo directed additional ground and
air units to move to the Philippines. Among these was the 1st Division, which had come from Manchuria to Shanghai as strategic
reserve pending activation of one of the *Sho* operations. By committing it to the Philippines, Imperial General Headquarters
underlined further its belief that *Sho*-1 would soon begin.

Then, on the 26th of September, the army general staff suddenly relieved General Kuroda as commander of the Fourteenth
Area Army. An officer sent from Tokyo to investigate the rumors
about Kuroda's activities had found considerable substantiating
evidence. The result was Kuroda's removal and the appointment
of Yamashita to succeed him. The change had come not only because of Kuroda's apparent ineptness but also because of
Yamashita's reputation as a commander. The situation in the
Philippines was critical, and Imperial General Headquarters, as
one of its members wrote later, "counted heavily" on Yamashita's
"military leadership."

The new Fourteenth Area Army commander spent a week in
Tokyo attending conferences on strategy and the defense of the
Philippines. Here he learned the details of *Sho*-1 and, in particu-

lar, of the differences of opinion between Marshal Terauchi and Imperial General Headquarters. Only a few days earlier the Southern Army staff had again recommended against waiting to fight the decisive ground battle on Luzon and had once more urged that this battle be waged wherever the Americans landed. Now the Tokyo staff explicitly informed Yamashita that the decision on Luzon still stood. All preparations would proceed on that basis.

Yamashita reached Manila on October 6, determined to carry out the policy directed by Imperial General Headquarters. That very evening he called a staff meeting at his headquarters at Fort McKinley, the former American army base just south of the city. Luzon, he told the assembled officers, would be the decisive battlefield in the Philippines, and here the fate of the Empire would be settled. Each man had a "heavy responsibility," and Yamashita expected all of them to fight boldly, "resolute and united" in their determination to triumph. "If we all remember this," he concluded, "the Japanese army must win in the end."

Although he spoke firmly and positively, Yamashita's inner feelings were less than optimistic. The Fourteenth Area Army was far from ready to wage a decisive battle, and its new commander could see this almost at a glance. Troop strength was inadequate, and even then many of the soldiers defending the Philippines still needed extensive training. Food, gasoline, and other supplies and equipment were noticeably deficient. Halsey's carrier raids had cut deeply into Japanese air strength and heavily damaged airfield installations. Even ground defenses, supposedly in an advanced state, were still a long way from completion. Communications were unsatisfactory and increasing guerrilla activity threatened to make it worse. Equally annoying to Yamashita was the fact that most of his top staff officers were recent replacements, unfamiliar with the situation in the Philippines. The chief of staff himself, on whom Yamashita would be greatly dependent, had been ill for some time and was still bedridden. Yamashita remedied this deficiency by arranging to have an old friend, the able Lieutenant General Akira Muto, brought from a division command in Sumatra to be his new chief of staff. But this scarcely even began to solve his many problems.

One condition that greatly disturbed Yamashita was his own

general unfamiliarity with the situation in his new command. Still more was he annoyed to realize that the imminence of an American invasion left him little time to acquire the necessary knowledge in depth. He was particularly disturbed by the fact that, with the exception of General Suzuki, he did not really know his own staff and subordinate commanders. "The source of command and coordination within a command," he said later, "lies in trusting in your subordinate commanders." In the Philippines he was forced to oppose a major invasion "with subordinates whom I did not know and with whose character and ability I was unfamiliar." As General Muto put it, Yamashita's assignment had been made "six months too late."

With characteristic vigor, nevertheless, Yamashita plunged into his new responsibilities. He reviewed and approved plans, studied reports, and questioned his subordinates on all aspects of the situation. He had no time to conduct his own inspections, but he dispatched staff officers to outlying units with specific instructions about the information he needed. At Fort McKinley the situation took on an air of haste and alertness never before evident. Morale at headquarters improved noticeably almost overnight.

By October 11, less than a week after his arrival, Yamashita had taken a firm enough grip on things to call a meeting of his major subordinate commanders. Carefully he described his plan of defense, emphasizing the Imperial General Headquarters policy of waging the decisive ground battle on Luzon. The objective in the central and southern Philippines would be solely to delay or, if possible, prevent American seizure of naval and air bases. With this understood, Yamashita ordered all preparations to be pushed as fast as possible for completion by late October. Everyone, he urged, should exert himself to the utmost and keep his spirits high.

Even as General Yamashita was issuing these instructions, however, events were taking place that would exert a major influence on the subsequent course of the *Sho*-1 operation. A few days earlier Admiral Toyoda, visiting Manila to confer on strategy, had predicted that Third Fleet carriers might strike in force at Okinawa, Formosa, or the Philippines as the opening round of an American invasion. How right he was! While the King-II forces assembled in two groups at the New Guinea base of Hollandia and on Manus Island in the Admiralties, a great air and sea campaign began to isolate the Philippines. Japanese strongholds in the Marshalls and Carolines felt the sting of land-based aircraft from the central and south Pacific. Formosa and the China coast were targets for army bombers operating out of western China. And from SWPA, the Far East Air Forces of Lieutenant General George C. Kenney hit again and again at Mindanao and the Indies. But while all this was happening, what turned out to be the most important role was played by Halsey's Third Fleet, just as Toyoda had foreseen.

Halsey's job was to neutralize the Japanese northern flank. Early on the morning of October 10, then, his carriers began a sustained attack on Japanese bases from Luzon to the northern Ryukyus. In a week of crowded and impressive activity, Vice Admiral Marc A. Mitscher's Task Force 38—the combat element of the Third Fleet—struck first at Okinawa, then at Luzon, and finally, for three intense days, at Formosa. Until this moment neither Okinawa nor Formosa had felt the impact of American bombs, and the repercussions of these attacks shook not only the targets but the whole Japanese Empire. At times more than 1,000 American aircraft were in action simultaneously, in a display of seaborne airpower the like of which had never been seen before. Certainly the Japanese had never witnessed or felt anything like this—which may possibly explain their reaction to it.

When the first air strikes began against the Ryukyus on the 10th, Admiral Toyoda was at Formosa, on his way back from Manila. But at Combined Fleet headquarters in the Naval War College in the Tokyo suburb of Hiyoshi, Rear Admiral Ryunosuke Kusaka, Toyoda's chief of staff, realized that a decisive moment was at hand. Under the original terms of the *Sho* plans, Imperial General Headquarters had reserved for itself the authority to implement them. In September, however, the high command had agreed to give Admiral Toyoda greater operational flexibility by allowing him to choose for himself the moment to launch naval air units against American task forces. Now Kusaka, acting on his own authority in Toyoda's absence, alerted all naval land-based air elements at about 9:30 for *Sho*-2, the defense of Formosa and the Ryukyus. Apparently unaware as yet of Kusaka's action, Toyoda, a few minutes after noon, alerted the naval land-based air forces for both *Sho*-1 and *Sho*-2.

In response to these orders, Japanese naval air units and attached army air elements on Formosa and in southern Japan—Vice Admiral Shigeru Fukudome's Sixth Base Air Force—began preparing for battle with Task Force 38. Halsey had planned to hit northern Luzon before turning on Formosa, and his execution of this plan on October 11 gave Fukudome's scout planes the opportunity to locate the American carriers and allowed the rest of the Base Force additional time to get ready. Meanwhile Toyoda, believing that Kusaka had issued the original *Sho*-2 alert only after close consultation with Imperial General Headquarters, waited impatiently for Kusaka to issue the *Sho* execute order on the same basis. Kusaka, however, now apparently expected the Combined Fleet commander to run things himself—and did nothing.

On the morning of the 12th, finally, as Task Force 38 struck Formosa, Toyoda acted. He cabled Kusaka to check first with Navy Section of Imperial General Headquarters and then issue to the base air forces the execute order for *Sho* Operations 1 and 2. At 10:30 Kusaka put out the order in Toyoda's name. A second order directed Admiral Ozawa to release the newly reconstituted flying groups of the Mobile Fleet to Fukudome, to operate from bases on Okinawa. This latter action effectively stripped Ozawa of the air units he had so laboriously built up and left Japan's main carrier striking force without a single operational plane.

Now the great Formosa air battle was joined. For three days the American carriers lashed at Formosa in a massive effort to knock out Japanese air strength there and to eliminate the island's potential as a staging base. Four fast carrier groups of Task Force 38—seventeen flattops in all, with battleship, cruiser, and destroyer escorts—sent their fighters and bombers into the clear sky over Formosa and the Pescadores.

On the 12th the American target was the Japanese fighter defenses. Destroy the airborne protection of the area, and Mitscher's flyers would have a clear shot at ground installations and shipping. When the attackers reached Formosa, they discovered Japanese fighters, alerted by radar, already in the air to meet them. Combat began immediately, and soon the sky was full of the rush and noise of aerial dogfights. Crouching in his command post below the scene of the heaviest action, Admiral Fukudome watched the confused drama with high hopes. When he saw planes fall from the sky, enveloped in smoke and flame, he clapped his hands and cried "Well done! Well done!" For surely these were American aircraft his noble eagles had thrown to the ground. But then, he recalls, "Alas! to my sudden disappointment, a closer watch revealed that all those shot down were *our* fighters, and all those proudly circling over our heads were enemy planes!"

When the fight was over the saddened admiral knew that he had lost a third of his aircraft, including many of his flight leaders, and had suffered great damage to ground installations, not the least of which was the destruction of his own headquarters. A second American strike knocked down still more Japanese fighters, so that the third raid found the sky empty of defenders. American losses were not light, but in a single day Halsey's flyers had assured themselves of air control of the area. That night Japanese torpedo planes struck at the task force. They accomplished nothing and took heavy losses themselves, but the surviving pilots returned home with exaggerated claims of American carriers sunk or set aflame.

Mitscher's men returned to their task on the 13th. This time they struck ground installations, primarily hangars, fuel dumps, shops, and parked or disabled aircraft. Damage was heavy and, having accomplished his mission, Halsey now made ready to retire from the area in accordance with his original plans. As the attackers returned to their carriers that evening, however, Japanese torpedo planes struck and made a crippling hit on the heavy cruiser *Canberra*. When the ship refused to sink, Halsey decided to tow it home. To cover this operation, he delayed his retirement and, the next morning, sent out a light attack on Formosa and northern Luzon. That evening, as the task force moved slowly east, the light cruiser *Houston* also took a torpedo in her side. She too was given a tow.

At the cost of only two cruisers badly hurt and a few other light scratches, Task Force 38 had inflicted tremendous damage on the Japanese. Not only had it wreaked great destruction on Formosan ground installations but it also sunk much enemy shipping, and destroyed nearly 600 aircraft, including those shot down as they attacked the task force. The northern flank of the

Leyte operation was now secure and, equally important, the hastily organized Japanese carrier flying groups, thrown precipitately into the Formosa battle, had been decimated, leaving Admiral Toyoda once again without carrier air forces.

To the Japanese, however, it appeared that the Empire had won a great victory. Japanese pilots returning from futile attacks on the American task groups reported tremendous success. Carriers, battleships, cruisers, and destroyers had been set aflame and sunk, they announced jubilantly. Task Force 38, completely shattered, was fleeing in disorder. These wild reports were the result of several factors. Undoubtedly wishful thinking was somewhat to blame. But the inexperience of the Japanese pilots, many of them in combat for the first time, was probably the real cause of the trouble. It is always difficult to identify an enemy warship in the heat and smoke of battle. At night the difficulty is compounded. And flyers, "aspiring to fame," in Admiral Fukudome's words, "were likely to exaggerate their achievements." Thus a destroyer was reported as a cruiser, a cruiser as a battleship or aircraft carrier. A near miss became a hit, a hit became a fatal blow. Two or more planes attacking a single target might each claim to have struck a different ship. Sometimes the bursting of a bomb or the flare of antiaircraft fire was mistaken for a shipboard explosion. A fire in the darkness which suddenly disappeared was seen as a vessel sunk beneath the waves. The most likely circumstance was that the flames of doomed Japanese planes, bursting as they struck the surface of the water, seemed like exploding ships, or silhouetted American vessels briefly against their glow, giving the warships themselves the appearance of being on fire. Even American spotters were fooled by this phenomenon.

Be that as it may, the reports that reached Japan—and those that Radio Tokyo spread over the airwaves—were incredible in their claims of victory. The Third Fleet had been destroyed as an organized striking force. All of Mitscher's carriers, or nineteen, or eleven—depending on which broadcast one listened to —had been sunk, along with several battleships and many cruisers and destroyers, not to mention a large number of ships which had merely been heavily damaged. Mitscher himself, announced the Domei news agency, had "vividly witnessed" it all from a "watery grave." The Emperor issued a special rescript to note the great triumph, mass celebrations were held in many cities and at scattered military headquarters, and Premier Koiso officially proclaimed that "victory is within our grasp." On board the battleship *New Jersey,* Admiral Halsey smiled at the enemy's gullibility and dispatched a simple, reassuring message to Admiral Nimitz in Honolulu. All of the Third Fleet ships that Radio Tokyo had reported sunk, said Halsey, had been salvaged, and were "retiring" at high speed "in the direction of the enemy."

To Admiral Toyoda, still watching events from Formosa, the Japanese claims were no joke. He, along with Admiral Fukudome and, undoubtedly, many other knowledgeable officers, realized that the reports were probably exaggerated. But no one had any idea of the extent of the exaggeration. It seemed reasonable to assume that perhaps a third of the damage claimed had actually been achieved—and the relatively weak strike, without a follow-up, that Halsey had mounted to cover his retirement on the morning of the 14th seemed to support this contention. Thus a victory, incomplete perhaps, and not so great as first reported, but a victory nonetheless, had been won. It merely remained to be exploited for the achievement of complete triumph.

Late on the 14th, then, Toyoda ordered all available Japanese naval air strength thrown at the supposedly crippled Third Fleet. He also directed Admiral Shima's 2nd Striking Force of cruisers and destroyers to sortie from the Inland Sea and mop up the remnants. Unknown to him, Halsey had deliberately withdrawn most of Task Force 38 from the immediate combat zone, leaving the damaged *Canberra* and *Houston* and their escorts as bait for the overanxious Japanese. Thus when Fukudome's search planes that afternoon reported only a few badly damaged ships—which they mistakenly identified as a carrier and two battleships—Toyoda felt even surer of victory and ordered the air and surface pursuit pressed to the utmost.

"Needless to say," recalled Admiral Fukudome after the war, "all this pursuit business ended in a fiasco." While Shima's force raced south at flank speed, Japanese aircraft tried in vain to locate the crippled remnants of Task Force 38 for the 2nd Striking Force to mop up. The 2nd Striking Force, however, was not unexpected. American radio monitors had picked up Toyoda's order to Shima, decoded it, and passed it on to Halsey. He, in turn, had immediately notified MacArthur that he was suspending his support of the Leyte invasion—then only a few days off—in order to seize the chance to destroy what he believed was a major portion of the Japanese fleet. Thus on the 15th most of Task Force 38 was maneuvering east of Formosa, just waiting for Shima to steam into range, while one group of carriers sent another strike against Luzon. Japanese aircraft on that island hit back at this carrier group, while Formosa- and Okinawa-based planes made vain efforts to bomb the rest of the task force. In all of these attacks the Japanese suffered heavily, but pilots returning that evening continued to report great success.

By now, however, Admiral Toyoda was getting somewhat suspicious of these claims. And when the regular morning search missions on the 16th brought in disquieting reports of large American carrier groups maneuvering in the Philippine Sea, he became even more concerned. He sent the bulk of Japanese naval aircraft based on Okinawa, Formosa, and Luzon to search for the carriers and sink them. Most of these planes never found their intended targets. Many that did find them were shot down before they could do anything. But a single aircraft that managed to slip through the American protective screen put another torpedo into the *Houston*—which still failed to sink that redoubtable warship.

By afternoon Toyoda was convinced that a sizable American fleet was still in existence—and that Admiral Shima's force was sailing directly into a fight against overwhelming odds. Shima had already been spotted and briefly attacked by two American planes. How many more were even now on their way for a second strike? With understandable discretion, Toyoda told Shima to put into the Ryukyus for fuel and then proceed south to the Pescadores, west of Formosa, to await further orders. The great Formosa air battle was ended.

For the Japanese the battle had been extremely costly. No two sources seem to agree on the size of their losses, but they apparently totaled well over 600 aircraft of all sorts shot down or destroyed on the ground. These losses crippled Japanese land-based air strength on Formosa and in the Philippines and ruined all chances that Admiral Ozawa's carrier groups could be reconstituted before the American invasion of Leyte. While a few hundred planes still remained in operation, the *Sho* concept of launching overwhelming land-based air strikes at the enemy land-ing force now appeared impossible of execution. To make matters worse, Shima's 2nd Striking Force had wasted tons of precious fuel in a fruitless operation and was now separated from Ozawa's Main Body, with which it had been originally scheduled to oper-ate. And then, of course, there was the fact that Halsey's losses had amounted to only two damaged cruisers and fewer than 100 planes destroyed.

In retrospect, the Japanese had blundered badly. Poor coordi-nation between Admiral Toyoda on Formosa and Imperial Gen-eral Headquarters in Tokyo had resulted in the premature initia-tion of part of the *Sho* plan on October 12. Had this taken place even one day earlier, Admiral Fukudome's planes could have hit Task Force 38 with their full strength while the carriers were engaged in attacking Luzon, and perhaps wounded at least some of the ships. Again, however, poor coordination combined with poor tactics held most Japanese aircraft at Formosa, to be de-stroyed there by Mitscher's flyers on the 12th. The further com-mitment of Ozawa's carrier groups only compounded the error. And the continued, futile attacks by outnumbered Japanese air-craft made a bad situation all the worse. By gambling that he could destroy the American task force and thus disrupt American invasion plans, the normally conservative Toyoda had needlessly crippled Japanese airpower and rendered it all but useless for the *Sho* operation that was now sure to come. Next to so great a mis-take, the misguided optimism that sent Shima's fleet scurrying south in a fruitless waste of vital fuel can only be regarded as a minor piece of nonsense.

Perhaps the most ironic result of the battle was that many Japanese believed the exaggerated victory claims broadcast by Radio Tokyo—or at least failed to discount them by a large enough percentage. This seems to have been especially true among army officers, who were less skeptical of the victory than Toyoda and some of his colleagues had become after a few days. Thus, even while Halsey's fleet was shifting south to cover the in-vasion of Leyte, many responsible Japanese felt that American landings in the Philippines would either have to be delayed or else undertaken without the support of strong carrier forces. This mistaken belief by the Army Section of Imperial General Headquarters, and by many lower echelons, would have a vital effect on Japanese plans for decisive ground operations.

Thus, no sooner had the Formosa air battle subsided than Marshal Terauchi again raised with Tokyo the question of where to fight the decisive land battle in the Philippines. Once more he urged an all-out contest wherever the Americans landed, instead of waiting for the assault on Luzon. This time the army staff of Imperial General Headquarters—with the supposed American losses off Formosa freshly in mind—was more willing to listen to him. A delayed invasion, or one attempted without heavy air cover, might well be defeated by Japanese ground forces wherever it came, even in the central or southern Philippines. Under the circumstances, however, there seemed to be ample time to study the situation in detail before reaching a final decision.

That decision was still pending when the first warships and transports of the American Seventh fleet entered Leyte Gulf on the morning of October 17. General Yamashita, who would have to implement the decision, was not even aware that it was under consideration.

≪≪≪≪≪≪≪≪≪≪≪≪≪≪≪≪≪≪≪≪≪≪≪≪≪≪≪≪≪≪≪≪≪≪≪≪≪≪

≫≫≫≫≫≫≫≫≫≫≫≫≫≫≫≫≫≫≫≫≫≫≫≫≫≫≫≫≫≫≫≫≫≫≫≫≫≫

v The Opponents

THE ISLAND of Leyte lies in the central Philippines, guarding the eastern approaches to the Visayan Sea. To the south is Mindanao, to the northeast Samar, and to the west the numerous other islands that make up the Visayas. The waters of Leyte Gulf wash Leyte's eastern shore and the southern coast of Samar. The gulf exits on the south to the Mindanao Sea via Surigao Strait, a broad channel formed by Leyte and long, thin Dinagat Island. Astride the eastern entrance to Leyte Gulf is Homonhon Island and, where the gulf becomes the Philippine Sea, the tiny isle of Suluan marks the transition.

Leyte itself, the eighth largest island in the Philippines, is about 115 miles from north to south, but barely 45 miles across at its widest and only 15 at its narrow waist. Its irregular shape has been compared to that of a large molar tooth, a roughhewn and slightly damaged Winged Victory of Samothrace, and, among other things, a misshapen hourglass. Perhaps the island is easiest to visualize by imagining a small dog running from left to right, forelegs amputated at the thigh, hindlegs outstretched, ears and tail flying, mouth slightly open. Now stand the dog on his heels, so that his head points north, his hindquarters south, and you get a fair approximation of Leyte's appearance on a map.

Nestled against the dog's belly is Leyte Gulf. Running northwest from the gulf, cutting the animal's forelegs at the upper thigh, is beautiful but narrow and swift-flowing San Juanico Strait, which separates Leyte from neighboring Samar. To the

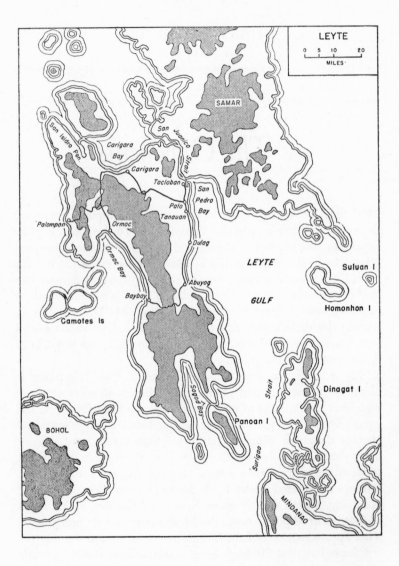

west the dog's head and ears are formed by the San Isidro Peninsula, of little military significance save for the ports of Palompon,
at the top of the head, and Ormoc, at the nape of the neck. Extending north from Ormoc to Carigara Bay, the Ormoc Valley
can be seen as a dog collar. East of this valley a heavily forested
central mountain range stretches from the animal's shoulder to
the high rugged country of his hindquarters and tail. This mountain range, with sharp spurs and ridges, and deep cuts, effectively
separates the thin western coastal strip, running south from
Ormoc along the dog's back, from the broad fertile plain of the
Leyte Valley, which constitutes the chest and belly between
Carigara Bay and Leyte Gulf.

Well cultivated and thickly populated, the Leyte Valley is less
a valley than simply a wide flatland extending unbroken to the
water. It is thus deceptively attractive for military operations.
Along the shores of Leyte Gulf and San Pedro Bay, at the southern entrance to San Juanico Strait, are some of the best landing
beaches in the Pacific. But once an invader has crossed the
beaches, he is faced with swamps, rice paddies, innumerable
streams, and a general sponginess underfoot—for in most places
the water table is only a few inches below the surface. Traffic, except on foot or animals, must stick to the roads, and these, in
1944, were not very good. They linked the island's major towns,
none of which was more than an overgrown village built around
the usual old Spanish church. The coastal road ran south from
Tacloban, Leyte's capital, on San Pedro Bay, through Palo,
Tanauan, and Dulag to Abuyog. From Tanauan and Dulag, two
narrow roads led inland several miles to other towns, and from
Abuyog a mountain trail zigged and zagged its way west across
the mountains to the coast, thence north to Ormoc. From here a
better road ran up the Ormoc Valley to Carigara Bay and then
east again to the Leyte Valley.

One of the most important things about Leyte from a military
point of view is its weather, especially in the fall. From September until early spring moist northeast trade winds bring heavy
rains to the eastern half of the island. From October until late
December, also, typhoons add their fury to the tropical downpour. The central mountain range blocks much of this rain from
reaching the western portion of Leyte, but the rest of the island

practically turns to mud during the fall. The ground, already soft
and marshy in many areas, becomes almost completely saturated.
These conditions could be expected to affect both Japanese and
American operations, although the Americans, planning to land
on the shores of Leyte Gulf, would get the worst of it. Even more
important was the effect the rain and the water-soaked ground
would have on American plans to build airfields and supply bases
on the island.

American staff officers were well aware of these problems.
Most of them anticipated a good deal of rain, although one
claimed to have visited Leyte twice during the rainy season without ever having had to don a raincoat. Nor is it clear that everyone really appreciated how unsuitable Leyte's marshy soil was for
construction. But one engineer officer, Colonel William J. Ely,
was concerned enough to submit an official warning. In a detailed
written analysis, he forecast rains and high winds on Leyte and
described in detail the island's spongy terrain, inadequate drainage, "unstable" soil, and poor roads and bridges. Under these circumstances, he warned, there were simply not enough engineer
troops available to build major air and supply bases within the
time required. To assume otherwise would only guarantee a delay
in future operations. Ely suggested three alternatives: assign
more engineer construction troops to Leyte, forget about using
the island as a major base and seize another area with fewer construction problems, or slow down the tempo of the strategic
offensive against Japan.

Ely's warning went straight to the top, and not without favorable endorsement along the way. But MacArthur's staff could not
accept any of the colonel's recommendations. Additional engineer
troops were simply not available, there were overriding reasons
for at least attempting to construct a base on Leyte, and the advance across the Pacific could not be slowed. If there was a risk
involved, it would have to be taken.

The decision in mid-September to assault Leyte two months
earlier than originally scheduled increased the engineering problem. Not only would the Americans have to fight their way across
the island during the worst part of the rainy period but now the
invasion would come squarely in the middle of the typhoon season, instead of at its end in late December. This advanced time-

table also cut severely into the period left for planning, training engineer troops, and assembling supplies and equipment. And, finally, the elimination of Mindanao as a steppingstone removed the possibility of supporting the invasion from nearby air bases. The nearest fighter base would be 800 miles away, bomber bases no closer than 1,000 miles. If weather or unsuitable ground conditions delayed construction of airfields on Leyte, air support would have to be almost entirely carrier-based for longer than anyone considered prudent.

Still, what were the alternatives? To return to the plan for invading Mindanao? To delay the Leyte invasion until December again? To give up the opportunity to hit the Japanese when they were evidently weak and off balance and provide them with an opportunity to rebuild their strength? No, if there were problems, they would have to be faced as best they could. A swift, bold stroke seemed infinitely preferable—and perhaps even safer in the long run—than a slow, cautious approach.

The first Western visitor to Leyte, himself embarked on a risky venture, was Ferdinand Magellan on his celebrated attempt to circumnavigate the globe. Magellan never actually landed on the island, but he took a good look at it in early 1521 when he sailed through Leyte Gulf and Surigao Strait before passing westward to his untimely death. Nearly four hundred years later, young Second Lieutenant Douglas MacArthur, conducting engineer surveys at Tacloban, nearly met his own untimely death. Sent with a small detachment to the island of Panay, westernmost of the Visayan group, MacArthur was ambushed on a jungle trail by two bandits. Only his speed and skill with a pistol saved his life, and a bullet hole in his campaign hat, barely an inch above his skull, showed how narrow was his escape.

Certainly the Japanese had reason to regret this inadequate marksmanship. By 1944 they had been so impressed with Mac-Arthur's victories, so awed by his imposing personality, so hypnotized by his relentless drive toward the Philippines, that many Japanese army officers were infected with a defeatist psychology whenever they thought of the American general. This was especially true in the Philippines. According to General Yamashita, many of his subordinates thought MacArthur could never be defeated, that he might be delayed but never really stopped.

Yamashita himself did not share this feeling. Nor, at any rate, did it prevent the Japanese in the Philippines from trying their best to halt MacArthur.

In mid-October, 1944, Japanese defenses on Leyte were in the hands of Lieutenant General Shiro Makino's 16th Division, some 20,000 strong, including attached service and naval guard troops. This force constituted one fifth the total strength of General Suzuki's Thirty-fifth Army, which was responsible for defending all of the central and southern Philippines. Other units of the Thirty-fifth Army were available to reinforce Leyte, of course— and, in the event of a major landing on the island, Suzuki planned to bring a reinforced division in through Ormoc to back up the 16th. Until help arrived, however, Makino's troops would have to do the best they could alone.

The 16th Division had been in the Philippines longer than any other Japanese combat unit. It had taken part in the original invasion of the islands in 1941 and had remained there. It was a division that MacArthur was "particularly anxious to get at," as he told a newspaperman, for he blamed it for the horrors of the Bataan Death March. "They've been living off the fat of the land for more than two years," he added, "and I believe they'll be a little softer now."

Actually, while the 16th Division had fought on Bataan, the extent of its participation in the Death March was probably small. In any event, it is doubtful if either General Makino or many of his men had ever even seen Bataan—except from the deck of a ship. Most of the division consisted of replacements and transfers from other units, with at least 25 percent of the troops being recent draftees. Makino himself had been in the Philippines only half a year. Nor had the living been particularly soft for his men, given the state of Japanese supplies and the increased activities of Filipino guerrillas on Leyte during 1944.

MacArthur was right, however, in assessing the 16th Division as relatively weak. Not only were many of Makino's troops inadequately trained, but at least one regiment had only recently been transferred to Leyte and its officers and men were still unfamiliar with the area they were to defend. On top of this, 16th Division defenses, which the troops had been feverishly building since the summer, were still incomplete. Only the first line of positions, facing Leyte Gulf around Dulag, was anywhere near finished. This line guarded the approach to most of the Leyte airfields, clustered to the west in the Leyte Valley, and faced that section of the coast where the Japanese expected MacArthur to land. Secondary and tertiary positions inland still were in need of considerably more work. The division signal net, moreover, was so poorly equipped that it would be difficult to shift troops around in the face of any sort of heavy attack.

Curiously enough, there were no coastal defenses around Tacloban, site of Makino's headquarters and his main supply dumps, as well as the location of one of the Leyte airfields. None of the Japanese had felt that the Americans would take a chance on deploying assault shipping in the confined and therefore dangerous waters of northern San Pedro Bay. General Suzuki eventually changed his mind about this and ordered Makino to shift his headquarters inland. But by this time, Makino had other problems and, unfortunately for the Japanese, waited too long before moving.

These "shortcomings," as one Japanese officer understated it later, were perhaps not so bad in light of the Japanese strategy for defending the Philippines. If the *Sho* plan worked, then Japanese air and naval forces would engage the invaders in a decisive battle before they could establish a beachhead. Hopefully, this would leave little of the enemy left for the 16th Division to handle. Even then, however, Imperial General Headquarters' choice of Luzon for the decisive land battle meant that only holding or delaying actions would be fought anywhere else in the Philippines. So all General Makino had to worry about was preventing the Americans from seizing the Leyte airstrips. If Japanese air and naval units were unable to thwart a major landing on the island, he might have a hard time holding the airstrips for long. But in view of the reported Japanese victory off Formosa, the 16th Division commander felt that his chances were pretty good. General Suzuki, for the same reason, was inclined to agree with him.

Perhaps the two would have been less sanguine if they had known the actual results of the Formosa air battle and understood, also, the true state of Japanese air and naval strength. On the eve of MacArthur's return to the Philippines, the number of

Japanese aircraft, both army and navy, available to defend those islands was pitifully small. As is often the case, precise figures are not available and there is wide disagreement even on the figures that can be assembled. But a safe estimate would probably be that there were perhaps 150 operational planes of all types in the Philippines, with an additional 300 navy aircraft under Admiral Fukudome ready to shift down from Formosa. Reinforcements were in process of moving in, from Japan as well as from forward areas, but the quality of both planes and men in these cases was less than might be desired. The only other planes available were about 100 carrier aircraft, flown by inexperienced pilots, that had been reassembled with Admiral Ozawa's carrier forces still anchored in the Inland Sea.

The strength of Japanese naval forces available for *Sho*-1, the First Mobile Fleet, was somewhat more reassuring, although, without adequate air cover, the security of the fleet was open to serious question. The most powerful group of warships in the fleet was Admiral Kurita's 1st Striking Force, at Lingga Roads: seven battleships, including the huge *Musashi* and *Yamato,* eleven heavy cruisers, two light cruisers, and nineteen destroyers. Admiral Shima's 2nd Striking Force, now refueling in the northern Ryukyus, consisted of two heavy cruisers, a light cruiser, and seven destroyers. The carrier element, Admiral Ozawa's Main Body, was a curious one. It carried relatively few planes and, since it was intended as a decoy force, consisted only of expendable ships and those carriers for which there were no trained air groups: one large carrier, three light carriers, two battleships partially converted into carriers, three light cruisers, and eight destroyers. About fourteen submarines were available to support the Mobile Fleet.

The Japanese command structure in the Philippines was a confusing and divided one. There was no single unified command for the islands, which made the integration of land, air, and sea operations extremely difficult. The army ground commander in the Philippines was General Yamashita. He commanded the Fourteenth Area Army but had no authority over General Tominaga's Fourth Air Army. Both officers reported to Marshal Terauchi, who, as Southern Army commander, was responsible for army forces throughout the Southwest Pacific. He was thus charged with the coordination and control of joint operations by ground and air commanders, including those of Yamashita and Tominaga. Terauchi did not, however, have any authority over naval forces, even those based or operating in his command area.

All Japanese naval forces, except certain units at home, on the China coast, or on escort duty, were under Admiral Toyoda's Combined Fleet. The major surface forces, organized as the First Mobile Fleet, were directly under Toyoda, as was a separate submarine command. The First Mobile Fleet, although it would fight in Philippine waters, was completely independent of the Japanese naval command in Manila, Vice Admiral Gunichi Mikawa's Southwest Area Fleet. Mikawa, also under Toyoda, controlled some miscellaneous vessels, base and guard forces, and air units scattered throughout the Southwest Pacific—including the important Fifth Base Air Force on Luzon. The Sixth Base Air Force, on Formosa, reported to Toyoda. With Toyoda, therefore, lay the responsibility and gargantuan task of coordinating all the various Japanese naval units—surface, undersea, and air—that would take part in the *Sho* operation, even as Terauchi had a similar task for the major army units involved.

But who would coordinate Toyoda and Terauchi? Theoretically this would take place in Tokyo, since each officer was responsible to his own service staff at Imperial General Headquarters. Yet Imperial General Headquarters was nothing at all like the American Joint Chiefs of Staff organization which, despite interservice friction, was, after all, a fairly unified arrangement. Imperial General Headquarters was, in fact, two separate headquarters, an army command and a navy command. The rivalry, animosity, and at times outright antagonism between the Japanese army and navy was so strong as to preclude any really joint headquarters setup or even any close coordination between the services. The Army and Navy Sections of Imperial General Headquarters were housed in separate buildings, developed separate plans, and issued separate directives to their services. When joint operations were conducted, they were carried out by means of "agreements" between the two service staffs, which put out their own orders to their respective units. If the Army and Navy Sections disagreed, there might be no operations at all or separate operations might be undertaken in different directions. Even when they did agree, a single joint commander was rarely appointed to control the entire operation, which was normally conducted by the two local service commanders "cooperating" under the terms of special "agreements."

Thus Marshal Terauchi and Admiral Toyoda had no one to coordinate their execution of the *Sho* plan. Each reported to separate headquarters, which might or might not agree on a course to follow. Or each might simply pursue a different course without too much consideration for what the other would do.

This, as the old saying goes, was certainly no way to run a war. And if the *Sho* plan was not already too complex for proper coordination and control, the divided command that would execute it offered little hope for improving matters.

By contrast with the relatively weak and disconnected Japanese land, sea, and air elements prepared to defend Leyte, the American invasion force for King-II was overwhelming—and considerably better coordinated. Over-all commander of this force was General MacArthur. As CINCSWPA, MacArthur did not directly command any troops, ships, or planes himself, but he had in his subordinate army, navy, and air force commanders three able and experienced leaders, all used to serving under him and to carrying out his directives. Each, of course, exercised command in his own right, and each was capable of decisive and independent action. For the Leyte operation, MacArthur controlled the American Sixth Army, Seventh Fleet, and Far East Air Forces. Admiral Halsey's Third Fleet, which was a part of Nimitz's Pacific command, as well as army air forces in the Marianas and China, would play a supporting role.

The Sixth Army was commanded by Lieutenant General Walter Krueger, a gruff, starchy veteran of the war in the Southwest Pacific. Born in Germany, Krueger had come to the United States early in life and fought as a private in the Spanish-American War. He had won his commission during the Philippine Insurrection and was now returning to the islands in a somewhat more responsible position than he had enjoyed on his first visit. As an army commander, he had a simple mode of operation. "I don't do much," he once said, "except think a lot, scold a little, pat a man on the back now and then, and try to keep a perspective."

The Sixth Army contained two corps commanded by Major

Generals Frank C. Sibert and John R. Hodge. Both men were seasoned leaders. Sibert's X Corps included the 1st Cavalry and 24th Infantry Divisions, Hodge's XXIV Corps the 7th and 96th Infantry Divisions. In addition, Krueger had the 32nd and 77th Infantry Divisions and the 6th Ranger Battalion to throw into the fight when necessary. The strength of the Sixth Army was over 200,000 men, twice the size of the entire Japanese Thirty-fifth Army and two thirds as many as the total number of Japanese ground troops in all the Philippines in mid-October.

Krueger's plan called for initial landings on Suluan, Homonhon, and Dinagat Islands, to capture Japanese radar there and secure the entrance to Leyte Gulf. Then on A day his troops would seize beachheads around Tacloban (where they were not expected) and Dulag (where they were). They would then quickly occupy the Leyte Valley and its all-important airfields. With air and sea bases in American hands, conquest of the rest of the island would be relatively easy—and the way would be open for operations elsewhere in the Philippines.

The job of transporting, landing, and supporting the Sixth Army was the responsibility of the Seventh Fleet, sometimes referred to as "MacArthur's Navy." Its commander was Vice Admiral Thomas C. Kinkaid. Kinkaid looked like a college professor and had seen duty at the 1932 Geneva Disarmament Conference. But he had also done his share of fighting in the Pacific. Strict and conscientious, imperturbable under stress, he was an ideal commander for the great task assigned to him. To carry it out he divided his fleet into three elements: Task Force 77, under his direct command, and Task Forces 78 and 79, the Northern and Southern Attack Forces under Rear Admiral Daniel E. Barbey and Vice Admiral Theodore S. Wilkinson. Barbey, who had put ashore so many invasions that he was called "Uncle Dan, the Amphibious Man," and Wilkinson, also a veteran, were each responsible for landing one of Krueger's corps. Task Force 77, which contained the bombardment, escort carrier, and other close support groups, would directly cover the landing.

The array of assault shipping, transports, and warships in the Seventh Fleet was tremendous. The combat element included no less than six battleships, five of them veterans of Pearl Harbor, eighteen escort carriers with about 500 planes, four heavy and four light cruisers, thirty destroyers, twelve destroyer escorts, and thirty-nine motor torpedo boats. Add to this hundreds of troopships, command ships, landing ships, minesweepers, tankers, supply vessels, and others, and the armada becomes even more impressive. It included, incidentally, a handful of Australian ships and one British vessel.

Initial air coverage of the Leyte invasion would be provided by carrier-based planes, but General Kenney's Far East Air Forces had a general long-range support function. Once the invaders had seized airstrips on the island, however, Kenney would move in fighters and light bombers and take over the close-support function from the naval aviators. Kenney had been Mac-Arthur's air chief for over two years. He was energetic, daring, and a successful innovator of air tactics. On the eve of the Leyte invasion he commanded more than 2,500 front-line combat aircraft. This included over 1,000 bombers and about 1,400 fighters of all types—more than enough to handle anything the Japanese had, once Kenney was able to bring them forward.

In addition to the impressive combination of land, sea, and air forces under MacArthur's command for the Leyte invasion, there still remained a sizable American naval force with a major support function. This was Admiral Halsey's Third Fleet, under Nimitz's command and operating by agreement with MacArthur. The Third Fleet consisted essentially of Vice Admiral Mitscher's Task Force 38, over which, in these circumstances, Halsey exercised direct tactical command. The Third Fleet was one of the most formidable naval striking forces ever assembled. It contained nine large, or fleet, carriers, as they were called, and eight light carriers, with more than 1,000 planes, as well as six new battleships, six heavy cruisers, nine light cruisers, and fifty-eight destroyers. These were organized into four powerful task groups of approximately equal strength, commanded by Vice Admiral John S. McCain and Rear Admirals Gerald D. Bogan, Frederick C. Sherman, and Ralph E. Davison. All these officers had seen enough salt-water fighting to qualify as hardy veterans.

Halsey's mission was to attack targets in the Philippines, Formosa, and Ryukyus in the week preceding the Leyte invasion—which, as we have seen, he carried out brilliantly—and to cover the landings themselves by hitting the central Philippines immediately before and during the amphibious assault. During this latter phase he would also provide "strategic support" of the operation by destroying Japanese naval and air forces that threatened the invasion force.

But Halsey's operation plan—as written by the Third Fleet commander and approved by his boss, Admiral Nimitz—also stated that if the chance to destroy a "major portion" of the Japanese fleet was "offered or could be created," then this would become the Third Fleet's "primary task." Giving this mission a higher priority than that allotted to the task of protecting the beachhead represented a divergence from the practice that the Pacific Fleet had been following all during the war. Up to this point the primary mission of naval units supporting an invasion had been just that: to provide protection and assistance to the amphibious forces. The previous June, however, American fleet units covering the Saipan operation had refused to chase a badly damaged Japanese naval force, sticking instead to their primary mission of supporting the invasion. For allowing the Japanese to escape, the American commander, Vice Admiral Raymond A. Spruance, had been severely criticized by some. Yet had he gone after his quarry he would have left the Saipan beachhead uncovered, vulnerable to attack by any Japanese force that might have slipped by him in the confusion of the chase. If this had occurred, and the invasion been crippled, Spruance would have received more than criticism—he would have been court-martialed.

The aggressive Halsey was well aware of these factors. Yet he was not one to ignore a chance to close with the enemy. He would cover the invasion the best way he knew: not by sitting idly by and guarding the beachheads, but by knocking off the Japanese fleet at the first opportunity. So he wrote his plan accordingly and, since MacArthur had no authority over him whatsoever, he was completely free to execute it as he chose.

This situation illustrated perhaps the only weakness in the American plan for King-II: the absence of a unified command. The arrangement, while less confused and disjointed than the Japanese organization, still found no single individual with authority over the entire operation. MacArthur controlled most of the forces—except Halsey. Responsible only to Nimitz, Halsey was free to support MacArthur when and as much as he pleased.

If he chose to withdraw his support, there was nothing Mac-
Arthur could do about it. Obviously, Halsey would not act
without good reason, but what might seem like good reason to
him might not appear so convincing to MacArthur. And in any
event the SWPA commander could never be sure just how much
he could depend on the Third Fleet.

This had been made quite clear during the Formosa air battle,
when Halsey had temporarily suspended his support of the
Leyte invasion armada, then already approaching the target area,
in order to set an ambush for the Japanese fleet. His action then
had left Admiral Kinkaid, who had direct command of the invasion force while it was still at sea, with a ticklish decision to make.
He could either delay the invasion or proceed with whatever extra assistance he might obtain from General Kenney's Far East Air
Forces and by assigning extra missions to the carrier planes of his
own Seventh Fleet. He chose the latter course, which proved sat-
isfactory. And Halsey was back on the job two days later, in
ample time to support the actual invasion. But, as these events
made plain, the Third Fleet commander was free to leave at any
time that he flushed more attractive game.

This situation was obviously a dangerous one. It could, and in
fact almost did, lead to disaster. And it would result in one of the
most controversial events in the whole Pacific war.

But this episode was still in the future as the mighty invasion
convoy approached the Philippines.

vi Activate Sho-1!

OCTOBER 17 dawned cloudy and sullen. Gusts of cold rain stung the surface of Leyte Gulf and a high wind whipped the waves into a white froth. On tiny Suluan Island, athwart the entrance to the gulf, the Japanese naval lookout stared at the gray ships that loomed suddenly out of the water before him. Within a matter of minutes a hasty uncoded message was on its way to all Japanese naval headquarters. "0700 hours," it read, "two battleships, two converted aircraft carriers, and six destroyers approaching."

This was a slight exaggeration. What the excited lookout should have reported was three minesweepers leading eight destroyer-transports and half a dozen light cruisers and destroyers. At about 7:45, the sweepers having completed their work, the cruiser *Denver* opened fire on Suluan's southern beaches. A few minutes later soldiers of Company D, 6th Ranger Battalion, on board the transport *Crosby,* began scrambling down cargo nets into four landing craft. At 8:05 hulls scraped against sandy bottom, landing ramps splashed down, and the men dashed onto the beach. No Japanese tried to stop them. But a second message, again in the clear, had already been dispatched: "Enemy elements have begun landing on this island."

At Formosa, where Admiral Toyoda still remained, the Combined Fleet commander promptly interpreted the news as heralding the start of a major invasion of the Philippines. Even before he had word of the actual landing he had alerted the entire fleet for *Sho*-1 and specifically directed Admiral Kurita to move the 1st Striking Force from Lingga Roads to Brunei Bay, on the northwest coast of Borneo, prepared to attack the American invasion force. A few hours later Toyoda ordered Admiral Ozawa's Main

Body to sortie from the Inland Sea in time to coordinate with Kurita's attack. He also directed Japanese submarine forces to move to the Leyte area to intercept the American fleet. Toyoda himself took off immediately for Tokyo. He was still not positive that an invasion was under way, but he would be ready if it was.

Other Japanese commanders were more skeptical—especially those in the Philippines who remembered the false alarm raised a month earlier. When word of the Suluan landing reached Manila at about 8 A.M., General Tominaga ordered Fourth Air Army units to reconnoiter Leyte Gulf and attack any enemy shipping they might discover. But the weather was so bad that flights were limited. Pilots who did reach the area found that they could see little anyway because of the rain and dense clouds. The lack of any sightings indicated to Tominaga, as well as to General Yamashita and Marshal Terauchi, that the report from Suluan might be another error. They changed their minds that afternoon when a naval reconnaissance plane broke through the clouds to spot American warships off Suluan. But they still doubted that this meant a full-scale invasion. For one thing, American air activity had been limited to a Third Fleet strike at Luzon—the weather had prevented any flights by Kinkaid's pilots—and this hardly seemed to indicate a coming invasion. And, for another, the Japanese in Manila still believed that American naval forces had been all but crippled off Formosa, which in itself would rule out a major offensive venture.

While the Japanese were making up their minds about the Suluan landing, the American rangers on that island had been efficiently going about their business. Moving quickly inland from the beach that morning, they had burnt some buildings which bore signs of hasty Japanese evacuation and destroyed an enemy radio transmitter. As they proceeded across the island, however, they ran into an ambush. Sudden shots, fired by Japanese hidden in the jungle, killed Private First Class Darwin C. Zufall and wounded Private First Class Donald J. Cannon, the first American army casualties in the battle for Leyte. One other ranger would be hit that day, but thirty-two Japanese would die. The island secured, D Company returned to the beach to re-embark but found that the high seas had broached the four landing craft. With none others available, the men dug in for the night and were taken off the next morning.

Other rangers had made a similar landing on Dinagat Island at about 9:30 on the morning of the 17th. They found no Japanese—which explains why their landing went unreported by the enemy—and quickly erected a navigation light to guide the Leyte invasion convoy. Still another landing had been scheduled for Homonhon Island that day, but gale winds and heavy surf forced a postponement until the next morning. By then the weather had lifted and the rangers went in. Again there were no Japanese to be found, and another navigation light went up. By noon of the 18th, then, the entrance to Leyte Gulf had been secured, the channel marked, and the first small phase of the invasion had been completed.

Meanwhile, in Manila, General Tominaga had been having second thoughts about the import of the Suluan landing. Earlier he had felt that the absence of heavy American air activity ruled out an invasion at this time. By the evening of the 17th, however, he concluded that the fact that any air strikes had been launched at all in the face of the day's heavy weather indicated that the Americans were beginning a major offensive action. Also, American radio traffic had increased greatly, and this too showed that something unusual was going on. His mind now made up, Tominaga ordered an all-out air strike the next morning against American shipping around Suluan and directed additional units of the Fourth Air Army to shift to fields in the Visayas. He also recommended to Marshal Terauchi that *Sho*-1 be implemented.

But Terauchi wanted more concrete evidence—and bad weather on the 18th kept Tominaga's planes grounded, precluding even a reconnaissance of the Leyte Gulf area. Nor had any word come from the 16th Division on Leyte itself. The storm on the 17th had really shaken up General Makino's unit. The fierce winds had knocked over buildings and installations, filled defensive positions with sand and water, and torn down wires and radio equipment. "The communications network," recalled one Japanese officer, "was like a broken spiderweb." So most of the division spent the morning of the 18th digging out, while lookouts strained their eyes peering intently across the dark waters of Leyte Gulf. Soon they discovered minesweepers and support ships of Task Force 79, moving in to sweep the gulf channels and cover a beach reconnaissance by underwater demolition teams. It was close to noon, however, before word reached General Makino over his still-crippled communications net. He immediately notified General Suzuki, at Thirty-fifth Army headquarters on Cebu, and General Yamashita in Manila. But Makino, like his superiors, was still under the impression that the Japanese had won a great victory off Formosa. And he noted in his message that the American ships in Leyte Gulf might simply be remnants of the fleet destroyed off Formosa, now seeking shelter from the storm.

Since Makino reported no hostile activity by the American warships, and in the absence of more solid intelligence, neither Suzuki nor Yamashita could reach any firm conclusion about American intentions. But the 16th Division report had convinced Terauchi. At about noon of the 18th he sent an urgent message to Tokyo recommending the immediate activation of *Sho-*1.

At roughly the same time Admiral Toyoda, anticipating word from Imperial General Headquarters, was issuing preparatory orders for *Sho-*1. These called for Kurita's 1st Striking Force—now en route to Brunei Bay—to advance through the central Philippines, pass through San Bernardino Strait, north of Samar, and then rush south to attack Kinkaid's invasion force in Leyte Gulf. Admiral Ozawa's Main Body would lure Halsey's covering fleet to the north and, if possible, engage and destroy it. Shima's 2nd Striking Force would not participate in the attack but would come under Admiral Mikawa's Southwest Area Fleet and convoy army reinforcements to Leyte. All land-based naval air forces would concentrate in the Philippines to strike at the American carriers and submarine forces would attack the convoys or try to pick off damaged American warships.

Toyoda originally had wanted to set X day—the date of the attack—as October 22, hoping to catch the invaders with one foot ashore and the other still on board ship. But Admiral Kurita had protested that this left him no time to refuel and replenish, and there were other logistical problems, so now Toyoda tentatively fixed October 24 as the target date.

By two o'clock on the afternoon of the 18th, meanwhile, there could no longer be any doubt about American intentions. At that hour the battleship *Pennsylvania* along with two cruisers and sev-

eral destroyers opened fire on the Dulag beaches. At about three
o'clock members of the underwater demolition teams left their
transports aboard motor-powered rubber landing craft and
moved in several columns toward the shore. As they approached
the beaches they broke formation to avoid giving the appearance
of an assault landing wave. This did not keep the Japanese from
opening fire, however. At about 3:15, 16th Division troops let
loose at the small craft with small-arms, mortar, and light artillery
fire. As some of the landing craft returned the fire with their machine guns, the whole flotilla swung within 200 yards of the shoreline.

Now the swimmers who were to make the reconnaissance
began slipping over the seaward side of the boats. Clad only in
trunks, a life preserver, and rubber fins, each man carried a face
plate for underwater observation, a pair of clippers, a sounding
line, and a knife. All expert swimmers and well trained in their
work, the men struck out individually for the shore.

No sooner had the swimmers entered the water than one of
the boats was hit and sunk. The destroyer-transport *Golds-
borough* swung in close to shore to take the Japanese gunners
under fire with her 4-inch guns—and received a direct hit on her
forward stack. Two men were killed, but no serious damage was
done, and she continued to fire away.

The swimmers, meanwhile, were doing the only thing they
could to avoid enemy fire: staying underwater as long as possible
and surfacing for air carefully and briefly. As they swam in to the
shore they took soundings and searched for mines and underwater obstacles. Two men actually reached the beach and
crawled along in the surf for about fifty yards. When they finished
their work they headed out to sea again, to be picked up by the
remaining landing craft.

All up and down the southern invasion beaches similar scenes
were taking place. Japanese fire was heavy but sporadic and not
overly effective. American supporting fire appeared to be equally
ineffective and was much lighter than the swimmers would have
wished. "The bombardment prior to the reconnaissance," complained one underwater team in its report, "can be described as
economical rather than efficient. The fire support during reconnaissance was very light and generally ineffective."

Part of the trouble was that the destroyers were unable to maneuver close enough inshore to use their 40-mm. guns effectively. And longer pre-operation bombardment from offshore might have given the Japanese enough extra warning time to prepare an even hotter reception for the swimmers. More critical was the fact that planes from Kinkaid's escort carriers, which should have been hitting and burning out Japanese shore installations, were fully engaged attacking the Leyte airfields originally assigned as targets for Halsey's flyers. Since Halsey at this time was busy trying to ambush Japanese naval units east of Formosa, planes from the Seventh Fleet had to take over the Third Fleet general support mission and were not available for close support of the pre-invasion reconnaissance.

Despite these difficulties, the reconnaissance on the 18th—and a second one on the northern invasion beaches the next morning—was entirely successful. The swimmers reported the complete absence of underwater obstacles or mines along the shore. The beaches appeared to be perfect for landing. Casualties were very low for this type of dangerous game: three men killed, twenty-six wounded, two landing craft sunk, and two destroyer-transports hit. Fortunately for the swimmers, they did not have to remove or destroy any mines or obstacles. Had this been necessary, the casualty list would undoubtedly have been much longer.

In Tokyo, meanwhile, the army and navy staffs of Imperial General Headquarters had been following developments closely. Convinced by noon of the 18th that a major invasion of the Philippines was about to begin, they sat down to decide what to do. The immediate conclusion was to activate *Sho*-1.

Then for the first time naval staff officers explained to their army counterparts the plan for the Combined Fleet attack on Leyte Gulf. The army staff thought it was a poor plan: there was little chance of success and, if it failed, the fleet would be destroyed and the Japanese war effort critically damaged. The attack, advised the army officers, should be called off. But, having stated their position, there was nothing else they could do. The navy liked the plan and the Combined Fleet would attack Leyte Gulf. If the army disagreed, it was regrettable—but of no consequence.

There was, however, complete agreement of activating *Sho*-1.

So the chief of the army general staff, General Yoshijiro Umezu, and the chief of the navy general staff, Admiral Koshiro Oikawa, went together to the Imperial Palace to make their formal report to the throne and go through the motions of getting the Emperor's approval of what Imperial General Headquarters had already decided to do.

Standing stiffly before their silent ruler, they bowed low, and one of the two officers—which, is not clear—started to speak in the clipped, formal language used only when addressing the Emperor. "We report to Your Majesty," he began, "on the commencement of the *Sho*-1 Operation." Next followed a description of the American actions, an estimate of enemy intentions, a statement of Japanese plans and alternatives, and the conclusion that *Sho*-1 should be activated. Then the speaker referred to the "severe losses inflicted on the enemy task force in the Formosa area." Because of these, Japanese officers and men were "of excellent morale" and anxious to destroy American forces attacking the Philippines.

> The decisive battle of the *Sho*-1 Operation [he concluded] is the most important operation affecting the fate of Japan. Officers and men will therefore be completely united in carrying out this operation and will exert every effort in accordance with the common policy of both Imperial General Headquarters and local forces and will bring a successful conclusion to Japan's decisive battle.
>
> Respectfully, we conclude this report.

Now it was the Emperor's turn to speak. His words were brief. "Since this is the important battle to decide the fate of the Empire," he declared, "the Army and Navy will work as one to destroy the enemy." The audience completed, the two officers bowed and retreated from the room. At a few minutes after five that afternoon, October 18, the Army and Navy Sections of Imperial General Headquarters issued separate orders activating *Sho*-1.

With the die cast in the Philippines, all that now remained to decide was where to fight the decisive ground battle. Army Section officers still had before them Marshal Terauchi's urgent recommendation that the location of the battle should be switched from Luzon to wherever the Americans first landed in force. The supposed Japanese victory off Formosa also weighed heavily on their minds. With almost half the American carrier strength believed destroyed or put out of action, the Americans appeared to be risking a major invasion with seriously reduced carrier forces. If this was so, then the time was ripe for a change in Japanese plans. Japanese losses in aircraft had admittedly been heavy. But these could be replaced a lot faster than the Americans could make up their losses. This, in turn, meant that the Japanese had a good chance of gaining at least temporary air superiority over the Philippines. The safe movement of Japanese troop reinforcements and supplies to Leyte would thus be possible. Since Japanese inability to reinforce the central or southern Philippines had been a primary reason for choosing Luzon as the decisive battleground, it now seemed clear that Leyte would do as well if not better. Also, despite their skepticism, army staff officers felt that the Combined Fleet's sortie against Leyte Gulf might just be successful enough to damage the American supply line seriously.

On the evening of the 18th, then, the Army Section of Imperial General Headquarters made the decision to shift the decisive battleground to Leyte and throw all available ground strength into the fight for that island. There were obvious disadvantages in such a last-minute change of plan, but the prospects of crushing the enemy with a simultaneous and concerted commitment of air, sea, and ground forces seemed to outweigh the drawbacks.

Despite the clear need for speed in transmitting this decision to Terauchi and Yamashita, the army staff did not send off an immediate radio to Manila. Instead, Colonel Ichiji Sugita of the Operations Division, with two other staff officers, left Tokyo for Manila on the morning of October 19 with word of the decision and a detailed plan for implementing it. Flying first to Formosa to brief the Japanese commander there, Sugita did not reach Southern Army headquarters until late on the 20th, a good eight hours after the first American troops had landed on Leyte. Until that time Terauchi and Yamashita continued to form their strategy on the basis of the standing instructions to fight only a delaying action in the central Philippines.

On the morning of October 19, even as Japanese commanders in the Philippines were issuing orders and taking other steps to implement *Sho*-1, the bulk of the Seventh Fleet close support and bombardment units moved into Leyte Gulf. The weather had finally cleared. The sea was calm and visibility perfect. Mine-sweeping was all but completed now—the Japanese had not sown many mines in the gulf itself, but had thoroughly mined the approach channels—and underwater demolition teams made their last reconnaissance early in the day, supported this time by heavy fire from battleships and destroyers. The 16th Division reported that it had repulsed a landing attempt, but all its gunners had done was to make things fairly warm for a few of the swimmers.

But it was also quite hot on shore. At about 8:30 in the morning battleships, cruisers, and destroyers of Rear Admiral Jesse B. Oldendorf's Fire Support Unit South began a heavy shelling of the beaches around Dulag, where the XXIV Corps was scheduled to land the next day. Half an hour later Rear Admiral George L. Weyler's northern fire support unit opened fire on the X Corps beaches around Tacloban. The big guns of the fleet poured a rain of destruction on the towns along the coast, smashing the flimsy buildings and setting fire to the debris. Most of the Filipinos, forewarned of the attack through messages sent to the guerrillas, had left the area, but the Japanese were forced to stay and take it. They fired back at their tormentors, though with little success, and crouched in shelters or foxholes to sweat out the bombardment.

While some of the fire support ships continued to shell the towns, others concentrated on the beaches, roads, and possible Japanese troop concentration points. The thick foliage along the shore made it difficult to spot targets, so the ships resorted to area fire, shooting at whatever could be seen, attempting to destroy camouflage on suspected Japanese positions, and then spraying the area in hopes of just hitting something. The underwater swimmers had reported a line of well-camouflaged pillboxes, trenches, and dugouts along the southern beaches, and Admiral Oldendorf's gunners tried their best to smash away at these targets. Overhead, in the haze and smoke that rose from the burning shoreline, floatplanes from the cruisers and battleships hovered unmolested to direct fire and report results.

In the middle of all this activity Filipinos in bancas and other native craft were busy paying visits to the American ships lying offshore. They had started these visits on the 18th, and now they came in increasing numbers until it seemed that every citizen of Leyte was intent on paying a social call. Some of the visitors were Filipino guerrillas, bringing welcome and valuable intelligence information, but most seemed to be self-styled "patriots," curiosity seekers, or simply people so delighted at the coming end of Japanese rule that they could not wait to thank their liberators. The American sailors were pleased with the welcome, but many of the ship commanders were skeptical. It was not beyond the realm of probability that at least some of the visitors were spies sent by the Japanese. So some of the ships simply held all their Filipino guests on board until after the main assault, while others just refused to receive any more.

At the same time that the fire support units were pounding Leyte's shore, the Seventh Fleet Escort Carrier Group, Rear Admiral Thomas L. Sprague commanding, was sending fighters and dive bombers against targets on Leyte, other islands in the Visayas, and northern Mindanao. With Halsey's support of the invasion still suspended, Sprague's planes once again had to take over the task of general support. This meant hasty shifts in plans and some confusion in their execution. Control of aircraft missions, Sprague reported later, was confused. Some flights were misdirected and others had difficulty locating targets that had not been specifically enough designated. As a result, some flyers dropped their bombs with little effect, while others missed really worthwhile targets. These problems were cleared up within a day or so, but they proved troublesome on the 19th.

Nevertheless, Sprague's pilots had a field day, with perfect flying weather. On Leyte they struck at the Japanese airstrips, which, strangely enough, appeared to be abandoned, and at defensive positions, ground installations, and vehicles. Elsewhere they hit at airfields and shipping and at any points from which Japanese reinforcements, ground or air, might come to threaten the impending landing. On Leyte itself, the 16th Division was soon almost out of antiaircraft ammunition. And in the air Japanese opposition was negligible.

The lack of Japanese air activity was significant and, for the

Japanese, critical. It indicated that the air phase of the *Sho* plan
was already disrupted, with possible fatal effects on the plan as a
whole. The *Sho* plan had called for mass air attacks against the
American invasion forces just before they reached the landing
area. Success in these attacks would leave only seriously crippled
troop elements to be dealt with by Japanese ground forces. Admiral Halsey, however, had thwarted this scheme of maneuver by
his early strikes against Japanese air bases—and Admiral Toyoda
had contributed to the Japanese losses by his mistaken decision to
activate the air portion of the *Sho* plan prematurely. The beginning of the Leyte operation before the Japanese could rebuild
their air strength and concentrate it in the Philippines meant the
complete frustration of Japanese intent.

On the eve of the invasion of Leyte the Fifth Base Air Force,
in the Philippines, was a negligible factor. The Sixth Base Air
Force, which had lost half its strength in the Formosa battle, had
not yet begun to redeploy south from Kyushu, Okinawa, and Formosa. And the Fourth Air Army, which had managed to keep a
respectable number of planes in operation, was widely scattered.
To operate effectively in the Leyte area, it had first to concentrate at forward bases in the Visayas, where it now maintained
only a handful of aircraft. But vigorous American opposition, bad
weather, and the miserable condition of many of the rain-soaked
Japanese airfields made Fourth Army redeployment both difficult
and hazardous. Under these conditions the movement might take
several days or a week. And in the meantime Japanese air opposition to the invasion would be light and ineffective. Certainly its
effect on the pre-assault operations was nil.

Not until October 19 did the Japanese attempt an air strike
against the American invasion fleet in Leyte Gulf. And even this
was only a limited one, since both the Fifth Base Air Force and
the Fourth Air Army were unwilling to commit major elements
until Japanese air strength had been fully concentrated for an all-
out decisive air battle. So, despite the clear skies and favorable
weather on the 19th and the profusion of inviting targets in the
Leyte area, only a handful of Japanese planes attempted to break
through American air patrols over Leyte Gulf. And these were
unsuccessful.

Japanese reconnaissance planes did manage a few quick looks, however. One pilot, in the morning, reported eighteen American transports in Leyte Gulf, shepherded by over thirty warships, including six carriers. Another flyer, late that afternoon, reported 100 transports in or near the gulf, six carriers, ten battleships, and thirty other warships. Some of Halsey's carrier groups were also spotted east of Luzon. Clearly, the invasion was about to start.

Despite all these reports, there were no carriers actually inside Leyte Gulf on the 19th—although Admiral Sprague's flattops were operating close at hand in the Philippine Sea—and the main body of transports did not begin to enter the gulf until nearly midnight.

On board the ships that evening chaplains held open-air services, and their prayers were broadcast over the public-address systems so that all could hear. The outdoor services were well attended, although some of the men remarked uncomfortably that they were being given the last rites.

Reveille was set for 3 A.M. But the number of soldiers who tried to sleep that night, or even went to bed, was probably not great. The evening was warm and the area belowdecks stuffy and, it seemed, particularly close. Seldom were so many minds occupied with such similar thoughts. Tomorrow was A-day.

vii A-Day

DURING the night the transports carrying the Sixth Army steamed through the channel between Homonhon and Dinagat Islands and across Leyte Gulf. Admiral Barbey's Northern Attack Force, carrying the X Corps, approached the narrow waters of San Pedro Bay while Admiral Wilkinson's Southern Attack Force, with the XXIV Corps, moved toward the palm-lined beaches between Dulag and Palo. The carriers accompanying them had already turned north to join the rest of Admiral Sprague's escort carriers cruising off Samar. Now the cruisers and destroyers that had entered the gulf with the convoy moved to join the bombardment and fire support ships already covering the landing areas. Two vessels picked up mines on the paravanes slung from their sides for just this purpose, but otherwise nothing disturbed the stillness and glassy calm of Leyte Gulf.

The sun rose, bright and hot in a cloudless sky, at about 6 A.M. on October 20. A single Japanese reconnaissance plane put in a brief appearance just beyond antiaircraft range and then disappeared. Almost at the same time the warships supporting the Southern Attack Force opened fire on the beaches with everything they had. An hour later the bombardment of the northern landing beaches began. In both areas the full fury of the seaborne arsenal was unleashed. Everything from the small 3-inch guns of the destroyers to the heavy 16-inch rifles of the battleships poured tons of high explosive on the shoreline, roads, and high ground.

Overhead, planes from two of Halsey's fast carrier groups, once more operating in support of King-II, and other aircraft from Sprague's escort carriers joined in the furious assault. Some bombed towns and installations, others struck at trenches and

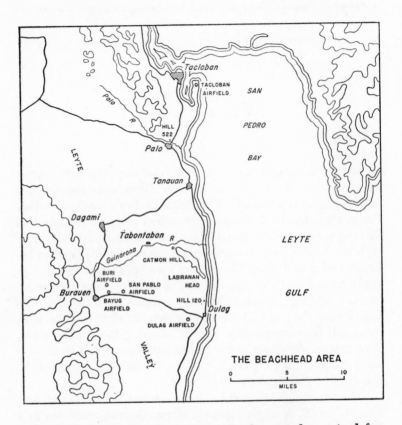

THE BEACHHEAD AREA

pillboxes along the beaches, while still others tried to strip defensive positions of their camouflage by dropping napalm, a newly developed incendiary mixture of oil and liquid rubber. Farther inland airstrips, supply dumps, and other targets received visits from the carrier planes. Few if any Japanese aircraft were in the sky. Only dust and smoke rose from the ground, along with the feeble, almost pitiful, cough of intermittent Japanese antiaircraft fire.

As H-hour approached, the bombing, strafing, and shelling reached a deafening peak—and held at that level. Aerial observers, reporting on the bombardment, could now see hundreds of tiny landing craft and amphibious tanks surrounding the ships below them, the small objects circling the mother vessels like so many waterbugs, their faint white wakes forming intricate patterns on the smooth sea. From the decks of these assault craft, the troops looked on approvingly as explosions ripped the shoreline. The men wondered if anything could survive the punishing fire. They clutched their weapons and rooted for the naval gunners and the fighter and bomber pilots to knock out Leyte's defenses and kill the Japanese who manned them. On board the transports other men scheduled to go in later watched with no less anxiety and anticipation. Each explosion, they hoped, each burst of aerial gunfire, each eruption of smoke and dust increased their chances of coming through alive on A-day.

By about 9:30 the assault waves had been formed, the control craft and guide boats jockeyed into position, and the close support vessels swung into line. A few minutes later the race across the line of departure began. It seemed an agonizingly slow race, at a speed of barely four knots, as the covering warships lifted their shelling inland and left the assault craft exposed to whatever defensive fire the Japanese on the beaches might have left. This was not long in coming. Almost immediately concealed enemy mortars opened up, followed by machine guns and other small arms. For a brief moment this fire remained unanswered and then, as the range to shore closed, the landing craft and amphibian tanks began to blanket the beachhead area with rockets, cannon, and machine-gun fire. Once again a heavy pall of smoke rose from the explosions on shore and the assault troops, crouching behind the front and sides of their landing craft, noted a gradual slackening in the Japanese fire. Almost exactly at ten o'clock, right on schedule, the men in the first landing craft felt a sudden, almost sickening lurch as their boats grounded on the Leyte coast. Ramps dropped noisily into the warm surf—a few, as always, jammed and the troops had to climb over or around them—and the men splashed hastily ashore. The first wave had landed on Leyte.

The landing caught General Makino at the worst possible time. Only the night before he had finally begun to move his command post from Tacloban south to Dagami, a more centrally located point nine miles inland on the road from Tanauan. Thus, at H hour Makino and his immediate staff were still in transit, with the remainder of the headquarters and rear echelon service

troops sitting in Tacloban, cut off from the 16th Division commander. It was noon before Makino could order reinforcements to
the landing sites and direct the rest of division headquarters to
pull out of Tacloban. Not until the next day was he able to set
himself up at Dagami.

The hasty evacuation of Tacloban by the division rear echelon
made a bad situation worse. All major communication facilities
had to be abandoned and, as a result, contact between the 16th
Division and higher headquarters was completely cut off for
nearly forty-eight hours. From late on October 20 until the night
of the 22nd, General Yamashita in Manila and General Suzuki on
Cebu were entirely out of touch with developments on Leyte.

On A-day, meanwhile, the Americans had taken full advantage of this situation. Within a few moments of H-hour soldiers of
four divisions were running, creeping, or crawling forward across
Leyte's sandy beaches. At the extreme north, on the right of the X
Corps area along San Pedro Bay, troopers of the 1st Cavalry
Division moved quickly over the White Beach, opposed by only a
few scattered Japanese. The 1st Cavalry, with a tradition going
back to the days of Indian fighting and the Civil War, had been
dismounted early in World War II and equipped and organized
as infantry. It had fought in the Admiralties earlier in 1944 and
now, commanded by Major General Verne D. Mudge, had the
immediate mission of seizing the area around Tacloban and the
shores of San Juanico Strait. Defending this sector on October 20
was a battalion of the Japanese 33rd Infantry Regiment and a
small number of naval troops.

Once ashore, the men of the 1st Cavalry pushed rapidly inland through the tangled jungles and swamps between White
Beach and the coastal road and then fanned out to overcome a
few minor pockets of Japanese resistance. The troopers knocked
out two pillboxes and killed more than a score of the enemy. By
midafternoon General Mudge was ashore and in his advance
command post. Within a few more hours the division objective
had generally been secured. The coastal road in the beachhead
area and the Tacloban airstrip to the north were in American
hands, all ships had been unloaded, and the division artillery was
in position and ready to fire.

Immediately to the south, on the left of the 1st Cavalry, the

24th Infantry Division had been encountering somewhat heavier resistance on Red Beach. Another historic army outfit, with honors dating back to the War of 1812, the unit had been at Hawaii when the Japanese struck Pearl Harbor and had been blooded on New Guinea in early 1944. On Leyte, under Major General Frederick A. Irving, its first task was to seize the town of Palo and nearby Hill 522, a steep, knobby height that dominated the division beachhead. Defense of this area was also the responsibility of the Japanese 33rd Infantry.

Among the men in the first boat of the initial assault wave on the right flank, the zone of the American 34th Infantry Regiment, were Private First Class Silas Thomas and Corporal Ponciano Dacones. Thomas, a North Carolinian, and Dacones, a Filipino, had won a lottery, giving them the honor of carrying the first American and Philippine Commonwealth flags to be returned to Leyte. As the ramps touched down, the two men splashed ashore quickly. No Japanese fire greeted them as they ran forward to a line of coconut trees at the edge of the beach and, side by side, planted the two flags firmly in Philippine soil.

For nearly ten minutes after the first wave landed there was no opposition on Red Beach. Then Japanese mortars and machine guns opened up on the troops ashore and on the still-incoming landing craft, inflicting numerous casualties. Colonel Aubrey S. Newman, the regimental commander, landed with the fifth wave to find nearly a battalion of his men pinned down on the sand. The big, redheaded officer stood erect and began to walk inland despite the heavy fire. "Get the hell off the beach!" he shouted to the men. "Get up and get moving! Follow me!" Noticing that the two flags erected by Thomas and Dacones were serving as aiming points for the Japanese gunners, he ordered the colors taken down until the area could be cleared.

Inspired by Newman's courage and leadership, troops of the 34th Infantry began to stream past their commander and move into the woods and swamps. They knocked out half a dozen Japanese pillboxes and pressed forward through foul-smelling water and slime often up to their waists until they finally reached high ground and the coastal road. By late afternoon they had secured the regimental objective and tied in on the north with troops of the 1st Cavalry.

The really heavy fighting, however, took place on the division left, where the 19th Infantry was driving toward Hill 522. The first waves of that regiment missed the planned landing point and the punishing Japanese fire that fell on succeeding waves added to the general confusion. Nevertheless, despite casualties, the troops pressed forward vigorously off the beach, overrunning Japanese pillboxes that filled the wooded area immediately inland. One soldier, Private First Class Frank B. Robinson, earned a Distinguished Service Cross by first crawling atop a pillbox to drop grenades inside it, then helping to set fire to another, and finally exposing himself to draw fire from still a third pillbox that American tanks were trying to locate. Examples like this inspired the other men and the regiment, fighting in squads and platoons in the deep swamps beyond the woods, continued to advance undeterred by its growing casualty list.

As dusk approached, most of the 19th Infantry beachhead area had been taken. But Hill 522, the key to the area, still remained in Japanese hands. On its steep slopes the Japanese had forced Filipino laborers to dig camouflaged caves, emplacements, and trenches, and from these positions General Makino's troops could fire down on the landing beaches, Palo, and the connecting roads. In the late afternoon three companies of the 19th Infantry began making their way up the approaches to Hill 522. Fortunately for them, the heavy pre-assault bombardment had driven most of the defending Japanese—about a company of the 33rd Infantry—off the height, and covering artillery fire had kept them off. So only the intense heat of the tropical day slowed the Americans as they climbed. It was not until twilight, as the first troops neared the top, that they began to receive fire from two pillboxes before them. Bypassing this resistance, another company pushed on to the crest of the hill and quickly began to form a defensive perimeter. Even as it did so, however, the men could hear the returning Japanese climbing the forward slope of the hill.

In the gathering dark a fierce fight broke out as both sides maneuvered for position and sought to occupy the crest. The Americans, however, had the advantage of both position and numbers, and succeeded in holding the hill. More than fifty Japanese died in this attack and in several lesser attempts during the night. The American company commander, First Lieutenant

Dallas Dick, appears to have had a charmed life. Wounded in the shoulder earlier in the day, he was hit again in the leg, and then had his carbine shot from his grasp. He lived, but others were not so fortunate. Their sacrifice, however, saved the hill and protected the southern flank of the X Corps beachhead. This beachhead now stretched comfortably for five miles from the outskirts of Tacloban to the top of Hill 522.

Some thirteen miles to the south, meanwhile, General Hodge's XXIV Corps had also been carving out a beachhead. Since the corps target area, around Dulag, was exactly where General Makino had expected the American assault, the Japanese were better prepared in this sector than anywhere else. Their defenses still left much to be desired, but the position was better fortified and there were more troops to defend it. The greater part of the 16th Division was dug in here, most of the 20th Infantry Regiment around Dulag itself and the bulk of the 9th Infantry farther north, guarding the approaches to Catmon Hill. This height, 1,400 feet of steep, grassy terrain, partially covered by trees, rose ominously to the northwest and dominated the entire beachhead. Most of the 16th Division artillery had been knocked out in the pre-assault bombardment, but one battery plus supporting mortars atop Catmon Hill still remained to back up the defenders.

The right, or northern, half of the XXIV Corps beachhead was the responsibility of the 96th Infantry Division. Commanded by Major General James L. Bradley, the unit was going into combat for the first time and the men, though well trained and experienced in working together, were perhaps just a bit more apprehensive than the battle-tested veterans in the other American divisions. As the troops of the 96th poured ashore, however, they were pleasantly surprised to find no Japanese opposing them. A few rounds of mortar and artillery fire from Catmon Hill killed and wounded several men, but otherwise nothing hindered the dash across Orange and Blue Beaches and into the woods beyond. Within an hour most of the division was two thirds of a mile inland. Hill 120, a small rise on the division left, was captured after a brief fight. First Lieutenant Clifford W. Mills raised an American flag atop the height—which proved an attractive target for Japanese shelling for some time thereafter.

By noon the division advance had slowed considerably. Japa-

nese resistance, scattered and generally ineffective, was less of a
hindrance than the terrain. As General Bradley's men pushed forward, they found themselves hip deep in marshes and swamps.
No roads led inland in the division sector, and vehicles, even
amphibious tanks and tractors, soon became mired in the grasping mud. Engineers quickly began building roads out of coconut
tree logs, but the infantry could not wait for such luxuries and it
was all the men could do to haul themselves over the soft ground
and through the water. They slogged ahead, often on hands and
knees in the muck, trying to keep their weapons dry and their
senses alert for the enemy. Many dropped their packs to ease the
effort of moving forward, but for those carrying machine guns or
mortars the advance was particularly exhausting. Fortunately for
the Americans, most of the defending 9th Infantry troops were
still dug in on Catmon Hill, and only a few scattered Japanese
riflemen attempted to oppose the 96th Division advance. By evening of A day, most divisional objectives had been taken, General
Bradley had set up his command post ashore, and unloading was
all but completed.

The last of the four major American units to go ashore on
October 20 was Major General Archibald V. Arnold's 7th Infantry
Division, assigned to Violet and Yellow Beaches. To the men of
the 7th, veterans of Attu and Kwajalein, fell some of the heaviest
combat of the day. Most of this fighting was on the division
right, in the zone of the 32nd Infantry Regiment. The 184th
Infantry, which landed south of the 32nd, encountered relatively
little resistance, either on going ashore or farther inland. One of
its battalions seized Dulag around noon and by evening the regiment was dug in on the edge of Dulag airstrip, a prime objective
in the corps area. It had encountered few Japanese and its only
casualties were three men overcome by the heat.

The 32nd Infantry was less fortunate. Even before it landed,
Japanese artillery fire killed or wounded more than a dozen men.
Then, as the troops crossed the beach, one company found itself
in the midst of a cemetery occupied by some very lively troops of
the enemy 20th Infantry. A brisk fight ensued and it was an hour
before the Japanese defenders could be overcome. Meanwhile,
other Americans were moving forward against sporadic rifle fire.
Soon the advance uncovered a cleverly concealed series of pill-

boxes, machine-gun emplacements, trenches, and foxholes, supported by a single 75-mm. field piece. This position remained hidden until the forward elements of the 32nd Infantry were almost on top of it. Then the defending Japanese poured machine-gun fire into the exposed Americans, inflicting many casualties and pinning down an entire company. A second company, advancing to the right of the first, was also quickly pinned down by the heavy fire. Five medium tanks then lumbered up to the rescue, but three of them were knocked out in quick succession by the Japanese field piece. Finally, after nearly three hours of fire and maneuver, a coordinated attack by the infantry and tanks enabled several men to get close enough to finish off the Japanese with grenades.

Similar actions were taking place elsewhere along the front and it was midafternoon before the advance could cross the main north-south road, barely half a mile in from the shore. Here the attacking troops ran into further well-concealed Japanese positions which they were unable to penetrate. During the fight Sergeant Alvino Cotta and Private First Class Quinton W. Gower distinguished themselves by braving enemy fire to drag a wounded comrade from the path of a retreating American tank. Both were hit, but all three men survived the incident.

By late afternoon it was clear that the 7th Division had pushed inland as far as it could. The men dug in for the night, having advanced a mile and a half on the left but less than a third that distance on the right. After dark the Japanese made several attempts to penetrate the American positions with small groups of medium tanks. Those tanks, supported by a handful of men from the 20th Infantry, struck down the narrow road that entered Dulag from the west. Although some of the tanks managed to push through 7th Division defenses, almost all of them were destroyed as they attempted to escape inland again.

Of the last group of three tanks, which attacked well after midnight, all were knocked out. A bazooka man stopped one with his first round as the tanks came in. The remaining two went on through the line, but on their return one was destroyed when it ran into an American supply detail. The crews of two 37-mm. guns tried without luck to knock out the last tank, and finally a bazooka team took it under fire and succeeded in halting it. By now the tank had attracted quite a bit of attention and a small crowd was gathered around it. As flames enveloped the tank, the Americans could hear the trapped Japanese screaming in agony. Some of the observers turned away, but one officer stood by yelling out his own hatred of the enemy. "Fry, you bastards, fry!"

Thus, by the evening of October 20, General Krueger's Sixth Army was dug in along Leyte's east coast from the outskirts of Tacloban as far south as Dulag. A gap of about ten miles separated Sibert's X Corps on the right from Hodge's XXIV Corps, but the initial Japanese resistance had not been strong and there was no reason to fear that the beachhead would remain split for long. In Sibert's hands were the Tacloban airstrip and vital Hill 522, while Hodge's men were in position to seize the airfield at Dulag. And in a separate landing seventy miles away the 21st Infantry Regiment, 24th Division, had secured the entrance to Sogod Bay, on Leyte's southern coast, providing a passageway for American PT boats to enter the Mindanao Sea. All of this had been accomplished at the cost of less than 250 casualties, mostly wounded. Future gains would not be so easy.

While the infantry had been carving out the beachhead, the less glamorous but equally important work of hauling thousands of tons of supplies and equipment ashore had been going on full speed. This was in many respects the most crucial part of the landing operation, for troops without supplies could neither advance nor repel an enemy counterattack nor, for that matter, even eat. All day long, then, ships' companies, naval beach parties, army engineers, and other service troops sweated at their work in the hot Philippine sun. Transport commanders brought their ships in as close as they dared. Then the crews moved supplies and vehicles onto landing ships and smaller craft which ferried them to the shore. Some of the latter vessels could move right up to the beach and lower their ramps on the dry sand. Others grounded 100 or more yards offshore, necessitating a further shift of their cargo to still smaller craft. On one beach bulldozers erected a ramp of earth thirty-five yards out into the water to reach grounded landing ships. Nevertheless, some supplies spilled into the sea and were lost, others reached shore in a water-soaked condition. One bulldozer operator attempted to drive directly to the beach from a landing ship grounded some distance offshore. He promptly found himself over his head in seven feet of water and had to be rescued from his sunken vehicle. Other vehicles, trucks and jeeps, churned shoreward through several feet of water only to stall on the edge of the beach, blocking further landing operations until they could be pulled out of the way.

Fortunately for the success of these efforts, few Japanese planes appeared and General Makino's artillery and mortar fire, while at times intense, was not too accurate. The Japanese gunners scored some hits, but did little in the way of major damage. Indeed, despite difficulties, cargo piled up on some beaches faster than it could be hauled inland, a situation not corrected everywhere until the next day. In one area amphibious trucks hauled supplies directly from ship to frontline user, making delivery within an hour of the initial request. By sunset of A-day, as the Seventh Fleet transports began laying smoke screens to counter any possible Japanese air raid, more than 100,000 tons of cargo had been hauled ashore, with most of it already dispersed to dump areas inland.

Unloading continued for three more days and was nearly completed by the evening of October 24. The entire landing operation placed ashore a total of over 130,000 men and more than 200,000 tons of supplies and equipment, enough to support the troops for a month. Roads, supply dumps, and airstrips were being carved out in the marshy terrain, and preparations were speeded to meet the Japanese air attacks which everyone knew could not be much longer in coming. The initial landings on Leyte, in the words of General Krueger, "had been accomplished much more easily than had been anticipated."

The invasion of Leyte was thus successfully launched. And those who participated in initiating it had a right to be proud. But for all the thousands of men who played a role in this great venture, October 20, 1944, was for one individual more than any other the culmination of hope and ambition. For Douglas MacArthur, A-day was a personal triumph.

On board the cruiser *Nashville*, the general had slept well the night before. He rose shortly before dawn and, as he dressed, reminisced with an aide about the last time he had seen Leyte, as a young engineer officer forty-one years earlier. He ate a hearty breakfast and then, corncob in mouth, strolled to the bridge to watch the first assault waves land on Red Beach. For a while he observed the 24th Division troops pour ashore and then, satisfied with what he had seen, returned to his cabin for an early lunch.

Shortly before two MacArthur walked out on deck wearing a fresh uniform, sunglasses, and the familiar gold-braided hat. In his pocket was an old-fashioned revolver, once his father's, which he carried as insurance against being captured alive. He descended a ladder to a waiting landing barge, already filled with staff officers and newspapermen. In this group, also, was Philippine President Sergio Osmeña, whose emotions must surely have matched MacArthur's.

Osmeña's presence, however, had not been completely voluntary. MacArthur's invitation to join the invasion forces had found him in Washington with the Philippine government-in-exile, and Osmeña had declined to leave. He was badly needed in the American capital, he said, and would be more valuable there. Actually, the Philippine president had serious doubts about returning to the islands under MacArthur's control rather than on the basis of some formal understanding with the United States government. But MacArthur was not one to take no for an answer. To change Osmeña's mind, he immediately dispatched Major General Richard J. Marshall, an important staff officer who had escaped from Corregidor with MacArthur, accompanied by a high-ranking Filipino officer carrying letters from guerrilla leaders to the effect that they expected Osmeña to return with the first troops. But Osmeña was still hesitant, and only after an interview with President Roosevelt did he depart to join MacArthur. Now he stood near him, with the Leyte beach just a few minutes away.

As the boat moved shoreward, a ripple of excitement ran through the passengers. They chattered animatedly, pointed to the beach, and checked their maps to orient themselves. MacArthur, an aide recalled later, "seemed as eager as a kid going to his first party." He smiled, turned to General Sutherland, his chief of staff, and announced triumphantly, "Well, believe it or not, we're here."

The barge grounded to a halt about forty or fifty yards offshore and the ramp went down into a foot of water. As cameras whirred away to record the historic scene, the tall, happy general, several officers around him, splashed impressively ashore on Red

Beach. The picture of this landing is one of the most famous of World War II and it has given rise to considerable controversy. In his memoirs MacArthur claimed that he had gone in with the third assault wave, a statement confirmed by one of his aides who was present. But other officers who were there and a great number of accompanying newspapermen have disputed this, and it is clear that at least four hours had passed after H-hour before the general went ashore. There was still, of course, considerable danger at this time, for Japanese artillery and mortar shells continued to drop along the beaches, and the landing area was well within range of stray small-arms fire. Indeed, after the war General Yamashita stated that had the Japanese been aware of MacArthur's presence on the beach, they would have thrown everything possible into a suicide air raid to kill the American general. But who would have thought MacArthur would take such a risk? Even the pictures published a few days after the landing had not convinced Yamashita. He had been sure they were fakes, posed in New Guinea, and that MacArthur was safely back in Australia.

Once ashore on Leyte however, MacArthur did not pause to admire the white sand. Watched by unbelieving American troops, he strode quickly inland to inspect the damage done by the bombardment. An old Filipino stepped up to greet him. "Good afternoon, Sir Field Marshal!" he exclaimed. "Glad to see you." Then MacArthur returned to the beach and stood before a microphone set up by army signalmen. In a voice deep with emotion, his hands trembling perceptibly, he began to speak: "People of the Philippines," he said, "I have returned!"

viii *Destroy the Enemy on Leyte!*

OCTOBER 20 was obviously an American day in the Philippines. But the Japanese had also been busy. At Thirty-fifth Army headquarters on Cebu, General Suzuki was still unaware of Tokyo's decision to fight the decisive land battle on Leyte. But he had received the order to activate *Sho*-1 and, in accordance with earlier plans for a delaying action, had already dispatched part of the Japanese 30th Division to reinforce General Makino. Informed of the actual invasion at about noon, Suzuki ordered additional 30th Division troops as well as small elements of the 102nd Division and the 57th Independent Brigade to move to Leyte immediately. He himself was preparing to advance his own headquarters to Ormoc, on Leyte's west coast. Communications with Makino, already bad, would go out entirely that evening, and for the next two days Suzuki would have to operate in the dark—as, of course, would Makino.

Along with ground reinforcement, Japanese air strength was shifting toward the Leyte area in preparation for an air assault in coordination with the planned fleet attack. An air strike on the eve of the naval assault was essential, not only to cover the approach of the fleet but also to dispose of part of the huge American naval force that the Japanese warships would have to face. From Formosa, then, Admiral Fukudome's Fifth Base Air Force was set to move to Luzon, while shorter-range planes of General Tominaga's Fourth Air Army were readying to concentrate in the Visayas. On October 20 however, only a few Japanese aircraft were based close enough and in adequate operational condition to attempt to hit the invaders. One plane put a torpedo into the cruiser *Honolulu,* but the rest did little damage. This situation could be expected to improve. By the evening of October 23 all available army and navy planes—some 400 or more aircraft of all types—would be in position, just in time to cover the approach of Combined Fleet units.

These warships were also on the way. Two hours before the first American soldier set foot on Leyte, Admiral Toyoda had issued the *Sho*-1 execute order for the Combined Fleet, confirming his previous preparatory directives. To allow sufficient time for all his forces to reach their proper positions simultaneously, Toyoda once more postponed the target date for the attack, advancing it from the 24th to the 25th. This would give the Americans additional time to clear the beaches, but the delay could not be helped.

Admiral Kurita's 1st Striking Force reached Brunei Bay at noon on the 20th and began refueling and other final preparations for the attack. Ozawa's Main Body sortied from the Inland Sea a few hours later on its decoy mission. And Shima's 2nd Striking Force was at Mako, in the Pescadores, awaiting orders to sail for Manila and escort army reinforcements to Leyte.

At the Philippine capital, meanwhile, neither Marshal Terauchi nor General Yamashita knew of the shift in Philippine defense strategy decided upon by Army Section of Imperial General Headquarters. They had only fragmentary information about the fighting on Leyte and Yamashita, at least, was primarily concerned with how events there would affect his preparations to defend Luzon. The latter were progressing slowly, especially since many of the newly arrived members of the Fourteenth Area Army staff were as yet unfamiliar with the general situation in the Philippines. As a matter of fact, General Muto, Yamashita's new chief of staff, had reached Luzon only that afternoon.

Muto's arrival was perhaps indicative of the generally disorganized state of affairs at Fourteenth Area Army headquarters. It was also an unhappy portent of things to come. His plane had landed for fuel on Palawan Island, southwest of Luzon, and been set afire on the ground by an American bomber. Muto managed to escape by throwing himself into a muddy ditch, but he lost all his baggage and arrived at Clark Field on the afternoon of the

20th with his uniform torn and begrimed. At Clark he found that he had not been expected and it was several hours before he could get a car to take him to Manila. In the blacked-out capital the driver picked his way carefully through the rutted, bomb-cratered streets before finally discovering that Yamashita's head-quarters were not in the city but rather at nearby Fort McKinley. As they drove the last few miles, Muto recalled later, the sky above was clear and "a new moon embraced a lone glittering star."

It was after ten when he reported to Yamashita, still wearing his muddy clothes. The army commander took one look at his chief of staff and suggested that he take a bath. Later, clad in clean clothes, Muto sat down to eat while Yamashita briefed him on the situation in the Philippines. Muto had much to learn. Indeed, when Yamashita told him about the landing on Leyte, the chief of staff had to conceal his embarrassment and explain that he had never heard of the island.

Within the next few months he would hear a great deal more about it. Even as Muto ate, Colonel Sugita, who had finally arrived from Tokyo, was filling in Terauchi's staff on the decision to make Leyte the decisive battleground in the Philippines. The conference at Southern Army headquarters ended shortly before midnight. Almost immediately a second meeting began between Southern and Fourteenth Area Army staff officers. As soon as it was over, Major General Toshio Nishimura, the Fourteenth Area Army assistant chief of staff, hastened to Fort McKinley to awaken Yamashita with the news. Terauchi's staff, however, did not interrupt his sleep.

In the morning Colonel Sugita made a formal presentation to the Southern Army commander. Terauchi, "in high spirits," as Sugita describes him, welcomed the change in policy as right and proper—naturally enough, since it matched his own previous recommendations. Not so Yamashita. At Fort McKinley news of the decision for an all-out battle on Leyte had come, in Muto's words, like "a bolt from the blue." The Fourteenth Area Army commander was shocked. Both he and his staff were committed to fighting on Luzon and they viewed this last-minute switch in plans as dangerous and completely wrong.

Since the decision had come from Tokyo, Yamashita could not

refuse to obey it. Yet, pending receipt of a formal order implementing the change, he and his staff were free to question it, at
least to Terauchi. In conferences throughout the 21st at Southern
Army headquarters they raised several objections. First of all,
they pointed out the difficulty of transporting reinforcements to
Leyte in the face of the powerful American carrier-based air
strength already in evidence in the area. Second, assembling the
troops and supplies and enough shipping to carry them to Leyte
would take so long that reinforcements could not possibly reach
that island in time to ensure success. Furthermore, it was still not
clear that Leyte was the primary American target in the Philippines. Betting everything on the defense of Leyte would leave the
strategically more important island of Luzon stripped of its defenses and an easy victim for invasion.

Finally, argued Yamashita, the decision should at least await
the outcome of the air and sea phase of the *Sho* operation. Success or failure in this would obviously determine the chances of a
land victory on Leyte.

Yamashita and his staff went to bed that night believing they
had at least gained a postponement of the Leyte decision until
after the conclusion of the forthcoming air and naval battle. But
the next morning, October 22, Marshal Terauchi summoned both
Yamashita and General Tominaga to his headquarters. He
handed them each a copy of a brief formal order:

1. The providential hour has come for the total
destruction of the proud enemy.

2. The Fourteenth Area Army, in cooperation
with naval and air forces, will muster all possible
strength to totally destroy the enemy on Leyte.

In accordance with the *Sho* plan, Tominaga had already
ordered an all-out air assault beginning on the 24th to support the
attack of the Combined Fleet. So he simply continued his preparations and made ready to fly down the next day to his advance
command post on the island of Negros. For Yamashita, however,
the Southern Army order meant a complete change in plans and a
tremendous amount of hard and complicated work to implement
it. When he returned to Fort McKinley his officers, recalled Muto,
"were at first dumbfounded and then highly indignant." Bitterly
they berated Terauchi and his staff and their unwillingness to lis-

ten to reason. Not only was the order a mistake, but, as one of them said, "it was well-nigh impossible to execute." Finally the angry Muto dispatched General Nishimura to Southern Army headquarters to make certain there was no error. Nishimura received a simple answer. The orders, he was told, were those of Imperial General Headquarters. The Emperor's orders must be followed.

That afternoon Yamashita sent General Suzuki an urgent message describing the change in plans. The Thirty-fifth Army would be strongly reinforced on Leyte with troops and supplies. Overwhelming Japanese air and naval strength would also descend on the area. "A concerted effort . . . may be expected," said Yamashita, "on the 24th and 25th of October."

Yamashita's words concealed his apprehensions about the course ahead. But these apprehensions were not shared outside his headquarters. Visiting Marshal Terauchi that evening, General Muto found the Southern Army commander and his staff "in extremely high spirits and very optimistic. . . . They seemed to believe that the Navy and the Air Force would, at any moment, destroy the American forces which had entered Leyte Gulf." And at Thirty-fifth Army headquarters on Cebu there was equal optimism. "We had hopeful discussions," recalled Major General Yoshiharu Tomochika, Suzuki's chief of staff. "We were determined to take offensive after offensive and clean up American forces on Leyte." Some of the officers talked about capturing MacArthur and then "demanding the surrender of the entire American Army."

Until the arrival of reinforcements, however, and the anticipated air and sea victory, all General Suzuki could do was to order the 16th Division to hold its forward positions. But even this was rapidly becoming impossible.

ix Expanding the Beachhead

DAWN of October 21—A plus 1—had found the Sixth Army beachhead looking very much like the disordered morning after the night before. Empty ration containers, ammunition boxes, gas masks, wrappers from cigarettes and candy bars, and still other reminders of the first day's activities lay scattered across the sand. Downed trees, felled and thrown about by the heavy shelling, marked the ragged edge of the beach, and improvised shelters and haphazardly parked trucks and jeeps completed the random pattern of the scene. A more regular design could be noted along the water. Here landing craft, ships, and barges lay grounded at right angles to the shore, their bows thrust into the wet sand, disgorging a steady flow of cargo, their sterns pointed out into Leyte Gulf, swaying gently in the easy current.

The beach itself was pockmarked with foxholes of all sizes and shapes. Scattered and intermittent but heavy rains during the night had formed pools in these and other depressions along the ground and the already stagnant water gave off an offensive odor. Farther inland a heavy, almost sweet smell rose from the wet, frequently decaying jungle vegetation. The whole area, reported one witness, "already looked as old and weary as war itself."

The American troops did not pause to consider such matters. They immediately began to push inland, intent on expanding the beachhead and preparing the way for the drive across Leyte. All four division commanders were firmly established in headquarters ashore, and Sibert and Hodge set up their corps headquarters shortly thereafter. The Sixth Army was now bent on securing the Leyte Valley and its important roads, airfields, and potential base sites before the Japanese could reorganize and offer firmer resistance, including, perhaps, a major counterattack.

The northern Leyte Valley was the target for General Sibert's X Corps. But first Sibert would have to secure his flank by seizing Tacloban and the shores of San Juanico Strait. At 8 A.M. on the 21st, then, part of the 1st Cavalry Division struck northward out of its beachhead toward these objectives. The troopers moved forward, hampered only by the swampy terrain, until they were stopped late in the morning by about two companies of Japanese dug in atop a small hill blocking the main road. While some of the attackers remained to handle this situation, the rest boarded amphibious vehicles and continued the advance over water. Having thus bypassed the last enemy resistance before Tacloban, forward elements of the cavalry division entered the Leyte capital shortly before noon.

Tacloban had been continuously occupied by the Japanese since May, 1942, but the Filipinos had not forgotten the United States. As the troopers moved cautiously into the town, they met a cheering reception committee. Happy Filipinos lined the streets, waving American flags and bestowing flowers, eggs, and fruit upon the surprised cavalrymen—who had never before had the pleasure of being greeted as liberators. Some of the citizens even provided the Americans with hefty drinks of "tuba juice," the local painkiller. Less than a week earlier the residents of Tacloban had been forced by the Japanese to participate in a "Victory Parade" to celebrate the supposed Japanese victory off Formosa. Now the Filipinos really had something to celebrate—and they showed it by the warmth of their welcome.

But not all of Tacloban could participate immediately. Parts of the town still remained in Japanese hands, and it took most of the day for the troopers, moving cautiously from house to house, to clean out the rest of Tacloban. Tanks and even field artillery had to be used before the last Japanese soldier could be dug from his hiding place under a native hut or in some local vegetable garden. Late afternoon found most of the city in American hands and General Mudge, the 1st Cavalry commander, made a triumphal tour in an open tank. At one point, after the general's tank had shouldered its way past an overturned truck used by the Japanese as a roadblock, Mudge came upon a Filipino guerrilla leader standing guard over some forty Formosan laborers. The Formosans stood quietly, hands upraised in surrender, apparently quite happy over their liberation from the Japanese.

Meanwhile, other 1st Cavalry units had been hammering away at the Japanese hill position still holding out below the town. Only partially successful that afternoon, the troops attacked again on the morning of the 22nd after a heavy bombardment by mortars, artillery, and planes from Admiral Sprague's escort carriers. This time the men gained the summit, and by evening the entire Tacloban area had been secured. Still other 1st Cavalry elements were occupying ground to the west of the city, a job completed without too much difficulty on the 23rd.

That day also witnessed another highly dramatic scene as General MacArthur officially re-established the Philippine civil government in Tacloban. MacArthur had been ashore daily since his first visit, walking along the shore, chatting jovially with troops and correspondents, asking unit commanders, "How do you find the Nip?" and enjoying himself hugely. Now, on the afternoon of A plus 3, MacArthur stood on the steps of the Tacloban municipal building to formally return the Philippine government to power. With President Osmeña at his side and high-ranking American officers grouped around them, MacArthur broadcast his restoration speech and his pledge to liberate all of the Philippines. For some reason few of the townspeople were present, either through ignorance of the event or because they were unaware that they might attend it. Those who did witness it, however, watched approvingly as a bugler sounded "To the Colors" and an honor guard from the 1st Cavalry slowly hoisted the American and Filipino flags.

Even as this ceremony was taking place, still other elements of General Mudge's division were pushing north of Tacloban along the Leyte shore of San Juanico Strait. Some of the men boarded landing craft to hasten the advance. Of this amphibious force, part went ashore on the Leyte side of the strait while the rest landed, unopposed, on Samar. Within a few days, the troops had consolidated the area against slight resistance and assured General Sibert of control of San Juanico Strait. The northern flank of the beachhead was now secured and the narrow strait closed as an avenue for possible Japanese amphibious reinforcements. All of this had been accomplished with relatively light losses. Japanese resistance, while occasionally stiff, had not been effective.

Indeed, so confused was the Japanese situation around Tacloban and so disorganized was General Makino's headquarters during its hasty withdrawal from the area that no one in authority in the 16th Division had any clear idea of the extent of the American advance in the north.

Japanese defenses against the 24th Division, on the left of the X Corps attack, were stronger and more effective. Here the greater part of the 33rd Infantry still remained to contest the American advance. Ironically, General Krueger and the Sixth Army staff had expected the X Corps to meet its heaviest resistance around Tacloban, rather than farther south. When he needed a regiment for the landing at Sogod Bay, then, Krueger had not chosen to weaken the 1st Cavalry Division but instead had taken the 21st Infantry from the 24th Division. General Irving's division was thus operating with only two regiments on Red Beach, and this proved a decided handicap in his initial efforts to move inland.

Just how difficult this might be was quickly apparent. Beginning about an hour or so after midnight of A-day and continuing until dawn, nearly a battalion of 33rd Infantry troops threw themselves at the front lines of Colonel Newman's 34th Infantry, which held the right half of the division perimeter. Attacking in the dark with machine-gun and mortar support, hurling grenades and firing as they came, screaming *"Banzai"* at the top of their lungs, the Japanese quickly overran or swept around several of the forward American positions.

For Newman's men it was a night of sheer hell. Even many of the veterans in the regiment had never had such a terrifying experience. They fought their attackers at close range, firing at shadows, the flash of a gun, the noise of shouting Japanese. Dodging grenades, they threw their own in reply and fired their weapons until they ran out of ammunition. As the Japanese swarmed around the American foxholes, the fight became a series of individual actions, in which groups of two or three defenders in separate positions fought off repeated attacks by squads of Japanese. When American machine-gunners fell, riflemen quickly shifted over to take their place. When men were wounded, their comrades tried to drag them to the rear. The defenders crawled on their bellies from position to position or slithered through mud and long grass to avoid Japanese charges or to outflank the attacking enemy.

Instances of individual heroism were numerous. One almost incredible example was that of Private Harold H. Moon, Jr. Isolated by the first Japanese charge, which killed all the men around him, he held by himself a key point on his company perimeter and beat back repeated enemy attempts to take it. During four hours of almost constant fighting, he threw grenades until they were gone, fired his submachine gun and the weapons of his dead companions, directed American mortar fire on a Japanese machine-gun position, and yelled curses and challenges at his attackers. Wounded in the leg, for one frightening hour he fought a personal duel with a single Japanese officer who circled his position and threw grenades until Moon finally shot him in the head. As dawn approached, he purposely exposed himself to draw fire from a Japanese machine gun so that other Americans could locate it and knock it out. Finally, an entire platoon of Japanese charged his foxhole. Sitting on the ground, his submachine gun between his legs, Moon killed eighteen of his attackers before they overran him. By now, however, other Americans had moved up and were able to drive off the Japanese and restore the perimeter line. For his heroism, Private Moon was posthumously awarded the Congressional Medal of Honor.

Similar events were taking place at many points on the 34th Infantry perimeter, and nowhere were the Japanese able to make a breakthrough. Shortly after daylight American artillery and carrier planes struck at the enemy, breaking up the attack and driving back the Japanese. The night assault had cost General Makino's forces more than 200 dead. American losses were surprisingly light.

This was the last counterattack against the 34th Infantry sector of the beachhead. After collecting the wounded, repairing equipment and issuing more ammunition, and eating breakfast, the regiment opened its own attack on the morning of October 21. The objective was a hill mass beginning about a mile inland from the beachhead and rising to the west and north. This high ground dominated the 24th Division's entrance into the northern Leyte Valley, and it was up to the 34th Infantry to clear the way. In four days of bitter fighting against well-entrenched and stubbornly resisting Japanese of the 33rd Infantry, Colonel Newman's regiment carved a tenuous strip across the southern slopes and peaks of the hill mass. With elements of the less-occupied 1st cavalry Division moving south to protect Newman's flank, the men of the 34th were free to concentrate on pushing forward.

The attack consisted of a series of fights for individual hilltops, each one defended by Japanese dug in on the peak and reverse slopes and supported by others who crept along the ridges and tried to encircle the American flanks. The Japanese, well supplied with machine guns and what appeared to be an unlimited number of grenades, fought bravely and well. But they could not resist the steady pressure of the 34th Infantry nor the heavy, continuous shelling of the supporting American artillery. By evening of the 25th the tactically important portions of the hill mass were in American hands.

Meanwhile General Irving's other regiment, the 19th Infantry, was just as busy. On the 21st the men fought their way over the rest of Hill 522 and pushed through Japanese defenses into the town of Palo. They beat off several 33rd Infantry counterattacks during the night and spent most of the next two days hunting out small pockets of Japanese in and around Palo and in hidden caves on the slopes of Hill 522. During the mopping up of the Palo area, First Lieutenant Harry F. Davis had the honor of capturing the 24th Division's first prisoner. Since very few Japanese allowed themselves to be taken, Davis's action was most gratifying to the division intelligence section.

The Japanese had made several night raids on Palo. The last and fiercest came at about 3 A.M. on October 24. Immediately beforehand, according to a 16th Division report, the Japanese "with great trepidation . . . committed the colors of the 33rd Infantry Regiment to the flames." Then the regimental commander, Colonel Tatsunosuke Suzuki, led a picked force of about seventy-five men against Palo. Herding a terrified group of Filipino civilians in front of them, the Japanese had penetrated to the center of Palo and begun to raise havoc. Knocking out some American guns and capturing others, the raiders set fire to trucks, shot up jeeps and slashed their tires, and fired wildly around the town square with two captured 50-caliber machine guns. From here they continued their charge through Palo. They threw explosives into houses and vehicles, set a supply dump ablaze, and killed several wounded Americans lying helpless in an evacuation hospital.

Suzuki's primary objective was to destroy the bridge over the Palo River, at the north end of town. A dozen men guarded this bridge, and most of them fell victim to the first volley of Japanese fire. By now, however, the Americans in Palo were beginning to get organized. The remaining bridge guards, reinforced by a platoon of engineers, put up a stiff defense, and Suzuki's men were unable to place explosives under the span. A few Japanese managed to get across the bridge, but they were quickly killed. As more and more American troops closed in on the area, Colonel Suzuki's chances of success grew smaller and smaller. Most of his men died at the bridge, their mission unaccomplished. He and a score of others were killed by an American machine-gunner named Frank Wisnieuski not too far from the Palo church. In the light of morning some sixty Japanese bodies were found scattered throughout the town, so many, in fact, that the Palo police chief posted a sign reminding the people that the police station was "not a Morgue" and that cadavers were "NOT to be deposited There.

This was the high-water mark of Japanese resistance in the Palo area. On the 24th and 25th, 19th Infantry troops drove tenacious Japanese defenders off high ground to the west, sent elements south to tie in with the 96th Division of Hodge's XXIV Corps, and pushed about a battalion well to the southwest. These efforts plus those of the 34th Infantry meant that the main road from Palo into the Leyte Valley was now open to the 24th Division. For all the heavy fighting of the past few days, casualties had not been excessive. "The morale of the men is high," reported General Irving. "They have had no rest, but they are in good condition."

While the X Corps had been pushing inland, the XXIV Corps had been executing a gradual turning movement, designed to capture the airstrips west of Dulag and close north against the left of the X Corps. This would also serve to open the southern doorway to the Leyte Valley.

The anchor for the X Corps turning movement, on the corps right, was General Bradley's 96th Division. Like the 24th Division, it was operating with only two regiments since General Krueger was still holding its third regiment in Sixth Army reserve. Fortunately for Bradley's men, they encountered somewhat less opposition than Irving's troops had had to deal with. The bulk of this opposition was provided initially by elements of the Japanese 9th Infantry entrenched on Labiranan Head, a small rise guarding the southern approaches to Catmon Hill.

The capture of Labiranan Head was the work of a single Battalion—Lieutenant Colonel Edwin O. List's 1st Battalion, 383rd Infantry—but supporting it were naval guns, most of the division artillery, and planes from the escort carriers. List's men had moved to the base of the head on A-day and in the process encountered their first Japanese, a soldier who leaped from the deep grass onto the back of Technician Fifth Grade Victor L. Glenn. Glenn shook him off, and a bayonet dispatched the Japanese before he could do any harm. But then Japanese machine guns held up any further advance.

The next morning, after an airstrike and a three-hour naval and artillery bombardment, the 1st Battalion attacked up the head. This proved a frustrating experience. The men moved forward against machine-gun and light artillery fire and seemed to be making good progress. Around noon, however, naval gunfire began to hit the hilltop. Colonel List had neither requested this shelling nor had much warning that it was coming. His forward elements had to fall back in a hurry and in the ensuing confusion almost came under American artillery and mortar fire before they made good their escape. With the 1st Battalion troops off the hill, the artillery fire continued through the night and well into the morning of October 22. This proved decisive. A second infantry attack that afternoon succeeded in taking Labiranan Head within several hours. A Japanese counterattack in the evening met the combined fire of three of the four division artillery battalions, sufficient to repel the assault. With the hill secured, elements of the 1st Battalion were now able to push up the coastal road to the east of Catmon Hill.

Meanwhile the rest of the 383rd Infantry had been moving northwest through deep swamps in an attempt to reach the northern approaches of Catmon Hill, preparatory to an attack by the entire regiment on that height from both ends. Trusting to the effectiveness of the swamps as a natural barrier, General Makino had placed no troops in this area. The American advance was thus unhindered save by the heat, occasional artillery fire from Catmon Hill, and the nocturnal activities of a few infiltrating Japanese riflemen. The only real contact came on the afternoon of October 23, when the lead American company flushed a group of Japanese bathing in the river. In the fight that followed, the regiment killed several dozen Japanese. It seemed a small and easy victory to the men and, as someone commented later, it "was at last more exciting than half-marching, half-swimming through the marsh." And it brought the regiment to the northern end of the hill mass dominated by Catmon Hill.

On the left of the 383rd Infantry, its sister regiment, the 382nd, had also been advancing unopposed through the swamps. By now, however, General Makino had become worried by this gap in his defenses and shifted the bulk of the 20th Infantry north from the Dulag area to fill the hole. The 382nd began encountering 20th Infantry troops on October 23 and the next morning drove two companies of Japanese out of fortified positions blocking the American advance. Continuing the push on the 25th, the regiment overcame several Japanese strongpoints. In one action, the attacking troops were astounded to see a Japanese officer charge an American tank and hack away at its bow gun with his saber. The officer quickly joined his ancestors while the tank, of course, remained undamaged.

By nightfall of October 25 the 96th Division had completely isolated Catmon Hill, all but surrounding it, had swung the right half of the XXIV Corps advance in a 90-degree arc so that it now faced north, and was in patrol contact with X Corps elements farther up the coast. The last remaining barrier to the division's advance into the Leyte Valley was the town of Tabontabon. This was a key Japanese supply center and trail junction, located about three miles northwest of Catmon Hill and defended by a reinforced battalion of the 9th Infantry. Fortunately for the Americans, the bulk of the 20th Infantry had been driven off to the west and would not participate in the defense of Tabontabon.

Patrols from the 383rd Infantry, moving west from the upper end of the Catmon Hill mass, had probed 9th Infantry positions in and around the town on October 24 and 25. Heavy Japanese small-arms and mortar fire had kept the Americans at their distance, however, and it was left for the 382nd Infantry to make the actual attack on Tabontabon. But the initial patrol action had revealed the Japanese defenses to be solid: a series of interconnected trenches and pillboxes throughout the town, backed up by mortars and artillery. The 382nd would have its work cut out for it.

Late on October 26, after an intensive artillery preparation, two battalions of the regiment forded the shoulder-deep Guinarona River, just south of Tabontabon. Despite intense machine-gun and rifle fire, they pushed their way into the town itself. Here the attackers were met by increasingly heavy fire from well-camouflaged Japanese positions in, under, and around the houses, and even in the steeple of the church. Ditches and trenches along the streets connected one strongpoint to another and provided additional firing positions for the 9th Infantry troops. At dusk the Japanese laid down a heavy artillery and mortar barrage and followed it up with a counterattack that swept the Americans back across the Guinarona. The two sides shelled each other during the night while the Americans cared for their wounded and prepared to try again in the morning.

A heavy artillery barrage preceded the attack on the 27th. Mindful of the previous day's failure, however, many of the infantrymen hesitated to plunge across the Guinarona. Finally the regimental commander, Colonel Macy L. Dill, decided to do something. He snapped his pistol from its holster, yelled at his men to follow, and, taking the boldest route, ran forward across a small, fire-swept bridge. Encouraged by his example, the men of the 382nd now pressed vigorously ahead. They fought their way into the town and began methodically to clean out the Japanese positions. By noon the entire regiment was in Tabontabon and by nightfall had occupied a large part of the town.

The fight ended the next day, but not before almost every house in Tabontabon had been destroyed in the effort to dig out the tenacious Japanese defenders from their underground positions. The victors counted some 350 enemy bodies, about ten times the number of American dead. Any wounded Japanese who lived had apparently escaped. These statistics and the grim, stubborn defense that caused them were a bitter foretaste of what could be expected in the long campaign ahead.

South of the 96th Division, on the left of the XXIV Corps attack, the 7th Division was learning an equally hard lesson. General Arnold's troops had pushed forward on October 21 against only scattered opposition, overwhelming several minor strongpoints to seize the Dulag airstrip and continue the drive to the west. The division was moving along both sides of the road from Dulag to Burauen, seven miles inland, with the primary objective of taking three airstrips located northwest of Burauen. The advancing troops were hampered by the heat and the difficulty of maintaining contact with each other in the deep swamps or in other areas where the thick cogon grass grew shoulder high. Supported by tanks and artillery, however, they experienced only minor problems in smashing Japanese defenses. Indeed, boasted one regimental report, "the reduction of pillboxes was right down our alley." The Japanese must have felt the same way. A 20th Infantry soldier wrote despondently in his diary of the apparently irresistible American advance and the constant "gunfire and bombardment." "I feel alive during the night and dead during the day," he noted. But then, becoming more resolute, he concluded: "Though life and death are separated by a thin sheet of paper, I will not die until I see the face of a Yankee."

Planes from the escort carriers, artillery, and tanks helped clear the way for the 7th Division advance on October 22. The 32nd Infantry, on the right, found the going somewhat slow, bogged down almost as much by the marshy terrain as hindered by the Japanese defenses. In the attack on one position, Second Lieutenant Carl F. Stellman, Jr., crawled within seventy-five yards of a Japanese field artillery battery defended by hidden machine guns. Locating the enemy artillery pieces, he directed fire on them from American tanks and remained in his exposed post until the tanks and accompanying infantry could close in and wipe out the entire position.

By evening of the 22nd the lack of strong Japanese resistance had convinced General Arnold that he could move rapidly if he pressed vigorously ahead. Accordingly, he decided to launch a full-scale attack with everything he had to capture the Burauen airstrips before the Japanese could get set to defend them. Although Arnold did not know it, the success of this attack would be aided by General Makino's decision to shift the bulk of the 20th Infantry from the Dulag-Burauen area to fill the gap in Japanese defenses farther north. This move, on the night of the 22nd, left only a few 16th Division elements to oppose the 7th Division advance, with the important task of holding the airstrips relegated primarily to the army and navy airfield defense units stationed there.

The 7th Division assault formation on the 23rd was designed for speed. Tanks formed the armored tip of a huge flying wedge, with infantry filling out the wings and backing up the tanks. In the fierce heat of the tropical day, the men on foot struggled forward through the swamps and thick grass and barely kept up with the faster-moving tanks on the road. Only a few scattered riflemen attempted unsuccessfully to contest the advance, as the 20th Infantry pulled north in accordance with Makino's orders. In the course of this withdrawal, Colonel Keijiro Hokoda, the regimental commander, lost his life trying to make sure that all his men got out safely. By evening the San Pablo airstrip, easternmost of the three fields, was in 7th Division hands. The lead tanks had reached the outskirts of Burauen, two miles ahead, but pulled back behind the infantry for the night. Failure to provide the tanks with infantry cover in their forward position meant that ground already taken had to be given up and would have to be fought for all over again in the morning.

Despite this blow to their morale, the tankers led off the attack on the 24th in good spirits. This time the infantry stayed close behind them and the assault swept over the Bayug airstrip and reached Burauen by midmorning. Here the advance was halted temporarily when some of the tanks were damaged by Japanese mines, blocking the road and forcing the others to move around them. A few men passed out in the heat, but only scattered small-arms fire hit the Americans. Soon the tanks and infantry had forced their way into the town. Within Burauen only a handful of defenders were left. Well dug-in in "spider holes"— underground excavations with several exits through which the defender could emerge to fire—the Japanese resisted bravely but futilely.

"Our formidable enemy," reported General Makino to Thirty-fifth Army headquarters, "is the enemy's tanks. We are now making desperate efforts to destroy them . . . but we regret that we have no weapons effective enough." At Burauen, these "desperate efforts" consisted of individual Japanese crawling from their spider holes and attempting to place explosive charges beneath or against the sides of the lumbering American vehicles. These suicidal missions were generally unsuccessful. By midafternoon of the 24th, the tank-infantry teams had dug out all the Japanese they could find and the town was secured.

The main Japanese resistance came at the Buri airstrip, a mile or so northeast of Burauen, where about 1,000 defenders were holding out. The Japanese were strongly prepared in mutually supporting and well-camouflaged pillboxes and entrenchments, generously equipped with machine guns. They had mined large portions of the airfield with 100-pound bombs, buried nose up, some of which could be set off electronically from nearby positions. The area, it was clear, would be a hard nut to crack.

The 32nd Infantry Regiment, Lieutenant Colonel John M. Finn commanding, drew the mission of capturing Buri airstrip. While the rest of the 7th Division advanced north and south through Burauen, Colonel Finn's men found themselves faced with increasing opposition. Their first attack on the airstrip on October 24 was halted by heavy Japanese fire. A counterattack then threw the American regiment back in a disorganized withdrawal. In the confusion of the action portions of the 32nd lost contact with each other and some of the units were heavily infiltrated by Japanese infantry who tried to capture the machine guns and turn them on the retreating Americans. Casualties were numerous. Major Leigh H. Mathias, commanding the 1st Battalion, was wounded by machine-gun fire while trying to locate a lost unit. Private Charles J. Kaczanowicz crawled on his stomach to the machine-gun position and knocked it out singlehanded with grenades so that Mathias could be evacuated. By late afternoon the situation had become so bad that Colonel Finn directed his regiment to fall back toward the San Pablo airstrip, where the men dug in for the night. Japanese attempts at infiltration under cover of darkness were driven off by artillery.

The next day's fighting proved somewhat more successful. Despite additional casualties, the regiment fought its way to the edge of the airstrip, repulsed a *Banzai* charge in the late afternoon, and held its position there during the night. The following morning artillery and tanks supported the attack, and the 32nd began to make solid progress against the enemy fortifications. With heavier firepower now backing them up, the infantrymen knocked out the Japanese pillboxes on the forward edge of the field and began moving across the airstrip itself. One of the tanks advanced ahead onto the airstrip, lumbering back and forth and spraying both sides of the field with machine-gun fire. When some of this fire began falling on the American troops, Private Jack McDuffie raced across the open field despite the rain of Japanese bullets, climbed atop the tank, and beat his rifle butt against the roof until the tank stopped firing and drove back within the American lines. The attack continued throughout the afternoon, with the tanks proving particularly effective. By nightfall of the 26th Colonel Finn's men had knocked out a substantial portion of the Japanese defenses and overrun a large part of the fortified area.

When they resumed the attack in the morning they discovered that the Japanese had fled. General Makino, realizing that he could no longer prevent the loss of the coastal plain to the invaders, had directed most of his forces to fall back to positions in the mountains west of the Burauen-Dagami road. Scattered elements still held out to the east, but by nightfall of October 27 the Japanese no longer presented any threat to the Sixth Army beachhead. The hundreds of Japanese bodies and the scattered wreckage of weapons and equipment on the Buri airstrip bore grim witness to General Makino's defeat.

The 16th Division commander's decision to accept American control of the east Leyte coastal area, while certainly justified by circumstances, was counter to General Suzuki's orders to hold forward positions in preparation for a decisive battle on the island. Perhaps Makino had not yet received these orders. A Thirty-fifth Army liaison officer, Lieutenant Colonel Toshii Watanabe, who himself had left Cebu before word of the change in strategy had arrived there, testified later that on the 26th Makino knew nothing about plans for a decisive battle on Leyte. Yet communications between the 16th Division and the Thirty-fifth Army had been re-established by the 23rd, and the new orders should have been among the first messages transmitted to Leyte.

Be that as it may, it seems doubtful if Makino could have acted otherwise. By October 26 the 16th Division had taken staggering casualties. Reduced to less than 5,000 men, the unit, in the words of Colonel Watanabe, "had already lost its capabilities to carry out organized actions as a division." A few of the first reinforcements dispatched by General Suzuki on October 19 and 20 were beginning to land at Ormoc. But they were still too far from the scene of battle to have any immediate effect.

Nor had the great air and sea battle of Leyte Gulf, on which so many Japanese hopes were pinned, as yet affected the action on the ground. This battle was now in its final stages, however, and its outcome would surely influence the course of the struggle ashore.

≪≪≪

≫≫≫

x First Blood

AT 8:13 on the morning of October 20, from his headquarters at Hiyoshi, Admiral Toyoda had issued the *Sho-1* execute order for the Combined Fleet. This directed Admiral Kurita's 1st Striking Force to "break through to the Tacloban area at dawn on the 25th" and "destroy the enemy transport group and its covering naval escort forces." In support of Kurita, Philippine-based air units would hit the American task forces on the 24th and Admiral Ozawa's Main Body would maneuver east of Luzon "to lure the enemy to the north" and, "if a favorable opportunity arises," attack it.

When he issued this order Toyoda's heart must have been heavy, for he realized the desperate nature of the undertaking and its small chance of success. Given the heavy Japanese plane losses during the Formosa air battle, the scattered disposition of the Combined Fleet, the fuel shortage that had forced this deployment, and the great American naval strength that he knew still faced him, the operation was a gamble. Yet without committing the fleet, said Toyoda after the war, there was no possibility of Yamashita's forces "having any chance . . . at all." "If things went well," he continued, "we might obtain unexpectedly good results; but if the worst should happen, there was a chance that we would lose the entire fleet. But I felt that that chance had to be taken."

First to sortie for the attack was Admiral Ozawa's Main Body, which lifted anchor on the afternoon of the 20th and began moving out of the Inland Sea. It was a curious, tragic group of seventeen warships, embarking on a suicidal but vital mission. The heart of the force consisted of three light carriers and the large carrier *Zuikaku*, which was Ozawa's flagship and, incidentally, the last surviving carrier of the Pearl Harbor attack. There were also two semicarriers—battleships with their after turrets removed to make room for aircraft lifts and launching catapults, but still boasting considerable gunpower forward. Three light cruisers and eight destroyers completed the grouping. Although essentially a carrier force, it contained only a third of its normal complement of aircraft. The planes and their trained pilots that Admiral Ozawa had so painstakingly assembled for his carriers during the late summer of 1944 had been lost during the Formosa air battle. By October 20 he managed to scrape together only slightly more than 100 replacement aircraft, with pilots so poorly trained that many of them could not even be trusted to make a carrier landing under less than perfect conditions. In these circumstances some of the carriers could well have been left behind, but they were purposely included in order to heighten the attractiveness of the force as a lure. The two semicarriers remained primarily because of their firepower.

Ironically enough, Ozawa had consistently opposed employing carrier aircraft from bases on land. The transfer of his planes to Okinawa on the eve of the Formosa air battle had been despite Ozawa's protests, and his worst fears were realized when his carrier striking force was crippled by the losses sustained in that battle. Earlier plans had envisioned the Main Body acting as both a decoy and an attacking force, as, indeed, Toyoda's *Sho*-1 execute order still indicated. Yet Ozawa's fangs had been effectively pulled by what he could only regard as Toyoda's misuse of his aircraft. He realized that without these planes his fleet could fulfill its mission only by exposing itself to complete annihilation. But he also understood that this sacrifice was essential to the success of the *Sho* plan. As he explained after the war, "I thought if Kurita's fleet ever succeeded in attacking your landing forces I would be satisfied, even though totally destroyed; if they destroyed the transports there in Leyte Gulf I would have been satisfied."

Ozawa's force slipped out of the Inland Sea under cover of

darkness on the evening of the 20th. To his surprise, no American submarines attempted to interfere. A group of subs, stationed in this area during the Formosa air battle, had observed so much shipping going into the Inland Sea that it appeared as if the Japanese fleet were fleeing battle rather than seeking it. So the submarines headed for other waters to hunt merchant ships, and were not on hand two days later when Ozawa sortied. He could not know, of course, whether or not a sub had sighted and reported his force. But he hoped not. It would not do to be discovered too early. Accordingly, once he reached the open seas he pursued a course just beyond the range of American search planes based on Saipan. At the proper moment Ozawa would allow himself to be found.

The next day was quiet. Scout planes went out but saw no American ships, and dusk fell without event. A submarine alarm on the 22nd alerted the entire force, but air searches made no sightings. In the afternoon the destroyers refueled from the larger ships about 800 miles east of Formosa, and Ozawa turned southwest for Luzon. The next day search planes again failed to encounter American warships. Yet, fearing that he had been sighted and reported by submarines, Ozawa shifted his cruising formation to provide better antiaircraft defense. The hours passed, still without incident. Then, late on the 23rd, he picked up a message that Admiral Kurita's force was under submarine attack. Continuing to press ahead toward Luzon, Ozawa ordered the *Zuikaku's* powerful radio to begin transmitting a long message. The time had come to draw the enemy on himself.

Far to the south the 1st Striking Force had dropped anchor in Brunei Bay at midday of the 20th. Destroyers and cruisers came alongside the battleships to be refueled. The next day the slower tankers arrived with fuel for the battleships. Not until five o'clock on the morning of the 22nd was refueling completed.

During this period Kurita and his staff had been going over a series of directives for the coming attack that they had been receiving from Admiral Toyoda. In accordance with these orders, the 1st Striking Force would henceforth operate directly under Combined Fleet headquarters, instead of under Admiral Ozawa. Ozawa was now responsible solely for commanding the Main Body and, given the mission of that force, would probably be in no position to worry about Kurita's ships anyway.

To reach Leyte Gulf from Brunei Bay, prudence—and, indeed, Admiral Toyoda—dictated a course through the Japanese-controlled central Philippines and San Bernardino Strait and then down the east coast of Samar to the target area. To reach San Bernardino Strait, Admiral Kurita considered three routes. The first and most direct one was northeastward across the Sulu Sea into the Sibuyan Sea and east to San Bernardino. This route, which Combined Fleet headquarters apparently assumed he would take, Kurita ruled out. It passed within range of American planes based on Morotai and might expose him prematurely to detection and air attack. The second, and longest, route was northwest past the reef-filled Dangerous Ground of the South China Sea, then east through Mindoro Strait and the Sibuyan Sea to San Bernardino Strait. This approach, while out of range of land-based American scout planes and, it seemed, less likely to be covered by carrier-based air searches, was safest, but far too long. It would have taken more time than the schedule allowed and would require refueling en route (although probably not until the return trip). The third choice was similar to the first. But it avoided the Sulu Sea in favor of Palawan Passage, west of Palawan Island, then turned east to pass through Mindoro Strait and the Sibuyan Sea. This provided a compromise on the matter of distance, and relative safety from air attack during the first stage of the approach, but it meant dangerous exposure to American submarines which were known to hunt the waters of Palawan Passage.

Thanks in part to the slowness of his tankers in reaching Brunei Bay, Kurita would be hard pressed to meet the target of dawn of the 25th. At the suggestion of Admiral Toyoda, therefore, but on his own decision, Kurita split his fleet. A small force under Vice Admiral Shoji Nishimura, consisting of two old and relatively slow battleships, *Fuso* and *Yamashiro,* and their escort of a heavy cruiser and four destroyers, would sail directly east across the Sulu Sea, through the Mindanao Sea, and thence north through Surigao Strait into Leyte Gulf. In order to enter the gulf at dawn of the 25th Nishimura would have to risk discovery and air attack while in passage. Kurita himself would take the bulk of the 1st Striking Force on the Palawan Passage route, trusting in luck and his ability to maneuver more readily without the slower warships to bring him safely through the submarine-infested waters.

The choice of Palawan Passage is questionable. By sailing east of Palawan Island, Kurita could have avoided the risk of submarine attack. And by transiting the southern waters of the Sulu Sea before daylight he would have greatly reduced his chances of being discovered by Morotai-based air searches. As a matter of fact, the Morotai search caught only one belated and fleeting look at Nishimura's force, which sailed all the way across the Sulu Sea, much of the time during the day. But this is being written with the benefit of hindsight. When the actual decision was made, Kurita and his staff were under the dual pressures of haste and concern about other factors bearing on the coming battle. In calmer circumstances they might have made a different decision.

The group of warships sailing with Kurita was a powerful one. It included five battleships, the mighty *Musashi* and *Yamato* and the *Nagato, Kongo,* and *Haruna.* In addition to this hefty aggregation, there were ten heavy cruisers, including Kurita's flagship, *Atago,* two light cruisers, and fifteen destroyers. In firepower this force was impressive and overwhelming. But it lacked the strongest and primary weapon of modern naval warfare: airpower. Ozawa's carriers, assuming they still had their planes, could have provided this aerial punch, assuming also that the difficult fuel situation had not split the fleet. Under the circumstances, however, the only available Japanese airpower consisted of land-based planes in the Philippines, and these were unavailable for operations before the 24th when, of course, they would be sent against the American task forces off Leyte and in the Philippine Sea. What Kurita's force needed most was a covering air umbrella, to protect him against air and submarine attack until he was near enough to close with the enemy ships and destroy them with his firepower. But this umbrella was precisely what he lacked, and its absence was to prove his undoing.

To make a bad situation even worse, before his sortie Kurita dispatched most of his floatplanes to bases on Mindoro. Two reasons lay behind this action. First, there was a serious need for additional scout planes at Philippine bases, and, second, in submarine-filled waters it would be impossible to stop to recover the floatplanes once they had been launched. Had the Kurita force included an aircraft carrier, either of these reasons might have been valid. But under the circumstances, the transfer of the float-planes left Kurita without eyes to warn of approaching danger. As the scout planes took off for Mindoro, then, one officer commented prophetically that he would "hate to be responsible for this decision when enemy submarines attack."

In addition to the dangers of air and submarine attack, the difficulties of navigating in narrow straits with treacherous currents, and the complications of divided approach on a difficult time schedule, there was one other factor that bothered many of Kurita's staff officers and subordinate commanders. This was the basic question of whether the game was at all worth the candle. The original *Sho* plan, developed in July, had stipulated that if an American invasion force could not be defeated before it began to disembark its troops, then the attacking Japanese fleet would "engage and destroy the enemy in their anchorage *within at least two days* of the landing, thus crippling the invasion effort." October 25, no one needed to be reminded, was five and not two days after the American landing, and many of Kurita's officers realized that most of the transports would have unloaded and withdrawn by this time. What was the point, they asked, of risking the entire Japanese battle line, the only striking force left of the once powerful imperial navy, for the sake of "a few auxiliary transports"? Was the "final effort" of the great fleet to be "spent in engaging a group of empty cargo ships"?

Many officers wrote notes or memoranda, some of them highly emotional, while others called in person on Admiral Kurita to protest the commitment of their ships to such an undertaking. "Our whole force was uneasy," recalled Kurita's chief of staff, Rear Admiral Tomiji Koyanagi. And "this feeling," he added, "was reflected in our leadership during the battle" that followed.

Late on the afternoon of October 21, finally, Kurita called a meeting of his division commanders and their staffs on board the *Atago.* Concealing his own apprehensions, he addressed his officers in moving tones, his brief words directly to the point. He knew, he said, that many opposed the mission. But Japan's situation was far more critical than any of those present could possibly understand. Should the fleet remain intact while the nation perished? Imperial General Headquarters had given them a glorious opportunity and, while there were no such things as miracles, who could say how the battle might end? "We shall have a chance to meet our enemy," he concluded. "We shall engage his task forces. I hope that you will not carry your responsibilities lightly. I know that you will act faithfully and well."

Kurita stopped speaking. The men around him, almost as if on signal, snapped erect. Elated, charged with determination, faces flushed, eyes staring at their commander, they shouted as one: *"Banzai! Banzai! Banzai!"*

At eight o'clock on the morning of the 22nd Kurita led his mighty flotilla out to sea. "After penetrating through San Bernardino Strait at sunset on 24 October," he announced, "I will destroy the enemy surface forces in night battle east of Samar and then proceed to the Tacloban area at daybreak on 25 October to destroy the enemy transport convoy and landing forces." Seven hours after Kurita's departure, Admiral Nishimura's small but powerful task force sortied from Brunei Bay. The two groups would enter Leyte Gulf simultaneously, although if this proved impossible each would attack alone.

By now, also, a third Japanese task force had entered the picture. This was Vice Admiral Kiyohide Shima's 2nd Striking Force, originally scheduled to participate in the attack and then shunted to troop convoy duty under control of Admiral Mikawa's Southwest Area Fleet headquarters in Manila. Consultations with General Yamashita's staff, however, indicated that Shima's warships were not yet needed. So Mikawa recommended that they be used instead as part of the attack on Leyte Gulf.

On the afternoon of October 21, therefore, Toyoda ordered Mikawa to send the bulk of the 2nd Striking Force "into Leyte Gulf from the south through Surigao Strait" in support of Nishimura's assault. When Mikawa then suggested that Shima be removed from his command and placed under Admiral Kurita, however, he received no answer from Combined Fleet headquarters. Two reasons have been offered by the Japanese for this lack of reply. First, Toyoda's staff felt that Kurita's plans were too far advanced for Shima's force to be integrated into the attack without a great deal of long-range radio communication, which might have compromised the secrecy of the operation. And, second,

Combined Fleet headquarters believed that Mikawa should continue to control Shima in case it became possible to begin troop transfers to Leyte sooner than anticipated. This may be so, but it still fails to explain why Toyoda kept Mikawa in the dark.

In any event, Shima left Mako on the morning of the 22nd with three cruisers and four destroyers, shaping a course for Coron Bay, in the Calamian Islands southwest of Mindoro, where he would refuel before pressing on. While en route he received his final orders from Mikawa and dropped anchor in Coron Bay at dusk on the 23rd. There was still no plan to coordinate Shima's attack with Nishimura's—a costly oversight as events turned out.

Meanwhile, Admiral Kurita's powerful flotilla of battleships, cruisers, and destroyers had been speeding north from Brunei. During the daylight hours of the 22nd the ships maintained a speed of from eighteen to twenty knots and zigzagged constantly. For a while a few planes from Borneo provided air cover. Kurita's fear of submarine attack was reinforced by three alarms, all of which turned out to be false, and the gunners were so nervous that they often opened fire at pieces of flotsam, mistaking them for periscopes. With the coming of darkness the covering aircraft departed and the task force slowed to sixteen knots, maintaining only a very simple zigzag.

By midnight Kurita was approaching the southern entrance to Palawan Passage and at this point two new characters entered the drama. Just inside the passage were the American submarines *Darter* and *Dace*, under Commanders David H. McClintock and Bladen D. Claggett. At this moment they were sailing leisurely along on the surface, their two skippers exchanging information and discussing plans through large megaphones. At sixteen minutes after midnight, just as the two had about finished their conversation, the *Darter* radarmen reported a contact. It was a doubtful one, a good seventeen miles away, and the operator thought it might be a rain cloud. A few seconds later he changed his mind. The contact was ships, and McClintock quickly relayed the word to Claggett. Both skippers then took their subs toward Kurita's force as fast as they could.

A few minutes before 3 A.M. on the 23rd the flagship *Atago* signaled a warning to the other Japanese vessels that an American submarine was in the area and had been detected sending a radio message. What *Atago* had intercepted was one of three contact reports that McClintock, the senior commander, had dispatched and which were promptly relayed to Admiral Halsey. These reports were the first indication American forces had of the whereabouts of Kurita's force since it had left Lingga Roads. Despite the increases in radio activity at Brunei, U.S. Naval Intelligence had been unaware of Kurita's arrival there—and of his departure. The sighting now meant that the Japanese battle fleet had at last been found, and Halsey's carrier pilots would be ready for it. This again points up the fatal importance of Kurita's decision to advance up Palawan Passage. By sailing east of Palawan and avoiding the submarines, he might have prevented his discovery for another thirty-six hours or so, with a consequent delay and reduction in the number of air assaults he would receive. And of course he would have missed the reception that Commanders McClintock and Claggett were now preparing for him.

At first light on the 23rd Kurita resumed his speed of eighteen knots and his zigzag course. His ships traveled in two sections, *Atago* and eighteen others in the first group and the remaining thirteen vessels a few miles behind. Each group sailed north in five columns, with the destroyers and cruisers providing flank and forward protection for the battleships. Despite the knowledge that there was at least one American submarine in the neighborhood, and probably more, Kurita had not established a destroyer screen in front of his columns, a careless and costly error. By now the two submarines were about ten miles ahead of the Japanese and preparing to close on their targets. The sky was clear and visibility excellent.

Shortly after six o'clock *Darter* and *Dace* submerged and made their approach. Coming at the Japanese columns head on, McClintock slipped inside the port column of cruisers, planning to attack from the east with the rising sun behind him. Claggett, in *Dace*, moved between the starboard cruiser column and its protecting line of destroyers. He, too, was east of his intended targets.

On board the Japanese ships all eyes kept a strict lookout for submarines. But neither periscope nor torpedo wake could be seen. Then, at about 6:30, McClintock opened his attack on the first cruiser in the column, Kurita's flagship. At a range so close he could scarcely miss, the *Darter*'s skipper emptied his bow torpedo tubes at the onrushing *Atago*. Two minutes later Admiral Kurita felt the sickening thud and powerful explosion of four torpedoes plowing into the side of his cruiser. McClintock, meanwhile, had swung the *Darter* around and now sent four more torpedoes from his stern tubes at the next cruiser in line, the *Takao*. Two of these missiles struck their target.

Before taking *Darter* all the way down to evade the destroyer attack he knew would come, McClintock took a rapid last look through his periscope at *Atago*. The cruiser, he noted in his report, "was a mass of billowing black smoke from the number one turret to the stern. No superstructure could be seen. Bright orange flames shot out from the side along the main deck from the bow to the after turret." The ship was "already down by the bow." Satisfied with his kill, McClintock took *Darter* into its dive. He had fired the first rounds in the battle of Leyte Gulf and drawn first blood.

To the east, Commander Claggett had observed the results of *Darter*'s attack with great glee. Standing by his periscope, he shouted out an excited description. "It looks like the Fourth of July out there! One is burning! The Japs are milling and firing all over the place! What a show! What a show!" By now, however, the *Dace* too had come within firing range, and Claggett began concentrating on his own targets. Observing the first two ships in the column before him, he correctly identified them as heavy cruisers and decided to let them pass in favor of what looked like a battleship immediately astern.

At 6:54 Claggett fired a salvo of six torpedoes from his bow tubes. Two minutes later, already into his diving escape, he heard four of them hit in a series of tremendous explosions. Two of these, which appeared to come from the ship's magazines, were especially loud. A soundman on *Dace* likened the noise to "the bottom of the ocean . . . blowing up." The victim of this attack was not, as Claggett had guessed, a battleship, but rather the heavy cruiser *Maya*, an almost equally attractive target. And since the *Maya* was literally blown to pieces by the four hits and sank in four minutes, Claggett had every right to be proud of his attack. For the record, however, had he let *Maya* go by with the first two cruisers, the next ship in line would have been the mighty battlewagon *Yamato*. But that nautical behemoth had so much armor on her that it seems doubtful if Claggett would have been anywhere near as successful as he was with *Maya*.

For the next half hour or so both submarines stayed deep and sweated out Japanese depth charges. Kurita's destroyers tore back and forth over the attack area, dropping their lethal payloads. Inside *Darter* and *Dace* the men heard the exploding depth charges and the sounds of the stricken Japanese cruisers breaking up in the water, and feared that their own ships had been hit. Neither was, however. *Dace* probably experienced the nearest misses. The depth charges, recalled Lieutenant Commander R. C. Benitez, *Dace*'s exec, "were going off all around us, and they were close. The boat was being rocked considerably. Light bulbs were being shattered; locker doors were flying open; wrenches were falling from the manifolds. The Japs were very mad—and we were very scared."

Soon the attacks ceased. Both submarines rose to periscope depth later in the morning and discovered that the cruiser *Takao*, McClintock's second victim, was still afloat. But it was impossible to get close enough to administer the coup de grâce, for screening destroyers and two or three planes flying cover made any approach out of the question. The two skippers decided to withdraw to a safer distance, trail the injured ship until nightfall, and then attempt another attack.

This, however, was not to be. When the submarines surfaced that evening they discovered *Takao* and two escorting destroyers shaping a slow course to the southwest. In maneuvering on the surface to follow and attack the cruiser, *Darter* suddenly went aground. Long hours underwater and the presence of obscuring clouds when surfaced had prevented the navigators from fixing their position accurately. Now a coral reef on the western edge of Palawan Passage showed McClintock that he had ventured too far into shoal waters. Hard aground, his ship resisted all efforts to free her. The men burned secret papers, smashed special equipment, and tossed ammunition and supplies overboard. A little after 4 A.M. on October 24, after fixing demolition charges, the *Darter*'s crew piled into rubber boats and paddled through the swift current to *Dace*. Commander Claggett turned his overcrowded submarine toward Australia. Eleven days later, his food

stocks practically exhausted, crew and passengers dirty and
weary of their sardine-like situation, Claggett brought *Dace*
safely into Fremantle harbor.

No safe harbor awaited Admiral Kurita. When the *Atago* was
hit, Kurita and the officers and crew of the flagship had only a
few minutes to abandon her. Nineteen minutes after *Darter*'s
torpedoes struck, the cruiser went down, leaving *Atago*'s passengers to flounder briefly in the water before they were picked up.
Kurita and his staff finally made it aboard the destroyer *Kishinami*, but well over 300 men died in the sinking.

Kurita hoped to transfer his flag from *Kishinami* to *Yamato*,
but fear of renewed submarine attacks put any further transfer
out of the question. Indeed, nervous lookouts continued to give
the alarm for several hours, and Kurita had to delegate temporary
command of the task force to Vice Admiral Matome Ugaki, on
board *Yamato*. The Japanese ships pressed forward at high speed
to escape the submarine area. But it was midafternoon, nine
hours after *Atago* had been hit, before it was safe enough for
Kurita and his staff to move from *Kishinami* to *Yamato*. An hour
later the admiral resumed command of the task force from on
board that mighty battleship. Ironically enough, Kurita and his
staff had initially wanted to raise the command flag on *Yamato*.
The huge vessel had been designed as a flagship and had better
communication facilities than any cruiser. But Admiral Toyoda,
expecting Kurita to fight a night action, had directed him to
choose *Atago*, since Japanese doctrine called for the commanding
officer in a night action to be aboard a heavy cruiser. Now, thanks
to Commander McClintock, Kurita had finally made it to *Yamato*.

The submarine action on the morning of October 23 had cost
Admiral Kurita two heavy cruisers sunk, *Atago* and *Maya*. The
crippled *Takao*, effectively out of action, limped back to Brunei,
accompanied by two destroyers. Since *Takao* thus removed two
ships from Admiral Kurita's already inadequate antisubmarine
screen, the damaged cruiser hurt the Japanese cause more afloat
than if McClintock had sunk her. Five of Kurita's thirty-two ships
were no longer present for the coming battle. Kurita himself was
uninjured, and most of his staff and communications men had
reached *Yamato*, so command of the task force remained in good
shape. But the morale of all hands—and this must have included

Kurita—had certainly been shaken. They had lost their first skirmish, their presence had been discovered, and by morning they would be well within range of American carrier-based planes.

xi Air Strikes and Maneuvers

ADMIRAL HALSEY had received Commander McClintock's first contact report shortly before dawn on October 23—at a time when only three fourths of his force was available for immediate action. The Third Fleet—Task Force 38 for this operation—had been at sea for more than two weeks, engaged almost constantly in offensive or defensive operations. The pilots had shot off a considerable amount of ammunition, dropped quite a few bombs, and, in general, were pretty tired. So when the Japanese fleet failed to contest the Leyte landings, Halsey decided to use this respite to rotate elements of his command on quick trips back to Ulithi in the Carolines, there to take on fuel and ammunition and let the crews stretch their legs ashore.

On the morning of the 23rd, Vice Admiral McCain's Task Group 38.1, strongest of the four groups that constituted Task Force 38, was en route to Ulithi. Task Groups 38.2, 38.3, and 38.4, under Rear Admirals Bogan, Sherman, and Davison, were about 260 miles northeast of Samar. Even without McCain's ships, Task Force 38 still packed considerable power, for each of the remaining task groups included two fast new battleships, three or four carriers, two to four cruisers, and about fifteen destroyers. In Bogan's group was the battlewagon *New Jersey*, Halsey's flagship, from which the Third Fleet commander exercised direct control of the entire task force. Vice Admiral Mitscher, the actual task force commander, was on the carrier *Lexington* in Sherman's group, and, with Halsey running the show, had little to do but observe it.

On receipt of the *Darter*'s report, Halsey ordered the three task groups to refuel from nearby oilers and move in close to the Philippines. For the time being, he allowed McCain to continue on toward Ulithi, but the other groups would launch search planes at dawn of the 24th over the western approaches to Leyte.

Daybreak found Task Force 38 in position, Sherman off Luzon, Bogan 140 miles southeast off San Bernardino Strait, and Davison another 120 miles farther southeast near Leyte Gulf. At about 6 A.M. the scout planes took off from each task group and two hours later made contact. At 8:10 one of Bogan's pilots, Lieutenant Max Adams in a Helldiver from *Intrepid*, spotted the unmistakable pagoda-like masts of Kurita's 1st Striking Force in Tablas Strait, southeast of Mindoro. Halsey immediately directed Sherman and Davison to close on Bogan at top speed. To McCain he sent an order to rendezvous with tankers, refuel, and hurry back toward the scene of action.

Kurita was almost certainly headed for San Bernardino Strait. But the strait was mined and the safe channels unknown to Halsey, so sending his ships through these dangerous waters for a surface battle was out of the question. And the strait was too narrow for the carriers to maneuver freely to launch and recover planes. But Task Force 38 was already well located to send an air strike against Kurita, and at 8:37 Halsey ordered his three task groups to attack. Yet, even as he did so, his northernmost elements were being hit by Japanese naval aircraft from Luzon.

October 24 was the date set for the all-out assault by Japanese land-based planes against American warships covering the Leyte invasion. The success or failure of this attack would have a crucial effect on the forthcoming naval battle. On Luzon all available naval aircraft—now organized as the First Combined Base Air Force under Admiral Fukudome—stood ready. In the Visayas, General Tominaga's Fourth Air Army was all set to go. Bad weather on the 23rd had prevented Japanese search planes from spotting any of Halsey's ships during the day, but around midnight a flying boat located Sherman's Task Group 38.3 as it approached Luzon. Despite the action of Sherman's night fighters, a few Japanese planes trailed the task group at a discreet distance through the night. And at 6:30 A.M. Admiral Fukudome sent the bulk of his force—more than sixty bombers and torpedo planes escorted by nearly 130 fighters—against Sherman.

At about eight o'clock on the morning of the 24th radar aboard Task Group 38.3 picked up the Japanese planes approach-

ing in three roughly equal waves. By now most of Sherman's aircraft were out on search to the west, but he hastily scrambled his
remaining fighters to meet the oncoming attack. Bombers and
torpedo planes readying for the strike order anticipated from
Halsey were returned to the hangar decks, and Sherman moved
his ships into the cover of a nearby rain squall "like soldiers," he
recalled later, "going into their foxholes."

First to meet the attackers were eight Hellcats flying combat
air patrol from the carrier *Princeton*. Though obviously greatly
outnumbered, they dove on the first wave of about sixty Japanese
planes, shot down several, scattered the rest, and kept Fukudome's pilots occupied for about fifteen minutes. By this time,
close to 8:30, Commander David McCampbell and six others in
Hellcats from the *Essex* arrived on the scene to take over. Mc-
Campbell, who had already run up quite a record of kills, proceeded to knock down nine planes, while the rest of his group got
another fifteen. The American pilots were far better trained than
their opponents, better flyers and deadlier shots. They quickly
chased off the Japanese bombers, forced the fighters into defensive maneuvers, and seized an altitude advantage that they never
relinquished. As more and more American fighters joined the
fray, the second and third Japanese waves also were driven back.
At the end of about an hour's fighting, roughly seventy of
Fukudome's planes had been downed as against a loss of only a
few American aircraft. Incredibly, not one ship in Task Group
38.3 had come under aerial attack.

By about 9:30 Sherman's radar screen indicated that there
were no Japanese planes within fifty miles. The task group left
the covering rain squall and moved into the wind to take the returning fighters back aboard. Eight minutes later a lookout on the
Princeton spotted a single Japanese dive bomber emerging from a
low cloud and making a shallow approach on the port bow. Guns
from the carrier and nearby ships opened fire and Captain William H. Buracker, *Princeton*'s commander, started to maneuver
the huge flattop. But there was not enough time. From less than
1,200 feet, the Japanese pilot dropped his 550-pound bomb
squarely on the carrier's flight deck, just in front of the rear elevator and slightly to port. The attacking plane passed on over the
stern where it was promptly shot down by fighters—too late,

however, to save the *Princeton.*

From his position on the bridge Captain Buracker could see only a small hole in the flight deck, which appeared to indicate no more than slight damage. He recalled later that he had "visualized slapping on a patch and resuming operations in a hurry." But this vision was swiftly erased by the heavy cloud of smoke that billowed up from the deck. The bomb had penetrated deep within the *Princeton* and gone off with a blast that quickly set the hangar deck afire. Burning gasoline spread the flames until they enveloped the waiting torpedo planes, still carrying their deadly missiles, and huge explosions rocked the stricken ship. Chunks of elevator and flight deck and other debris hurtled through the air. A great column of smoke rose into the sky like a volcano's plume. The interior of the *Princeton* filled quickly with smoke and heat and crew members in the stern section were forced to jump overboard. Soon gas tanks on other planes began to explode, sending more flaming gasoline into the raging conflagration. At 10:10 Captain Buracker ordered all but about 500 men off the ship. Ten minutes later he directed half of these to go. The rest remained to fight the fires.

By now the *Princeton* was practically dead in the water. Buracker had swung her almost into the wind, so that the smoke and fire were blown aft and to starboard, leaving the forward part of the flight deck and its catwalks clear to facilitate the crew's escape. Three destroyers closed in to pick up survivors. The gun platforms jutting out from *Princeton*'s sides kept these rescuers at a slight distance, and the crew members had to jump into the water and swim or float about thirty feet to the nearest destroyer. No boats could be lowered from the carrier, but the destroyers placed some into the water to help. This was fortunate, for sharks had already put in an appearance. Machine-gun fire from one destroyer helped discourage these predators.

Now two cruisers appeared on the scene, the *Reno* to provide antiaircraft protection should the Japanese attempt another raid and the *Birmingham* to try to assist in extinguishing the *Princeton*'s fires. Water pressure in the carrier's fire mains had failed shortly after ten o'clock and one of the destroyers had been playing its own fire hoses into the forward part of *Princeton*'s hangar. Now *Birmingham* moved in close and ran hoses over onto the carrier, where they were manned by Captain Buracker's fire fighters and volunteers from the cruiser. Another destroyer closed in on the other side to do the same, and these combined efforts gradually forced back the flames. By 1 P.M. the fire was contained in the extreme rear of the hangar, and it seemed that everything would be under control in twenty or thirty minutes.

Before this could be accomplished, however, someone made a sound contact on a submarine and radar picked up Japanese planes coming in from the north. The ships helping *Princeton* immediately pulled clear so as to be free to maneuver and better protect the carrier. But the submarine contact turned out to be a false alarm and the air raid proved a dud. The planes were from Admiral Ozawa's decoy force, fifty-six in all. Only half this number, from *Zuikaku,* managed to get anywhere near Sherman's task group, and these were easily shot down or driven off. By 1:45 the *Birmingham* was back assisting the *Princeton,* but in the interval the flames had gained headway again. They were especially fierce near a reserve bomb and torpedo stowage area in the after part of the ship.

This area had been worrying Captain Buracker all day. Unable to jettison the ammunition stored there because of the smoke and intense heat, he had been keeping his fingers crossed and hoping that there would be no more explosions. Suddenly at 3:23 a great blast, "as surprising as it was terrifying," in the words of one survivor, roared up from the flames. The whole rear portion of the flight deck and much of the stern of the ship erupted into the air and fell back into the water. Great, jagged fragments of steel burst upward and outward and then fell back in a deadly rain on those below. Almost everyone still on the *Princeton* was killed or wounded.

The full force of the explosion hit the *Birmingham*. That gallant ship, her deck crowded with repair parties, fire fighters, engineers, and gunners, was directly in the path of the fatal shower of metal and debris. The effect was devastating—as if a broadside of shrapnel had hit the cruiser. Everywhere lay the dead, dying, and wounded. Several arms, legs, hands, and horribly mutilated bodies were scattered across the decks. Badly wounded men sprawled helpless as a river of blood flowed across the cruiser's topside. More than 200 men had been killed instantly, and twice as many were wounded: total casualties that exceeded by far all of those suffered aboard the *Princeton*.

The crippled *Birmingham* was forced to pull clear of the stricken carrier to tend her wounded and repair her own injuries. Left alone, *Princeton* now blazed brilliantly again and her saddened captain reluctantly ordered her abandoned. Himself the last to leave the ship, Buracker climbed down her side just after 4:30. The effort to save the carrier had lasted seven hours, a brave but costly and futile attempt. Any further endeavor would probably be useless and might well endanger the rest of the task group.

On Admiral Mitscher's orders, Sherman directed that *Princeton* be sunk. This almost caused another tragedy. The destroyer detailed to sink her had been engaged in the original rescue operations, and, in bumping against the carrier, had damaged her torpedo director. As a result, only one out of six torpedoes fired hit the *Princeton,* three missed altogether, and the remaining two followed a boomerang course that brought them back at the destroyer that had fired them. They missed, but the mission was turned over to cruiser *Reno,* which put the carrier under with two torpedoes. With this unpleasant task accomplished, Sherman regrouped his ships and, as darkness fell, finally began heading toward the other elements of Task Force 38.

Despite the destruction of *Princeton* and the wounding of *Birmingham,* Admiral Fukudome's air effort had been a failure. His all-out strike at Task Group 38.3 had so exhausted his resources that he was unable to do much else in the way of offensive action. His planes had spotted but were unable to hit Admiral Bogan's group off San Bernardino Strait, and Bogan, as we shall see, more than made up for the loss of *Princeton* in the damage he inflicted on Kurita's force. Nor did Fukudome's pilots even come close to finding Admiral Davison's task group near Leyte Gulf. The *Sho* objective assigned to the land-based naval air units—to destroy enough American warships to clear the way for the Japanese fleet—had not been even partially achieved.

The Fourth Air Army portion of the attack on October 24 fared even worse. Beginning at eight o'clock that morning, General Tominaga sent practically every operational plane he had—a total of perhaps 150—in a series of strikes against Seventh Fleet units in Leyte Gulf. So heavy were these attacks and at such frequent intervals that planes from Admiral Sprague's escort carriers had to temporarily suspend support missions of the Sixth Army in order to beef up the combat air patrol over shipping in the gulf. But this was the extent of the damage.

Sprague's flyers kept all but a few of the Japanese planes from penetrating their screen, and those attackers that did get through were downed before they could exploit their position. One American eyewitness recorded his impressions of the initial attack, as first one Japanese plane went down on fire atop a ridgeline near the coast, then another "fell flaming along the shore," and still a third, trailing smoke and heading out into the harbor, "suddenly fell off on one wing and crashed into the water alongside a Liberty ship." Then, "all the guns in the harbor opened up with a terrific barrage. . . . Flaming enemy aircraft literally rained from the sky." One bomber, smoking heavily, "swerved to the right, bounced twice and hit the side" of a large landing craft, "engulfing the ship in flaming gasoline." Nearby "a mine sweeper burst into flames." But only a few vessels suffered hits like this and by the day's end nearly seventy Japanese planes had been destroyed, a heavy price for Tominaga to pay for so small a return. Like Fukudome, he had failed in his mission. And this double failure boded ill for the success of the remaining portions of operation *Sho*.

Compounding this troublesome situation for the Japanese on the 24th were the punishing attacks by Halsey's flyers on the two naval forces driving toward Leyte Gulf. The first blow came at about 9:15 in the morning and was directed against Admiral Nishimura's flotilla of seven warships, then at the eastern edge of the Sulu Sea. Planes from Admiral Davison's Task Group 38.4 had spotted Nishimura about ten minutes earlier and now about twenty of them from the carriers *Enterprise* and *Franklin* swooped in to attack. Without friendly air cover, Nishimura had to rely solely on his antiaircraft guns for protection. And this was not enough. One bomb struck the battleship *Fuso* near her catapult, setting a fire that raged for an hour and destroyed her only floatplane. Destroyer *Shigure* also took a bomb on her No. 1 gun turret. This killed or wounded all of the gun crew, although it failed to knock out the weapon. Other than this, the attackers caused no damage and, in consideration of their dwindling fuel supply, the planes broke off the engagement and returned to their carriers. Admiral Nishimura sent a message to Kurita that *Fuso* and *Shigure* had sustained light damage which had not affected their navigability. He was continuing on toward Leyte Gulf in good order.

Nishimura was not attacked again during the day, since Davison moved north to join forces with Bogan and planes from the Seventh Fleet escort carriers had their hands full with General Tominaga's planes in Leyte Gulf. Admiral Shima's force, which had left Coron Bay before dawn that day, was spotted by a Morotai-based Fifth Air Force bomber at noon but was not attacked. Shima was still about 100 miles behind Nishimura and pushing forward rapidly. Meanwhile, some 300 miles to the north, Admiral Kurita had been receiving the brunt of the American attack.

The commander of the 1st Striking Force had eaten an early breakfast, which would be his last meal until late that evening. He was somewhat more fortunate than most of the crewmen, whose breakfast was interrupted by a call to general quarters and who missed lunch for the same reason. The first alert came at dawn, when radar picked up American planes approaching from the east. These were Admiral Bogan's flyers, who made the initial contact with Kurita shortly after eight. At this time the Japanese force was moving along rapidly at twenty-four knots in two large circular formations, the first centered on the huge *Yamato,* now Kurita's flagship, the second on the battleship *Kongo.* Other battleships and cruisers were ringed around each of these and, to guard against submarines, a screen of destroyers formed the outer circle. The whole formation bristled with antiaircraft weapons—*Yamato* alone boasted 150 antiaircraft machine guns—and was prepared to throw a wall of fire in front of the expected American bombers. When the first contact produced no air attack, however, Kurita slowed to his normal cruising speed of twenty knots and, having learned his lesson about submarines, resumed zigzagging. The men remained at general quarters, hungry and anxious. Blips on the radar screen appeared to indicate American scout planes, and spotters reported a periscope. An air of nervous anticipation covered the whole force.

Shortly after nine o'clock carriers *Intrepid* and *Cabot* of Bogan's group launched their planes, two dozen dive and torpedo bombers and almost as many fighters. Half an hour later Kurita's radar picked up the attackers and just before 10:30 the battle was joined. The Japanese put up a heavy curtain of antiaircraft fire, which proved embarrassingly ineffective and became even more so when the ships had to break formation and scatter under the air raid. The fight lasted twenty-four minutes, but most of the damage was done in the first three. The great battleship *Musashi* took a torpedo on her starboard side and a bomb struck her deck. Neither blow even shook the huge vessel, whose thick armor gave her ample protection. The heavy cruiser *Myoko*, however, was not so fortunate. A torpedo struck a damaging blow on the starboard side aft, slowing her to fifteen knots and forcing her to fall back out of formation. Since *Myoko* could obviously no longer keep up with the rest of his force, Kurita ordered the ship back to Brunei. But he could spare no destroyers to act as escort, and the cruiser would have to run the gantlet of American submarines on its own.

The rest of Kurita's force resumed formation and pressed forward rapidly into the Sibuyan Sea. Submarine alerts continued to startle the Japanese and force evasive action, although no American undersea craft were actually in these waters. Meanwhile a second strike of planes had been launched from *Intrepid*, *Cabot*, and *Independence* even as the first attack was ending. This second blow, in about the same strength as the first, hit Kurita shortly after noon. The American pilots concentrated on *Musashi*, and this time their efforts were more successful. Three torpedoes and two bombs, as well as several near misses, slowed the huge battleship to twenty-two knots, which in turn reduced the speed of the entire formation.

By now Admiral Kurita was understandably worried. Without air cover and with half the day still ahead of him, he anticipated continued carrier attacks and mounting losses. He had received no word about the effect on the American fleet of either Ozawa's decoy force or the land-based air raids. And, judging from the air assaults on his own force, he felt that Nishimura's report of light damage was a serious understatement of the heavy blows he must have been receiving. At 1:15, then, he sent an urgent radio to both Admiral Ozawa and, in Manila, Admiral Mikawa:

> I am receiving repeated torpedo and bomb attacks by enemy carrier aircraft. Request immediate information concerning situation as regards attacks on or contacts with the enemy by your forces.

Hardly had Kurita dispatched this message when two dozen planes from *Essex* and *Lexington* of Sherman's group—all he could spare from air defense of the stricken *Princeton*—began a third attack, again concentrating on the wounded *Musashi*. Several more torpedoes exploded against the side of the limping giant and four bomb hits shattered her superstructure. Beginning to flood badly, her nose settling low in the water, speed reduced even more, she fell slowly astern of the formation. At the same time her sister ship, *Yamato,* also was hit by a torpedo, but this single blow did not even slow that great vessel.

The fourth attack of the day, shortly after 2:30, came swiftly on the heels of the third. Delivered by sixty-five planes from Admiral Davison's group, it caused relatively little damage. Battleships *Yamato* and *Nagato* were struck by bombs, which slowed them slightly, but otherwise no harm was done. *Musashi,* unhit in this attack, was nevertheless now in too crippled a condition to continue. Her bowplates ripped outward, her nose pressed down, she plowed heavily through the sea and raised a huge furrow of water that slowed her more and more. Inside the ship, machinery had been flooded, steam lines cut, and still other damage sustained. Clearly she could no longer continue, and at three o'clock Kurita sadly ordered her to head for Coron Bay escorted by two destroyers.

For several hours now Kurita had been radioing frantically to Manila for land-based air support, either to defend his ships or to attack the American carriers sending planes against him. His pleas, however, were to no avail. Admiral Fukudome, indeed, ignored Kurita's requests for air cover because he felt he could be of more use by concentrating his forces against Halsey's carriers. In this latter effort he had tried and failed and, having shot his bolt, had practically nothing left with which to try again. He did finally send a handful of planes to defend Kurita, but only a few had pilots sufficiently skilled to pick their way through a heavy east-west front that blocked the area south of the central Luzon airstrips. Perhaps four of the land-based planes reached the scene of battle, and all were shot down.

Shortly after three o'clock, finally, came the last attack of the day on Kurita. This, the heaviest so far, included planes from five carriers representing all three task groups. A large number concentrated on the retreating *Musashi* and hit her almost at will. Other planes struck at the rest of Kurita's force, inflicting minor damage on a number of ships.

Musashi was now clearly dying. She had taken a score of torpedo hits and almost as many bombs, and sailing her even as far as Coron Bay was by this time out of the question. Her wounded commander, Rear Admiral Toshihei Inoguchi, attempted to beach the sinking giant on the nearest shore, but with power lines ruptured, uncontrolled flooding, and her bow almost underwater, he had lost all control. Only one engine remained in operation, and with this Inoguchi could barely move the huge vessel. The ship began listing to starboard and, as the crew frantically shifted every movable object to port, the bow went completely under, leaving the forward main turrets still exposed like two island fortresses. It was now close to seven o'clock. Inoguchi ordered "abandon ship" and stood calmly on the bridge to await his end. Some forty minutes later *Musashi* rolled suddenly to port and sank. A great column of smoke marked her grave.

Admiral Kurita, meanwhile, had been counting his wounds. "We had expected air attacks," recalled Admiral Koyanagi, his chief of staff, "but this day's were almost enough to discourage us." Besides the loss of *Myoko* and *Musashi*, two destroyers had remained with *Musashi*, and several other ships had been hit. Although the damage to these vessels was relatively light, their speed had been somewhat reduced and this might prove fatal in a major fleet engagement. Almost unbelievably, antiaircraft fire had been able to down but 18 of more than 250 attacking planes, a loss completely out of proportion to the damage inflicted.

Despite everything, Kurita still had a formidable body of ships: four battleships, six heavy cruisers, two light cruisers, and eleven destroyers. Yet he had lost more than 25 percent of his original force, primarily in heavy units. And there seemed to be no end in sight. Ozawa and Fukudome had failed to prevent air attacks, which could be expected to continue. And several false periscope sightings attested to everyone's concern about the continuing submarine threat. A message from Admiral Toyoda in Combined Fleet headquarters warning about possible submarine attacks and directing Kurita to "be alert" did nothing to improve the admiral's state of mind. More and more Kurita had the feeling, expressed earlier by his staff officers at Brunei Bay, that the battleline of the Japanese fleet was being thrown away for nothing. And to this was now added the suspicion that he was facing the bulk of the American fleet alone.

With the exception of some brief rearward maneuvers to support damaged ships during the fourth and fifth air raids, Kurita's force had not once flinched from its eastward advance. At 3:30, finally, as the ships neared the narrow approaches to San Bernardino Strait, Kurita suddenly reversed course. Reasoning that another air assault in the confined waters ahead might well finish off most of his ships and permanently block his own scheduled attack, he had decided to fall back for a while into the more open waters to the west. In a long message to Admiral Toyoda, he explained that under the circumstances, if he attempted to force his way through San Bernardino Strait at one hour after sundown as originally planned, "we would merely make ourselves meat for the enemy, with very little chance of success." He was therefore "temporarily" retiring "while awaiting the results of our other operations and standing by to cooperate as developments warrant"—by which he meant that he still hoped for a shattering blow by Japanese land-based planes against the American fleet. On the chance that it might do some good, Kurita also sent this message to Admiral Fukudome. But Fukudome, of course, was no longer in a position to help him, and there the matter rested.

For an hour and a half Kurita withdrew slowly. During this period no further air raids struck him, and he soon concluded that the Americans were intent on recovering all their planes before sundown and would attack him no more. He had still received no reply to his message to Toyoda and was becoming uneasy about meeting his original time schedule in case Toyoda should order the assault executed as planned. At 5:14, then, Kurita put about and headed once more for San Bernardino Strait.

At Combined Fleet headquarters, meanwhile, Toyoda had not yet received Kurita's dispatch. But, concerned by the messages that had been coming in all day, he sent out a brief, strong order to all naval units engaged in the *Sho* operation: "All forces will dash to the attack, trusting in divine assistance!" This reached Kurita an hour after he had reversed course to the east, although for some reason his own dispatch did not arrive at Combined Fleet headquarters until nearly 8 P.M. On its arrival, Toyoda briefly considered ordering Kurita to continue his retirement but then simply dispatched a short acknowledgment in which he restated his previous order to attack. Kurita responded that he would "break into Leyte Gulf and fight to the last man." At the same time he sent off another request to Manila for air support in the morning.

The freedom from air attack that Admiral Kurita had enjoyed after midafternoon was not, as he believed, due solely to a desire on Halsey's part to recover his planes before sundown. What in fact had happened was that the Third Fleet commander had finally spotted and taken the bait offered him in the form of Admiral Ozawa's decoy force.

Ever since the discovery that morning of the Kurita-Nishimura-Shima forces headed toward Leyte Gulf, Halsey had been convinced that the Japanese, as he put it, "were committed to a supreme effort." But if this was so, then where were the carriers, the ultimate striking arm of any major naval attack? There was good reason to believe that they had been in Japanese waters a week earlier, but neither submarines nor search planes had spotted them since. There was some chance the enemy carrier force might be in the South China Sea, preparing to follow and support the rest of the Japanese fleet. But Halsey and most of his staff and commanders felt that the carriers would have to come from the north, along the shorter, more direct route from Japan. Just before noon, then, the Third Fleet commander ordered Admiral Sherman, the northernmost of his three commanders, to launch a search to the north. But Sherman, with the stricken *Princeton* on his hands and another air raid coming in, was forced to delay the hunt for nearly two hours.

Meanwhile Admiral Ozawa had been doing everything possible to draw attention to himself—and for a while he must have been wondering if Halsey wasn't ignoring him on purpose. Since the previous evening he had been sending radio messages that he hoped would be intercepted, and he continued to sail rapidly into the range of Halsey's search planes. As it turned out, however, Ozawa found Halsey first. Shortly after eleven, one of Ozawa's scout planes spotted Admiral Sherman's group and reported its strength and location. Ozawa pushed south for about forty-five minutes, to shorten the range to 150 miles, and then launched the air strike that hit Sherman about 1 P.M. Since the Japanese pilots were green at executing carrier landings and the weather was none too good, Ozawa instructed them to continue on to fields on Luzon. Most of the survivors did so and were of no further use to him. The raid itself, as we have seen, was unsuccessful. Even worse, from Ozawa's viewpoint, was the fact that it failed to draw Halsey down on him. At about 2:40, then, in a final, desperate attempt to attract the enemy, Ozawa directed Rear Admiral Chiaki Matsuda with the two battleship-carriers, *Ise* and *Hyuga,* escorted by four destroyers, to push ahead and attack Sherman that night. This, he knew, could not be ignored.

During the afternoon Ozawa sent Admiral Kurita two messages, the first reporting the departure of the air strike, the second the dispatch of Matsuda. Significantly, neither message reached Kurita, perhaps because of trouble with *Zuikaku*'s transmitter, and that unhappy commander continued in ignorance of what Ozawa was doing.

Meanwhile, at about 3:40, two pilots from Admiral Davison's group, ranging far to the north, spotted Admiral Matsuda's force. And in another hour, a flyer from the *Lexington,* in Sherman's group, finally found Ozawa himself. This sighting—which, incidentally, had caused Mitscher to order the sinking of the crippled *Princeton*—was what Halsey had been waiting for. To use his own words, he "now had all the pieces of the puzzle." Only the solution remained.

The situation as Admiral Halsey saw it on the late afternoon of October 24 was this: three Japanese naval forces were converging on Leyte Gulf. The Southern Force, as the Americans called it—actually two forces, Nishimura's and Shima's, but regarded by the Americans as a single command—appeared to be the weakest. It was the smallest of the three, had already suffered some damage (although not as much as the attacking American pilots had reported), and could easily be handled by Kinkaid's larger and more powerful units. The Center Force, Kurita's, had been under heavy air assaults during the day and, according to the flyers' reports, had suffered one battleship sunk, four heavily damaged, at least three heavy cruisers badly damaged, a light cruiser sunk, and one destroyer sunk and four damaged. And when one added the damage previously inflicted by *Darter* and *Dace,* it was not difficult to conclude that, as Halsey reported, the Center Force had been "tremendously reduced in fighting power and life." Certainly it appeared that Kurita's ships "had been rather badly mauled . . . and that their fire control would be poor." By thus accepting exaggerated pilots' reports, Halsey was making the same error that Admiral Toyoda had committed after the Formosa air battle—and with almost as disastrous results.

But it was Admiral Ozawa's carrier units, the Northern Force, that really interested Halsey—and which, given the Third Fleet commander's background and nature, would probably have attracted him in any event. It included the bulk of Japan's carriers with, as far as Halsey knew, all of their aircraft. It appeared to constitute the strongest and therefore the most dangerous of the three enemy forces descending on Leyte Gulf. Its destruction would also remove for a long time, perhaps forever, the Japanese carrier threat in the Pacific.

Given this estimate, Halsey felt his choice was obvious. There was no point in remaining to guard San Bernardino Strait. This would leave the initiative to the Japanese and allow them to shuttle planes between their carriers and airfields in the Philippines, with the Third Fleet in the middle. The movement of Ozawa's pilots to Luzon after attacking Sherman underlined this possibility. On the other hand, American flyers had reported Kurita's vacillations and his hesitancy before San Bernardino Strait. And even if the Center Force did come through, it could at best, in Halsey's words, "merely hit-and-run." Besides, he felt, it was now so weak that Kinkaid could handle both it and the Southern Force.

An alternative would have been to leave strong elements to guard San Bernardino Strait and go after the Northern Force with the rest of the Third Fleet. This Halsey rejected—partially for the reasons already given, partially because he felt that dividing his fleet would leave the San Bernardino forces without sufficient air cover and the rest of the units without adequate antiaircraft defense, and partially because any weakening of his attack on the Northern Force would lessen his chances of dealing Japanese carrier power a crushing, decisive blow.

So, for all of these reasons, Halsey decided to uncover San Bernardino Strait and strike with his full power at Admiral Ozawa. This course, he wrote later, "preserved my Fleet's integrity, it left the initiative with me, and it promised the greatest possibility of surprise." He was not only seeking to meet head on the most dangerous threat to the whole Leyte invasion, but he was also fulfilling his original orders to assume as his "primary task" the "destruction of a major portion of the enemy fleet" if this opportunity arose.

Shortly before eight o'clock on the evening of October 24 Halsey made his decision to hit the Northern Force with everything he had. "Given the same circumstances," he has since written, "and the same information as I had then, I would make it again."

Halsey ordered Bogan and Davison to move north, Sherman to join them, and McCain to complete refueling and close with the rest of the fleet as soon as possible. San Bernardino Strait was wide open. Halsey had swallowed the bait. The Japanese plan, for all its difficulties, apparently had worked.

xii The Valley of Death

OF ALL the actions that made up what has come to be known as the Battle of Leyte Gulf, none actually took place within that body of water. But the battle fought in Surigao Strait in the dark, predawn hours of October 25 came closest.

October 25, 1944, was the ninetieth anniversary of the "Charge of the Light Brigade," immortalized in the famous lines of Alfred Tennyson. On that date in 1854, on the outskirts of a dirty Crimean town named Balaclava, 600 gallant British horsemen had galloped in a brave but futile assault on a Russian ridge position strongly held by artillery and infantry. Through the "valley of Death" they had charged, "into the mouth of Hell." "Someone," indeed, "had blundered." Now, nearly a century after that glorious catastrophe, on the very same date, Admirals Nishimura and Shima would lead their forces in an attack through Surigao Strait no less courageous, no less magnificent—and no less futile.

At 8:30 on the evening of October 24, as Admiral Kurita's warships headed for San Bernardino Strait, the 1st Striking Force commander received a message from Admiral Nishimura. The Nishimura Force, now well within the Mindanao Sea, expected to push through Surigao Strait and be deep within Leyte Gulf by 4 A.M. The time originally scheduled for Kurita and Nishimura to meet in the gulf was dawn—actually first light—or about 4:30, and it was important that the two forces arrive as close to simultaneously as they could. But as a result of Kurita's backing and filling in the Sibuyan Sea, this was no longer possible. Yet Nishimura, spurred by Toyoda's order for "all forces" to "dash to the attack," was still advancing in accordance with the original plan. So Kurita informed Nishimura that he did not expect to enter Leyte Gulf until about 11 A.M., and directed him to push through Surigao Strait as scheduled and join forces with him northeast of Suluan Island, at the eastern entrance to Leyte Gulf, at nine o'clock. Thus, Nishimura's attack was denied the assistance of a simultaneous blow by Kurita. He would have to penetrate Surigao Strait unsupported—unless, of course, Shima's 2nd Striking Force could catch up in time to help him.

The reception committee for Nishimura was every bit as strong or stronger than that which had awaited Lord Raglan's gallant cavalry at Balaclava ninety years earlier. In Surigao Strait, Admiral Kinkaid knew the Japanese were coming—and he was loaded for bear!

Kinkaid had been aware of the approach of the Southern Force since the morning sightings of both Nishimura and Shima. He reasoned correctly that they were headed for Surigao Strait and his preparations to receive them were as near perfect as possible. At 12:15 on the 24th Kinkaid had alerted all units of the Seventh Fleet to the probability of a major battle that evening. Two and a half hours later he directed Rear Admiral Oldendorf to block the northern exit of Surigao Strait with the entire Seventh Fleet Bombardment and Fire Support Group. Secure in the belief that Halsey was covering San Bernardino Strait and that his northern flank was protected, Kinkaid gave Oldendorf the fleet's entire heavy gunnery force: six old battleships, four heavy and four light cruisers, and twenty-one destroyers.

This force Oldendorf disposed in a manner best calculated to destroy anything coming up through Surigao Strait. At the northern end of the strait he placed his battleships, cruising back and forth in position to fire a devastating simultaneous broadside at anything that ventured into range. Here, also, the big ships would have ample room to maneuver and, furthermore, could be easily shifted if necessary to cover the eastern entrance to Leyte Gulf. In front of and on the flanks of this battleline Oldendorf stationed his cruisers, steaming parallel to the battleships. On and ahead of both flanks were the destroyers, ready to perform their classic mission of high-speed torpedo attacks on the approaching enemy. And in front of the whole arrangement, in the southern entrance to Surigao Strait and out in the Mindanao Sea, were thirty-nine PT boats, improved versions of the craft that had taken MacArthur from Corregidor to Mindanao. The mission of the PT boats was first of all to detect and report the approach of the Japanese force. Their secondary mission, which many of the PT commanders preferred, was to attack.

The only weak spot in this whole arrangement was a slight ammunition problem. The Seventh Fleet bombardment elements had been originally armed for pre-assault shelling in the since-canceled invasion of Yap. Consequently, they carried primarily "high capacity" shells for shore bombardment, and only a small proportion of armor-piercing projectiles, which were necessary to penetrate armored decks and hulls in any fleet engagement. Furthermore, more than half of their "high capacity" ammunition had been fired at shore positions on Leyte. To make up for this weakness, the captains of the battleships planned to withhold their fire until targets reached the relatively short range—for a battleship—of ten to twelve miles, to increase the chance that every shot would count. They were also ready to shift from armor-piercing to "high capacity" shells if anything smaller than an enemy battleship poked its nose into range. Oldendorf's destroyers also were somewhat short, with no replacement torpedoes and, after the pre-assault bombardment, only about 20 percent of their initial shell load for the 5-inch guns.

Despite these drawbacks, there is no gainsaying the tremendous power of Oldendorf's force nor the advantage of its position. Against this mighty armada, Nishimura had but two old battleships previously regarded as fit only for training purposes, a heavy cruiser, and four destroyers. Shima's force of one light and two heavy cruisers and four destroyers was even weaker. And both would have to come head on into the teeth of the Seventh Fleet. The Japanese ships, moreover, lacked effective fire-control equipment, while the Americans were carrying the very latest equipment. But as Admiral Oldendorf observed after the battle, he believed in the old saying, "Never give a sucker a chance." By this he meant that "if my opponent is foolish enough to come at me with an inferior force, I'm certainly not going to give him an even break."

On came Nishimura. Perhaps he anticipated his fate. That morning his only floatplane had reconnoitered Leyte Gulf and returned with a sobering report of American naval strength. The admiral was an experienced hand and well knew what his chances were. Possibly he consoled himself with the thought that in a night action he would be spared the punishing air attacks that Kurita had suffered that day. In any event, he was apparently determined to do all in his power to divert American seapower away from Kurita, who, with his stronger force, had a much better chance of breaking into Leyte Gulf. Nishimura had lost his only son, a brilliant naval academy graduate, only a short while before, and now he may have anticipated that he would soon join the young officer. By none of his actions did he indicate that he was not reconciled to this end.

At about 9 P.M. Nishimura sent heavy cruiser *Mogami* and three destroyers on ahead to scout the entrance to Sogod Bay, on the north flank of the Japanese approach, where American PT boats were thought to be based. Nishimura's intelligence was good, but by this time all the PT's had left their base and were deployed in three-boat sections astride his course and at the entrance to Surigao Strait. Thus, while the scouting force proceeded unopposed, Nishimura's flag group soon encountered the southernmost PT's.

At about 10:15 radar on PT 131 picked up this group and the torpedo boat and two others immediately drove forward to attack. Approximately half an hour later, before the small craft were within torpedo range, a light haze lifted, revealing both sides to each other. Nishimura immediately turned toward the PT's, presenting a narrow target. The destroyer *Shigure* illuminated the area with star shell, and both she and battleships *Fuso* and *Yamashiro* opened fire. Their shells straddled the three small craft, which zigzagged, made smoke, and continued to press the attack. But the odds were too great. One PT was hit on her bow gun and another took a shell that passed right through without exploding. Obviously una▨▨ ▨▨get within torpedo range, the PT's soon broke off the ▨▨▨▨ ▨▨ withdrew to send off a contact report. All their radios had ▨▨▨ knocked out, but the three boats joined another PT section, which relayed the news to Admiral Oldendorf. Oldendorf got this word not too long after midnight, his first specific report on Nishimura for more than half a day.

By now the *Mogami* group had flushed a section of PT's, just before midnight. This time the PT's managed to get off two torpedoes, but both missed, and the three boats retired, making smoke and zigging and zagging back and forth to escape the Japanese shells. A few minutes later the two Japanese groups joined each other again and Nishimura radioed Kurita and Shima—the latter about forty miles behind Nishimura—that he expected to enter Surigao Strait at 1:30 A.M. The weather was not good and he knew nothing of American dispositions aside from the few PT boats he had driven off.

At about 2 A.M. on the 25th Nishimura turned north into Surigao Strait, half an hour behind his earlier estimate. Almost immediately he came under attack by another PT section, shot his way through this ambush, knocking out one boat in the process, and then pushed through another group of PT's just before 2:30. This was his last encounter with the small craft, and so far Nishimura had suffered no damage. One by one he had brushed aside his attackers. Each PT section that he had encountered had been alerted by the lights and gunfire before it, had sent off a contact report, attacked, missed with its torpedoes, and then fled from the Japanese searchlights under cover of smoke while Nishimura's gunners laid down a hail of not very accurate fire. The PT crews had not had a chance to make torpedo attacks in over a year, so their misses can be excused for lack of practice. But the poor shooting of the Japanese, who hit a few boats but only one fatally, is much harder to explain.

Nevertheless, Nishimura's advance had been neither stopped nor hindered. If he was beginning to wonder about the lack of solid opposition, his questions would soon be answered. The PT contact reports had given Admiral Oldendorf ample warning and already Captain J. G. Coward, commanding the forward picket destroyers, had warned the PT's to get out of his way. He was attacking.

Shortly before three o'clock Nishimura ordered his ships into the formation in which they would push through the strait. This was a single column: the four destroyers, flagship *Yamashiro*, *Fuso*, and, finally, *Mogami*. His reasons for this formation are not clear and, as events turned out, his decision was an unfortunate one for him. It brought his ships forward in a long single column perpendicular to the American line of battle, as if Oldendorf's line formed the cap on the letter T and Nishimura's column the upright. For a naval force to thus "cap the T" of an enemy

column is a rare and most welcome situation. It enables the defenders along the crosspiece of the T to concentrate broadsides
from all their ships against each enemy vessel in turn as it comes
into range—while the attacking warships can only bring to bear
the guns in their forward turrets. Four decades earlier the Japanese Admiral Togo had capped the Russian T at Tsushima, and at
Jutland, in 1916, Admiral Jellicoe had done the same without
knowing it to a German fleet. Now Oldendorf was about to do it
to the Japanese—that is, if Nishimura could fight his way within
range of the battleships.

Just as Nishimura's ships were completing their shift into column formation at four minutes to three, a lookout on destroyer
Shigure, the fourth vessel in line, reported three ships four miles
off the starboard bow. These were three of Captain Coward's destroyers, speeding down Surigao Strait on a course that would
bring them between Nishimura's column and the Dinagat Island,
or eastern, shore of the strait. Two minutes later the three began
to turn away from Nishimura and, just after three, still turning,
launched their torpedoes. They deliberately refrained from firing
their guns, in order not to give away their position with the
flashes, but Japanese searchlights and star shells quickly illuminated them. Nishimura's gunners immediately opened fire, but
missed, and the three attackers steamed swiftly up the strait and
out of range. Nishimura, for some reason, made no effort to evade
the torpedoes that he should have realized were coming, and a
moment or so later the *Fuso* took at least two of these lethal fish
into her starboard side. The battleship slowed, but limped along
with the rest of the column.

While all this was going on, two more of Captain Coward's
destroyers were attacking down the west, or Leyte, side of Surigao Strait. Nishimura spotted these just as they were about to attack and brought them under heavy but inaccurate fire. At 3:11
the destroyers launched their torpedoes and, despite evasive action by Nishimura, hit three Japanese destroyers and *Yamashiro*.
Michishio, the lead destroyer, was crippled, and *Asagumo*, next in
line, lost her bow but remained afloat. Both fell out of the column
and attempted to retire. The third ship, *Yamagumo*, blew up and
sank in an instant, while *Yamashiro* was apparently not seriously
hurt. Meanwhile the attacking destroyers whirled about and

roared north to safety.

The first destroyer attack, skillfully executed, halved Nishimura's force. Only *Shigure* and *Mogami* had not been hit. *Yamashiro* was still in good shape, but *Fuso,* although Nishimura apparently failed to realize this, was dying and three destroyers were out of action. The admiral sent a brief report to Kurita—which, for some reason, did not reach him until eleven hours later—and an order to his remaining ships to "proceed independently to the attack."

But it was not the Japanese who were attacking. Beginning at 3:15 and continuing for half an hour, six destroyers led by Captain K. M. McManes struck at Nishimura from their stations off the Leyte shore. Charging down on the Japanese port flank, they launched spread after spread of torpedoes against the confused column. Most of these missed their mark, but one hit the already wounded *Yamashiro* and slowed the flagship to five knots. Gunfire from the American destroyers also struck the Japanese column, falling especially on the crippled *Michishio* and *Asagumo,* which were limping to the rear. A spread of torpedoes finally put *Michishio* out of her misery. The destroyer exploded and went down at once. The return fire of the Japanese force continued to be inaccurate.

Even before Captain McManes' attack was concluded, nine more destroyers under Captain Roland N. Smoot came driving down from their position in front of the east flank of the American battleline. Smoot's squadron hit Nishimura's column on both flanks and from dead ahead. Pressing close despite a heavy rain of shells from the Japanese ships, the destroyers swung in, launched their torpedoes, two of which slammed against *Yamashiro,* and then turned and hightailed it out of the way.

By now, however, the Japanese had come within range of Oldendorf's battleline and the American battleships and cruisers had at last opened fire. Some of Smoot's destroyers were thus exposed to shells from both sides. At seven minutes after 4 A.M., the inevitable happened. A shell—whether Japanese or American no one knows—struck the destroyer *Albert W. Grant,* to be followed within a few minutes by a dozen and a half more, most of them from the 6-inch guns of an American light cruiser. One shell hit the *Grant* at the waterline, flooding forward areas. Another ex-

Left, Admiral William F. Halsey, Third Fleet. *At right,* Vice Admiral Jesse B. Oldendorf, Battleship Squadron One

Left to right, Major General Verne D. Mudge, General Douglas Mac-Arthur, Lieutenant General R. K. Sutherland, General Walter Kraeger, and Lieutenant General G. C. Kenney on Leyte, October 22

U.S.S. *Princeton* afire, as seen from U.S.S. *Birmingham*

Part of landing fleet at Dulag Bay

A-Day at Dulag. *Below*, Landing ships at Tacloban Airstrip

77th Division heavy machine guns north of Ormoc

1st Cavalry Division Patrol in Tacloban

7th Cavalry Regiment motor pool

Engineers trying to repair White Beach access road

A forward aid station

Filipino porters supporting 1st Cavalry Division near Carigara

155-millimeter long toms near Carigara

Elements of the 24th Division at Pawing Hill

Japanese ships under air attack in Ormoc Bay

ploded in an ammunition storage area and started a fire. Another burst on the starboard boat davit, another on the port motor whaleboat, another in the galley, and still others on the forward stack. And still they came: one in the scullery room, one in the after crew's berthing compartment, one in the forward engine room. All lights, communications, radios, and radars were out, fires raged in several areas, and the killed and wounded were everywhere to be seen. The ship lay dead in the water. Just when it seemed that the next shell must surely finish the *Grant*, Admiral Oldendorf received word of her predicament and immediately ordered his heavy ships to cease fire. The destroyer *Newcomb* dashed in, rigged a tow, and pulled the stricken vessel back up Surigao Strait. Despite her injuries, the *Grant* lived to fight another day.

As much could not be said for Nishimura's force. At 3:51 A.M. the American cruisers and, two minutes later, the battleships that formed the cap of the T had finally opened fire on the Japanese ships still in the upright. *Fuso* had exploded and split in two by this time and the wounded *Asagumo* was creeping south along the western shoreline of the strait. So only *Yamashiro*, *Mogami*, and *Shigure* were left, the latter two still unhit. From the time the battleline opened fire until the *Grant*'s predicament brought a halt to the shelling, eighteen minutes elapsed. In this period the big American ships fired almost 300 rounds of 14- and 16-inch projectiles and over 4,000 rounds of 6- and 8-inch shells at the three Japanese ships. So many shells hit their mark that it seems incredible Nishimura's warships did not sink from the sheer weight of projectiles striking them.

But the Japanese vessels died slowly. Firing bravely, tending their wounded, making what repairs they could, the commanders of the three ships pressed gamely on "into the mouth of Hell." Yet it was more than flesh and blood and steel could take. At five minutes before four *Mogami*, badly hurt and on fire, reversed course and began to move south. Still firing and launching torpedoes, she pulled away as more and more shells crashed into her. Just after four a salvo hit on her bridge, killing the commander and staff, and seconds later additional hits slowed her almost to a halt.

By now, also, Nishimura had turned *Yamashiro*. The battleship continued to fire, but she was aflame from one end to the other and had absorbed so many hits that she was practically unnavigable. Nevertheless, when Admiral Oldendorf ordered ceasefire, *Yamashiro* seemed to catch her second wind and increased speed as she fled south. For several minutes she proceeded on course, smoke billowing skyward from the flames that wreathed her. But at 4:19 she rolled over and slipped beneath the sea. Admiral Nishimura and most of the crew went down with her.

Meanwhile the destroyer *Shigure* appeared to be leading a charmed life. She zigzagged through an increasingly heavy rain of shells, none of which struck her. "I was receiving a terrific bombardment," her captain, Commander Shigeru Nishino, recalled later. "There were so many near misses that the gyro compass was out. The ship was constantly trembling from the force of near misses, and the wireless was out." At about four o'clock, convinced that *Shigure* was the only surviving Japanese ship, Nishino turned the destroyer south. A moment or so later *Shigure* took her first hit, an 8-inch shell which pierced her deck but failed to explode. Nishino continued south past the burning *Mogami*.

Meanwhile Admiral Shima's 2nd Striking Force had been following Nishimura at high speed, to support him if possible and, in any event, to join in the scheduled morning rendezvous with Kurita off Suluan Island. With no orders to coordinate with Nishimura and, if he was to maintain radio silence, unable to communicate with him, Shima could only press ahead and await developments.

Forewarned as early as midnight by intercepts of messages from the embattled Nishimura, and later by the easily visible flashes of gunfire, Shima knew he was in for a fight. As he turned north into Surigao Strait at about 3 A.M. he pushed two destroyers forward as a screen and formed his remaining five ships in a column. Shima led in his flagship, heavy cruiser *Nachi*. Then came heavy cruiser *Ashigara*, light cruiser *Abukuma*, and the other two destroyers. Once clear of the entrance to the strait, Shima ordered his forward screening destroyers to fall back, and now he himself was at the head of the attack.

Just before 3:30, as the two destroyers moved to the rear of the column, Lieutenant Mike Kovar, Commanding PT 137, launched a torpedo at one of them from his station off the western shore of the strait. His torpedo missed its target but ran on and struck *Abukuma,* suddenly and unexpectedly, in the port side amidships. The blow came near the forward radio room and killed practically everybody there as well as several other crewmen nearby. Down at the bow, *Abukuma* slowed to ten knots and fell out of formation. Kovar had the distinction of being the only PT skipper actually to hit a Japanese ship in the entire battle of Surigao Srait.

Undismayed by the loss of *Abukuma,* Shima plunged on at increased speed through the heavy smoke of battle that drifted down from the north. Half an hour later he passed the burning halves of *Fuso,* sillhouetted by their own flames and blazing furiously. He took these to be two ships, *Fuso* and *Yamashiro* by their size, and his fears for the condition of Nishimura's force were suddenly magnified.

Next Shima came upon the *Shigure.* Commander Nishino had halted the destroyer's southward retirement to repair his rudder lines, damaged by several near misses, and *Shigure* lay still in the water. Nishino flashed a request for identification and received the answer, "I am the *Nachi.*" He himself then replied, "I am the *Shigure.* I have rudder difficulties." Nishino offered no further information about the rest of Nishimura's force, because, as he explained later, he "had no connection with [Shima] and was not under his command." Thus Shima continued north, still unaware of the fate of Nishimura or of the location of the American warships.

By now Shima must have been quite worried. The darkness and the heavy screen of smoke drifting south reduced visibility practically to zero. Even radar failed to reveal anything. At about 4:20, finally, the radar screen showed a group of ships, apparently American, some six to eight miles north. At the same time the burning *Mogami,* evidently dead in the water, appeared ahead and to starboard. Shima immediately ordered an attack on the American ships. The *Nachi* and *Ashigara* swung hard to starboard, to pass just short of *Mogami,* and launched eight torpedoes each. The four destroyers sped past the port side of the cruisers, heading north to strike at close range.

As *Nachi,* the lead cruiser, completed its torpedo launch, Shima and the others on the bridge were horrified to discover that the ship was nearing *Mogami* at an alarming rate and heading straight for a collision. Instead of being dead in the water, *Mogami* was actually creeping south at about eight knots. The burning ship was out of control, rudder useless, her entire command section dead on the bridge, and being desperately navigated from her engine room. At 4:30 *Nachi's* captain gave her hard right rudder and stopped his engines. But it was too late. The flagship plowed into *Mogami* at an angle, tore a hole in her own bow, began to flood, and slowed to eighteen knots. *Ashigara* managed to avoid a collision, but *Nachi* ran south for about ten minutes to investigate her damage before her captain judged the ship was in shape to turn north again.

Meanwhile none of the sixteen torpedoes launched by the cruisers had hit anything, and the four destroyers rushing north had failed to make any contact. Admiral Shima still had not located the American ships, which he knew were somewhere ahead of him in great numbers. He had lost one cruiser while another, his flagship could do no more than twenty knots, too slow to make an attack. And, finally, he still did not know what had happened to Nishimura's force, although he now had good reason to fear the worst. "At the time," Shima wrote recently, "things flashed in my head were thus: . . . If we continued dashing further north, it was quite clear that we should only fall into a ready trap." Shortly before 5 A.M. he decided to fall back, regroup, and reconsider.

Shima ordered his destroyers to "turn and head south to join us," and the entire force, including the crippled *Mogami,* began to withdraw under a smoke screen. To Admiral Kurita, Shima reported the "complete destruction" of *Yamashiro* and *Fuso,* the heavy damage to *Mogami,* and his own intention to retire "from the battle area to plan subsequent action."

As Shima withdrew, the first light of dawn revealed *Shigure* far ahead of him. The destroyer had completed her repairs and was now pushing south again at good speed. Shima made no attempt to communicate with her as she passed from sight. Commander Nishino apparently did not even notice Shima behind him, although even if he had he probably would have done nothing about it. Two days later *Shigure* dropped anchor in Brunei Bay, the sole survivor of Nishimura's force.

Meanwhile, at about 5:30 on the morning of the 25th, cruiser *Abukuma* rejoined Shima at the southern end of Surigao Strait, and the entire force proceeded into the Mindanao Sea. Hard behind them came Admiral Oldendorf with nearly a score of cruisers and destroyers. Now three of the American cruisers opened fire on *Mogami*, at the end of Shima's column, and hit her several times. But *Mogami* appeared unsinkable. Burning furiously, she refused to go down, and then was spared further punishment when the cruisers turned away to avoid Japanese torpedoes. Shima's force continued south, attacked several times without success by the plucky PT boats, but no longer menaced by the larger American ships, which had turned north again to concentrate in Surigao Strait. There, at about 7 A.M., more than half a dozen of Oldendorf's ships caught the crippled destroyer *Asagumo*, the last Japanese vessel still in the strait. A torrent of shells fell on her. Like a desperate animal at bay, she fought back viciously, but never had a chance. Fifteen minutes later, still firing as she sank, the valiant destroyer went down.

At about the same time Admiral Shima spotted American carrier planes and an hour and a half later, at 9:10, he came under attack by nearly a score of aircraft from Sprague's escort carriers. The attackers hit *Mogami* again. This time the blow was fatal. Dead in the water, ablaze, incapable of further navigation, the cruiser's luck had run out. A destroyer pulled alongside to take off survivors and then sent her to a well-deserved rest beneath the waves with a skillfully placed torpedo.

Now Shima made his final decision. In the face of American air action, another attempt to penetrate Surigao Strait—this time in daylight—would almost certainly lead to disaster. Two of his cruisers were already badly damaged, and all of his ships were getting low on fuel. Nishimura's force had apparently been destroyed and Shima had heard nothing of Admiral Kurita for nearly twelve hours. To renew the attack under the circumstances seemed senseless. Shima therefore ordered his ships to continue their retirement. *Abukuma*, however, was sunk by Fifth Air Force bombers the next day. *Nachi* made it to Manila, only to be destroyed by carrier planes within two weeks. *Ashigara* managed to stay afloat by putting into Palawan, and only the four destroyers were able to get all the way back to Brunei Bay. Thus, of two

Japanese battleships, one light and three heavy cruisers, and eight destroyers that entered Surigao Strait only a single heavy cruiser and five destroyers were left afloat two weeks after the battle.

The Battle of Surigao Strait, the valiant charge of Nishimura "into the mouth of Hell," the brave but more discreet maneuverings of Shima "through the jaws of Death," had brought the Japanese no gain whatsoever. The attack had failed to reach Leyte Gulf, had damaged only a few PT boats and, indirectly, one destroyer, and had not in any way, as we shall see, eased Kurita's planned entrance into Leyte Gulf. Who was responsible for the Japanese failure? Was it Balaclava all over again? Had someone "blundered"?

American naval strength would probably have proved sufficient in any event, but a series of unfortunate Japanese decisions —beginning with Toyoda's loss of his naval air strength in the Formosa air battle—inevitably made the fight a one-sided affair. Ignoring, however, those factors that affected the Battle of Leyte Gulf as a whole and concentrating for the moment on Surigao Strait, there were several events that led to the Japanese defeat in those dark waters.

The first was the decision to split the 1st Striking Force, sending Nishimura against an obviously superior foe. Had Nishimura remained with Kurita, and had Shima joined them, the combined force would have been a truly powerful unit, unlikely to be defeated, as it was, in detail. Kurita's choice of routes for his own approach to the battle was equally unfortunate for the Japanese. It left him open to attacks that delayed his advance and prevented a joint descent on Leyte Gulf from opposite sides, in which at least one of the Japanese forces might have been successful. The handling of Shima's unit was no less damaging, for the least that might have been expected was some coordination between Shima and Nishimura. By refusing to place Shima under Kurita's command, Toyoda effectively prevented any close cooperation between the two Japanese forces in Surigao Strait. And this being the case, Shima's warships might have been better employed with Kurita's force than they were as a separate element behind Nishimura.

A considerable amount has been written about supposed jealousies between Shima and Nishimura based on their relative ranks, and about whether or not Nishimura increased his speed (he apparently did not) in order to avoid coming under Shima's command. The basis for this speculation appears to be unsound. Indeed, the statement of Commander Nishino of the *Shigure* about his own lack of cooperation with Shima would seem to be more revealing: "I had no connection with him and was not under his command." If ever divided command was a significant factor in increasing the magnitude of defeat it was at Leyte Gulf.

Both Nishimura and Shima have also been criticized for their tactics in Surigao Strait, Nishimura for maintaining a column instead of zigzagging in a staggered formation, Shima for the collision with *Mogami* and his failure at least to damage some of Oldendorf's ships. But Nishimura did not survive to defend himself and it is not at all clear that a different formation would have produced different results in a battle so obviously one-sided. Shima, in turn, has explained his discretion, although not the *Mogami* incident, with reasonable arguments, and he did manage to get most of his ships safely out of Surigao Strait. Despite criticisms to the contrary, also, it is certainly not obvious that either Nishimura or Shima could have timed his entrance into Surigao Strait any better. The fault in the timing would appear to be Kurita's or, in a larger sense, Toyoda's. And given the overwhelming American naval strength, it is very doubtful that better timing would have given the Japanese victory in Surigao Strait.

If an observer on the shores of Surigao Strait during the first dark hours of October 25, 1944, had been able to view the whole glorious fiasco of the Japanese attack, he might have been moved to remark like the French General Bosquet at Balaclava ninety years earlier, "It's magnificent, but it's not war!"

xiii *Taffy* 3

THE MISSION of destroying the American invasion force in Leyte Gulf now lay with Admiral Kurita—supported by whatever diversion could be provided by Admiral Ozawa's decoy force. Shortly before midnight on October 24, Kurita began his final approach to San Bernardino Strait. For the run through these confined waters and the narrow strait itself he formed his ships in a single column. Friendly lights flashed from the shore to guide him and, thanks to a clear night, visibility was excellent. Navigation thus presented no problem and the Japanese force sped forward at twenty knots.

Since Kurita had no reason to think otherwise, he fully expected to have to fight his way out of the strait. His tense crews were at battle stations, the lookouts straining their eyes for the first sign of the enemy. The events of the past two days had clearly tired everyone, from the admiral down to the lowest seaman, and while the anticipation of coming battle lifted spirits noticeably, the strain and fatigue had taken their toll. It was with relief and incredulity, then, that Kurita debouched into the Philippine Sea at thirty-five minutes after midnight and found no enemy before him. He quickly shifted his force into night combat formation and sped east. Within a few hours he had turned the northeast corner of Samar and was running almost due south about ten miles off the island's coast. As yet he had encountered no American ships, an unbelievable stroke of good fortune.

By now, meanwhile, Admiral Halsey was nearly 250 miles to the north, his taste for battle whetted by reports from night search planes that had spotted the two halves of Ozawa's force attempting to rendevous another 200 miles or so farther north. The decision to go after this force had not, however, been re-

ceived enthusiastically in all quarters. Even before Halsey issued
the orders implementing this decision, a night search pilot had
discovered and reported Kurita's force heading once again
toward San Bernardino Strait, a report confirmed by a second
pilot only a few minutes after the orders went out. This in no
way bothered Halsey, who had taken this possibility into consid-
ration when he made his decision. But others were concerned.

On board the carrier *Bunker Hill* Admiral Bogan had received
not only the reports about Kurita but also the further, disquieting
information that the long-darkened navigation lights in San
Bernardino Strait had been turned on. Since Halsey, on *New Jersey*, was sailing in Bogan's task group, Bogan called him over TBS
(Talk Between Ships, a short-range, line-of-sight voice radio, unlikely to be intercepted by enemy listeners) to pass on this additional intelligence. He apparently did not talk directly with
Halsey and whoever did speak with Bogan merely told him, "Yes,
yes, we have that information." Bogan had intended suggesting
that strong elements be left to guard San Bernardino Strait. Now,
however, feeling that his recommendations were not wanted, he
decided not to make any.

A second dissent was entered by Vice Admiral Willis A. Lee,
who commanded Halsey's battleships and was himself a passen-
ger aboard the battleship *Washington* in Davison's task group,
then sailing in company with Bogan's force. Lee, too, had been
disturbed by the reports about Kurita and even more so by his
own conclusion that Ozawa probably commanded nothing more
than a weak decoy force. Lee sent two messages to Halsey, the
second stronger than the first, but received nothing more than an
acknowledgment in each case. Like Bogan, he also made no further effort to change Halsey's mind.

Admiral Mitscher, meanwhile, on the *Lexington* in Sherman's
group, had apparently been growing increasingly unhappy over
the fact that Halsey rather than he was running Task Force 38.
Halsey's order to move north and subsequent other instructions
now convinced Mitscher that he had in effect been relieved of
tactical command of the task force. He therefore decided to go to
bed and leave everything to Halsey. Two hours later, however,
his chief of staff and operations officer awoke Mitscher with the
information that Kurita was definitely headed for San Bernardino

Strait. Shouldn't they tell Halsey to turn around? Mitscher asked
if Halsey had the search plane reports. "Yes, he does," was the
reply. "If he wants my advice," said Mitscher, "he'll ask for it."
And he went back to sleep.

An hour later, just before midnight, the three task groups ren-
dezvoused east of central Luzon and pushed north. No one else
questioned this action.

In the meantime, what did Admiral Kinkaid know about Halsey's dispositions and Kurita's advance? From the start of the
King-II operation, Kinkaid had assumed that Halsey would protect him against any Japanese naval force approaching from the
north. He had no reason to change this assumption and, indeed,
was reinforced in it at midafternoon of the 24th when he intercepted a message from Halsey to his subordinate commanders.
This message, which Halsey dispatched shortly after the last carrier attack on Kurita that day, was aimed at the possibility that
Kurita, despite the beating he had absorbed, might still try to
come through San Bernardino Strait. Labeled a "Battle Plan," it
stated that four battleships and a score of cruisers and destroyers
from Task Force 38 "will be formed as Task Force 34"
under Admiral Lee and "will engage decisively at long ranges."
"This dispatch," Halsey wrote later, "I intended merely as a warning to the ships concerned that if a surface engagement offered, I
would detach them from Task Force 38, form them into Task
Force 34, and send them ahead as a battle line. It was definitely
not an executive dispatch, but a battle plan, and was so marked."

Halsey meant the order to be simply "preparatory," as he
afterwards explained, and several of its recipients so interpreted
it. But Admiral Kinkaid, who intercepted the message although
he was not an addressee, and Admiral Nimitz in Hawaii and the
deputy chief of naval operations in Washington, who received information copies, interpreted the words "will be formed" as an
order rather than a plan for future action. They assumed that
Task Force 34 was indeed being formed. None of the three, however, was in position to intercept a subsequent more precise TBS
message that Halsey sent his task group commanders two hours
later: "If the enemy sorties, Task Force 34 will be formed when
directed by me." The "Battle Plan" was still a plan.

Kinkaid nevertheless believed, as he wrote after the war, that

Halsey had "set up a plan to guard San Bernardino . . . which was perfect in concept and perfect in composition of the forces assigned." Nor did he receive any message to disabuse him of this conclusion. Shortly after 8 P.M.—Halsey having made his decision to move north—Kinkaid intercepted Halsey's implementing orders to his task group commanders. He also received a message from Halsey that he was "proceeding north with three groups to attack enemy carrier force at dawn." By this message Halsey meant that he was taking Bogan, Davison, and Sherman's task groups with him—including of course all the ships tentatively assigned to the as yet unformed Task Force 34. He did not mention McCain's group, which was still refueling to the east and would join him later. But Kinkaid, believing that Task Force 34 was already in being, concluded that Halsey was going north with three carrier groups and leaving Admiral Lee with Task Force 34 and the fourth carrier group to guard San Bernardino Strait. This disposition made good sense to Kinkaid and, to quote him again, "it was inconceivable that Halsey could have scrapped a perfect plan" and left the strait unguarded.

Believing that Task Force 34 was covering San Bernardino, and preoccupied with thoughts of the approaching battle in Surigao Strait, Kinkaid all but forgot about his northern flank. But, as a matter of routine and, as he said, "mostly out of curiosity," he ordered a northward search by PBY's, amphibious aircraft, equipped for night flights. Only one of these planes came anywhere near Kurita, but missed him because of unfortunate timing. The PBY took off from a bay in Leyte Gulf after sunset, flew up the east coast of Samar, passed over San Bernardino Strait around 10:30 P.M., before Kurita had reached that passage, and then lumbered down the western shore of the island while the Japanese force was actually steaming through and out of San Bernardino Strait.

Kinkaid had no night-search planes on his escort carriers, but he did direct Admiral Sprague to launch a northward search at dawn. This was delayed by the difficulty of shifting planes at night on a flight deck made slippery by rain. It was thus nearly 7 A.M. on the 25th before the search got off, too late to give Kinkaid any advance warning of Kurita's approach.

Indeed, it was just about then that the Seventh Fleet commander was shocked to learn from Halsey that San Bernardino Strait was wide open. At 4:12 A.M. Kinkaid had informed Halsey that he was "engaging enemy surface force [in] Surigao Strait." At the suggestion of his operations officer, Captain Richard H. Cruzen, he added the question: "Is TF 34 guarding San Bernardino Strait?" For some inexplicable reason—possibly an overloaded communications net—this message did not reach Admiral Halsey until 6:48. Confused by the question, since he was unaware that Kinkaid had intercepted his earlier "Battle Plan," Halsey replied: "Negative." Task Force 34, which he had finally formed just before three o'clock to use against Ozawa, was driving north with him.

By the time Kinkaid received Halsey's answer, however, he already knew the worst. At four minutes after seven a frantic message came in from the Seventh Fleet escort carriers off the southeast coast of Samar: four enemy battleships and a host of cruisers and destroyers were firing on them at a range of seventeen miles!

The Japanese gunners were shooting at a highly vulnerable group of targets. The escort carriers—or CVE's, as they were abbreviated—were small, slow, unarmored, and lightly gunned ships, built by throwing a short flight deck atop a merchant ship or tanker hull. They were developed early in the war to provide air cover for convoys or antisubmarine patrols and they quickly gained added value as a ready means of furnishing air support to amphibious operations. Each carried a dozen torpedo bombers and twelve to eighteen fighters. Security restrictions and the glamour surrounding the handsome big carriers kept the role of the CVE's relatively unpublicized, but if the larger ships got most of the credit, the little escort carriers did more tedious work and took on the greater part of the day-to-day routine. Never designed for a stand-up fight, the thin-skinned CVE's were called "baby flattops" or "jeep carriers" in polite parlance and "Kaiser coffins" (after one of their builders), "buckets of bolts," and a lot worse otherwise. Many of their crewmen swore emphatically that CVE really stood for "Combustible, Vulnerable, Expendable."

On the morning of October 25 the sixteen escort carriers—two of the original number having departed for Morotai the night before—of Rear Admiral Thomas L. Sprague's Task Group 77.4 were organized in three elements, or task units. These task units were referred to as Taffy 1, Taffy 2, and Taffy 3, after their voice radio call signals. Each included four to six CVE's, three destroyers, and four destroyer escorts, the latter as lightly armored as the jeep carriers and designed primarily for antisubmarine work. Taffy 1, commanded by Sprague himself, was operating off Mindanao, Taffy 2, under Rear Admiral Felix B. Stump, was east of southern Samar, and Taffy 3, under Rear Admiral Clifton A. F. Sprague (no relation to the task group commander), was another twenty miles farther north. Until now they had been flying routine support missions for the Leyte landings, covering the beachhead and the transport areas, maintaining antisubmarine patrol, and, since the captured Leyte airstrips were not yet ready to receive army aircraft, furnishing tactical support of ground operations on the island.

As Kurita approached, Taffy 1 had just sent off planes to help mop up Japanese remnants in Surigao Strait, Taffy 2 had launched the northward air search ordered by Admiral Kinkaid, and Taffy 3 was flying cover over Leyte Gulf as well as antisubmarine patrol. It seemed like a routine day, and the furthest thought from anyone's mind was that a Japanese battle fleet could be just over the horizon.

Kurita's force was still steaming in night scouting formation at the fuel-preserving speed of eighteen knots. Daybreak was masked by low black clouds and squalls, limiting visibility, but just before 6:30 A.M. *Yamato's* radar screen showed unidentified aircraft. A few minutes later lookouts spotted an American patrol plane. Kurita immediately ordered the fleet to change to antiaircraft formation, a circular or, as the Japanese put it, "ring-like" disposition.

Even as the admiral gave this order, the pilot above him, Ensign George Brooks, was shouting a hasty report over his radio to Taffy 3, the nearest group of escort carriers: "Enemy surface force of four battleships, eight cruisers, and eleven destroyers sighted twenty miles northwest of your task group." On board his flagship, the CVE *Fanshaw Bay*, Admiral Clifton Sprague thought Brooks had mistaken part of Admiral Halsey's force for Japanese ships. He ordered another check. Just then, however, antiaircraft guns on *Yamato* and *Haruna* opened fire on the patrol plane and, almost simultaneously, lookouts in both fleets sighted each other's masts. It was now about 6:45.

The sight of the telltale pagoda masts and of a heavy pattern of antiaircraft puffs above them was enough for Admiral Sprague. He knew what he was up against in his slow-moving, thin-skinned escort ships, and he wasted no time. Quickly he ordered a course change to the east, opening the range and at the same time heading at full speed for the cover of an inviting little rain squall. Simultaneously he sent all his planes aloft, radioed those aircraft on ground support missions to get back on the double, and directed every vessel in his task unit to throw up as much protective smoke as it could. A fortunate northeast wind enabled Sprague to launch his planes without shifting course and the warm, moist air held the smoke low over the fleeing ships. A few minutes later, just after seven o'clock, he sent out a plain-language radio call for help. Already Japanese shells were splashing down astern.

But if Sprague's decision was an obvious one, Kurita's was not so simple. The unexpected meeting with the enemy was, as his chief of staff put it later, "indeed a miracle." Undetected by radar, unopposed by warships, the Japanese had suddenly come upon an American carrier group at close range. Their unbelieving eyes seemed to behold what Kurita described as a "gigantic enemy task force": half a dozen large carriers, many cruisers and destroyers, and perhaps even one or two battleships. Not for a moment, either then or throughout the engagement with Taffy 3, did Kurita realize that all he faced was half a dozen puny escort carriers, three destroyers, and four destroyer escorts.

What should he do about this sudden target of opportunity? The previous day's experience had left Kurita most wary of American carrier planes, especially since he had no air cover himself and his antiaircraft gunners had shown little skill or effectiveness. The enemy force also represented a diversion from his primary mission of destroying the shipping in Leyte Gulf. But Kurita could not ignore what lay before him. The carriers could be expected to retreat out of gunfire range, but they would also certainly try to destroy him from the sky. Whether he liked it or not, he would have to close with the enemy and sink him lest his own fleet be demolished.

Now his course was plain. He would "take advantage of this heaven-sent opportunity" and pursue the enemy at top speed.

First he would concentrate on the vulnerable carriers, knocking them out swiftly to prevent an all-out aerial attack on his own exposed warships. Then he could turn and destroy the other American vessels. It was thus essential that he shorten the range as quickly as possible, bringing his fire to bear at close and punishing quarters. His ships were still in the midst of changing to their "ring-like" formation, but before they could complete this maneuver Kurita ordered "General Attack!" There was no time, he felt, to regroup. Thus, instead of forming his battleships and cruisers in a battleline and sending his destroyers forward for a torpedo attack, Kurita threw the whole force into a wild, disorganized charge. Already engaged in a complicated shift in disposition, the Japanese warships now plunged forward in an uncoordinated and confused scramble to reach Taffy 3. Two minutes later, at 6:58, *Yamato*'s huge 18-inch batteries opened fire. The other battleships quickly joined in.

As the Japanese ships pressed southeast toward their prey, they tried to regroup in some sort of coherent formation. This was not easy in the midst of a hot pursuit, but by about 7:15 they had achieved a somewhat better organized disposition. Battleships *Yamato* and *Nagato* were in column with *Haruna* nearby to port and the fourth battlewagon, *Kongo,* running independently in the same direction but some seven miles farther to port. The six heavy cruisers were slightly ahead and to port of the main group while the light cruisers and destroyers, to conserve fuel, were falling back to the rear for pursuit at slightly reduced speed. Charging ahead at thirty knots, Kurita's heavy units were rapidly closing on the slower American ships.

But it was difficult for the Japanese to keep their targets in sight. The smoke and scattered rain squalls provided good concealment for Taffy 3, and Kurita's fire-control radar was ineffective. Thus his gunners had to interrupt or cease firing completely for want of something to shoot at. For a while only *Kongo,* sufficiently far off on the flank to avoid the drifting smoke, was able to continue throwing shells at Sprague's formation. Equally annoying were the attacks of American carrier planes. By now every available aircraft from all three Taffys was beginning to reach the area of combat. The planes came in small groups, piecemeal, unable to coordinate their hasty strikes. And not all were carrying torpedoes, for many had been loaded with bombs for ground support attacks while still others were so armed in the interest of speed and convenience. The planes headed for the battleships, attacking them almost without letup for about twenty minutes. These strikes caused little damage, however, primarily because there was no time to organize them properly. But they did disable some of the Japanese ranging equipment, confuse and distract the gunners, and, most important, force Kurita's ships to take evasive action. Thus, fifteen minutes after opening fire, the Japanese had yet to score a hit and Clifton Sprague, who had originally entertained some grave doubts that his force would last even this long, had had a chance to think about his next move.

Taffy 3 was still running east, but now Sprague decided to change course under cover of a protective rain squall. By swinging south and then southwest, he could get closer to any help that might be coming up from Leyte Gulf. This maneuver would also keep Taffy 3 between Kurita and the gulf, whereas if Sprague continued east there was always the chance that the Japanese would ignore him and press ahead toward the landing areas. The great danger in shifting south and southwest was that Taffy 3 would thus be moving figuratively along the outer edge of a piecrust—and if Kurita chose to cut across the center of the pie he could easily intercept Sprague and blow him from the water as Taffy 3 came out of the covering squall. To help shield his maneuver, then, Sprague ordered his three destroyers to make a torpedo attack on the Japanese. This, as one of the destroyer officers commented, was like sending "little David" against Goliath—only "without his slingshot."

But little David was already in action. The destroyer *Johnston* had been closest to Kurita when he appeared on the scene and was the first to begin laying smoke. For several minutes she was the target for much of the Japanese fire. The Japanese shells contained a dye—different colors for different ships—so that the gunners could pick out their own shell splashes during an engagement and more readily correct their fire. Now the *Johnston* was surrounded by a veritable rainbow of colored splashes. "The red, green, purple and yellow colors might have been pretty under different circumstances," recalled the destroyer's gunnery officer, "but at this moment I didn't like the color scheme." At about

7:10, when the range was close enough, *Johnston* began to return the fire with her relatively puny 5-inch guns and scored a number of hits. Japanese marksmanship was incredibly poor, but it seemed only a matter of minutes before the multicolored explosives would begin to find their mark.

Shortly after 7:15 Commander Ernest E. Evans received Sprague's orders to attack and immediately started *Johnston* on her torpedo run. The destroyer headed straight for the lead Japanese ship, heavy cruiser *Kumano*, and bore down on her rapidly in the face of continued heavy fire. Still she remained unhit, although near misses were splashing her deck with colored spray. Not wishing to push his luck too far, Evans fired a full torpedo salvo at a range of about five miles, and then swung the destroyer around and pulled out under a heavy smoke screen.

Only one torpedo scored a hit, but this was a crippling one. *Kumano* fell astern, where she was joined by another heavy cruiser that had been damaged by air attacks, and both dropped out of the fight. But *Johnston* now paid heavily for her temerity. At about 7:30 three shells from battleship *Yamato* landed squarely on the destroyer and a few seconds later a Japanese cruiser also scored some hits. *Johnston* shook as if slammed down by a giant hand. The deck was full of holes, considerable equipment and power was knocked out, engines and steering were seriously damaged, the radar mast snapped off, and many men were killed. "The bridge," recalled a survivor, "looked like a kid's B-B target." Admiral Kurita, who was consistently off in his identifications, informed the rest of his force that he had sunk a heavy cruiser. But *Johnston* was far from done for. She reeled back at reduced speed into the shelter of a fortunate rain squall and set about repairing what damage she could.

By now a second destroyer, the *Hoel*, also had completed her torpedo attack. She had made her run on the battleship *Kongo*, exchanging long-range gunfire and sustaining a punishing hit on the bridge before getting close enough to launch her fish. At about a five-mile range she emptied half her tubes at *Kongo*, but the big warship managed to avoid the torpedoes by making a sharp turn. A minute later *Kongo's* shells began landing on the plucky destroyer, knocking out the port engine and three of her guns and badly damaging her steering mechanism and fire control. Somehow *Hoel* managed to stay afloat amidst the increasing rain of Japanese shells while continuing to fire at the many targets around her. Her skipper, Commander Leon S. Kintberger, shifted to hand steering and pressed forward on a single engine to launch his remaining torpedoes at the Japanese cruiser column. One or more of these may have struck the target but, if so, without inflicting serious damage. Whatever the results, Kintberger did not linger to investigate. He swung *Hoel* around to run the gantlet of enemy fire into which he had thrust himself.

But with his speed reduced he could not escape. The faster Japanese warships closed in on *Hoel*, hitting her again and again as they shortened the range. To fight back, the destroyer had only two forward guns, and these were difficult to train on her pursuers. For nearly an hour the one-sided fight continued. *Hoel* zigzagged frantically and attempted to outguess the Japanese gunners. Most of the Japanese rounds were armor-piercing and passed right through the ship without exploding. But *Hoel* took more than forty hits. She was holed and flooding beneath the waterline, her fantail was aflame, the superstructure was torn by repeated explosions, and most of the officers and crew were dead or wounded. At about 8:30, finally, she went dead in the water, listing and settling at the stern, her remaining engine out of action. Her few survivors went over the side and within half an hour she capsized and went down.

The third destroyer, *Heermann*, had been unable to join the attack until a few minutes before 8 A.M., by which time Admiral Sprague had already ordered a second torpedo strike. *Heermann* plunged into the fray, following *Hoel*, and launched her fish at heavy cruiser *Haguro* and battleship *Haruna*. None struck its mark, but some of *Heermann*'s torpedoes—or possibly those fired at the same time by *Hoel* at *Kongo*—drove Kurita from the scene. To avoid the torpedoes, the flagship *Yamato* turned away, to the north, and then was caught between two parallel spreads and forced to run in that direction for nearly ten minutes before it was safe to reverse course. Had *Yamato* turned toward the oncoming torpedoes, instead of away, she could have maintained her pursuit of Taffy 3. Turning tail, however, had just the opposite effect. The decision was apparently Kurita's, and it was a bad one. It sent *Yamato* some seven miles to the rear, well astern of the Japanese disposition. It not only removed the heaviest Japanese warship from the center of the action, but it deprived Kurita of his close view of what was going on and seriously hampered his tactical control of the already disorganized Japanese force.

The destroyer *Heermann,* meanwhile, was heavily engaged in a running exchange of fire with Kurita's other battleships and heavy cruisers. Incredibly enough, the plucky little ship was hit by nothing more than a few shell fragments. Somehow or other her skipper, Commander Amos T. Hathaway, managed to fight his way out, and *Heermann* retired unscathed under a protective smoke screen.

In response to Admiral Sprague's orders for a second torpedo strike, the destroyer escort *Samuel B. Roberts* had joined the attack, while the damaged *Johnston,* her torpedoes expended, had gone along to provide fire support. Neither did much harm, and both escaped, dodging Japanese salvos and firing frantically themselves. Two other destroyer escorts, *Raymond* and *Dennis,* also made torpedo attacks and, in turn, encountered a storm of Japanese fire. The torpedoes scored no hits, but they forced the Japanese to take evasive action and caused further disorganization in Kurita's formation. *Raymond* and *Dennis* got away without damage, laying smoke as they went.

By now, shortly after 8 A.M., the battle area was a scene of complete confusion. Shell splashes, torpedo tracks, the wakes of careening ships, and spouts from aerial bombs tore the surface of the already weather-roughened sea. Rain squalls, clouds, and smoke limited visibility. Warships maneuvered frantically at high speed, often missing each other at close quarters and suddenly backing or making emergency turns to avoid collision. It was this confusion perhaps as much as the incredibly bad Japanese gunnery that continued to protect Taffy 3 from what had appeared to be certain extermination. But the Japanese were closing fast.

The six jeep carriers in Taffy 3 had emerged from the rain squall at about 7:30 and, continuing to follow the edge of the pie-crust, headed generally southwest—although steady Japanese pressure forced the fleeing ships to shift back and forth several points on either side of this course. To his surprise, Sprague noticed that the Japanese had made no attempt to cut him off by slicing across the center of the pie but instead had followed him around the rim. Kurita was trying to drive the carriers away from the wind, in order to prevent Sprague's launching of his planes, so preferred to chase the American ships to the southwest. Yet by this time most of Taffy 3's aircraft had already taken off. These planes were doing their best to hit the heavy cruisers in the van of the Japanese attack, and one very quickly scored on *Suzuya*, which fell astern with *Kumano*. The four remaining heavy cruisers continued to press forward, however, despite the gallant attacks of the destroyers and destroyer escorts and the pitifully weak fire of the single 5-inch gun on each carrier.

The Japanese were traveling much faster than the escort carriers could possibly go and, as the range narrowed, attempted to cut off Taffy 3 and surround it. The heavy cruisers were coming up on the port quarter, trying to prevent the carriers from escaping to the south. The battleships were closing astern, laying down a heavy volume of fire. So far the Japanese destroyers had taken no part in the action but now they were beginning to form up beside the battleships, preparatory to charging down on Taffy 3's exposed northern, or starboard, flank.

The rate of Japanese fire continued to increase and the shell splashes came closer and closer to the fleeing carriers. "At one point," recalled Admiral Sprague, "it did not seem that any of our ships could survive for another five minutes." *Kalinin Bay* and *Gambier Bay*, the two carriers closest to the Japanese, began to take hits, despite smoke, evasive action, attempts by the American destroyers to distract the Japanese, and some surprisingly good shooting by gunners on the two ships themselves. *Kalinin Bay* managed to stay afloat and firing, despite holes below her waistline, damage to her power plant, several fires, and the complete loss of her steering control. *Gambier Bay* was not so lucky. Aflame, flooded below, with almost no power, and listing heavily, she began to fall astern. The other four escort carriers were more fortunate. Sprague's flagship, *Fanshaw Bay*, was hit several times, but kept going. *White Plains* took only a few hits and the remaining two ships took only near misses. The skillful American ship-handling and damage-control operations and the continued poor shooting of the Japanese kept the over-all damage minimal. And where hits were scored, another factor helped save the CVE's. The Japanese, still thinking they were fighting a force of large carriers and heavy warships, continued to shoot armor-piercing shells—and most of these passed completely through the thin-skinned escort carriers without detonating.

Shortly before 8:30, in another effort to keep the Japanese away from the carriers, Sprague ordered his destroyer escorts to attack the cruisers again. The plucky little ships, now with almost all their torpedoes expended, closed with the heavier Japanese vessels and boldly exchanged fire with them. Near misses grazed the *Raymond* and *John C. Butler*, which retired to lay covering smoke. *Dennis* took several hits which knocked out her guns and forced her to fall back under smoke, but still failed to sink her. Less fortunate was the *Roberts*. At almost point-blank range, Japanese shells began crashing into the little ship just before nine o'clock. Explosions tore her side, knocked out all power, ruptured fuel tanks, and started blazes on the fantail. A single gun remained in action, manned by a crew that loaded, rammed, and fired it by hand in the absence of mechanical power—with the full knowledge that failure of the gas-ejection system meant almost certain danger of an explosion. When this explosion came, it killed or seriously wounded all but a single member of the gun crew. Even then, one mortally wounded sailor, his body torn open from neck to thigh, was still trying to push a shell into the wrecked gun when other crewmen entered the shattered gun-mount after the blast. The *Roberts* remained afloat, continuing to absorb hits, for almost another hour, during which time most of her surviving crewmen managed to escape into the water. Shortly after they abandoned her, the battered, flaming wreck twisted over and went down by the stern.

Despite the game sacrifice of the *Roberts*, the plight of the escort carriers grew steadily worse as the Japanese pressed in on the all but helpless fugitives. CVE *Gambier Bay*, under steady fire from heavy cruiser *Chikuma*, now had a 20-degree list and obviously was not long for the fight. On board the wounded *Johnston*, Commander Evans noticed what was happening and began shelling *Chikuma* to draw her fire from the carrier. Boldly the destroyer closed with the heavier Japanese ship and scored several hits, but *Chikuma* continued to concentrate on the sinking *Gambier Bay*. The Japanese skipper, Captain S. Norimitsu, probably could have sunk both the American ships, but refused to be distracted from what he thought was a large carrier and therefore a prime target.

A moment later he changed his mind when the as yet uninjured *Heermann* joined the attempt to save *Gambier Bay*. When *Heermann* opened fire on *Chikuma*, Norimitsu swung around and concentrated some of his guns on his new attacker. The lucky *Heermann* managed to remain unhit until finally a salvo of 8-inch shells caught her squarely forward and drove her bow deep into the waves. One shell tore a jagged hole at the waterline, flooding the forward magazines, while the others compounded the damage. Adding insult to injury was one projectile that struck a locker full of beans, converted them instantly into a hot, gooey paste, and literally buried the paymaster, Lieutenant Bob Rutter, in the sticky mess.

By now, however, *Chikuma* was under heavy air assault and was soon so severely damaged that at about nine o'clock she fell out of the attack. Heavy cruiser *Tone*, which then took up the fire on *Heermann*, also was driven off by planes. But at about the same time *Gambier Bay*, now under attack by several Japanese ships, was completely helpless and still in the water. Without power or steering, flooding, and heeling over, she was little more than a battered target for Kurita's gunners. Shortly after nine, most of her crew having escaped, she rolled over and went under.

Meanwhile the damaged but plucky *Johnston* had got herself into another fight—this one her last. At about the same time that *Heermann* was engaging *Chikuma*, Commander Evans aboard *Johnston* noticed the Japanese light cruiser *Yahagi* and four destroyers charging down on the north flank of the escort carriers. He immediately moved to intervene. At ten minutes before nine Rear Admiral Susumu Kimura, commanding the Japanese squadron, was astonished to see a lone American destroyer closing rapidly on him, guns blazing. A moment later, after both *Yahagi* and *Johnston* had taken several hits, Kimura moved the cruiser out of the fight with a sharp turn to starboard and ordered his destroyers to attack. Commander Evans shifted his fire to these new targets, scored some hits, and then was pleasantly surprised to see the destroyers turn away and break off action. As the Japanese steamed away Evans strutted back and forth on his bridge, unable to believe his eyes. "Now," he announced grandly,

"I've seen everything."

Once out of effective range of *Johnston,* Kimura wheeled around and his squadron launched torpedoes at the carriers. But by now, about 9:15, the Japanese were well astern of their targets and, since the CVE's were moving along at a good clip, actually out of range. The torpedoes were already losing speed when they approached the carriers. One was destroyed by a strafing carrier plane, another by shellfire, and the rest sank by themselves without hitting anything. Admiral Kimura, however, reported that he had sunk two enemy carriers and three destroyers. Japanese commanders normally tended to overinflate their battle claims, but this assessment surely deserves some sort of award for hyperbole.

Evans had done a good job in thwarting Kimura, but his bold maneuver now placed him between Kimura's squadron and the remaining Japanese heavy cruisers. For about half an hour the lone American destroyer fought off first the cruisers and then the destroyers, engaging the two groups in turn, and striving desperately to keep them from closing on the carriers. Now shells began to land on *Johnston* with increasing frequency. Guns were out of action, ammunition blew up, decks were ablaze, and the bridge no longer tenable for Evans. The bold skipper himself had been hit by a shell burst which cut off two of his fingers and inflicted minor wounds all over his body. Still he persisted, crouched on the fantail, shouting orders through an open hatch to the men below turning the rudder by hand.

By 9:45 *Johnston* was motionless in the water, Japanese destroyers ringing her like mounted Indians circling an isolated covered wagon, while Evans and the crew hastily went over the side. Twenty-five minutes later the ship capsized and started to go down. A Japanese destroyer closed in to short range and pumped a final shot into her as she sank. Of the American survivors, nearly half died of their wounds while in the water or were never picked up. Among the missing was the gallant Commander Evans.

The sinking of *Johnston* brought to four the number of vessels in Taffy 3 lost to the Japanese. *Hoel, Roberts,* and *Gambier Bay* were the others. But their sacrifice had destroyed much of the cohesiveness of a Japanese attack that had been disorganized from the start. The bold charges by the light ships of Sprague's screen had forced Kurita's vessels into evasive maneuvers, split the Japa-

nese units, reduced visibility by the effective use of smoke, and
sent Kurita's flagship on an embarrassing flight out of action that
further reduced the admiral's tactical control of his forces.

To these courageous endeavors must be added the effective
work of the planes from the escort carriers. While Sprague's
plucky destroyers and destroyer escorts had been thwarting Japanese surface attacks, all the air strength of Taffy 3, backed by
planes from Admiral Stump's nearby Taffy 2 and a few planes
from Thomas Sprague's Taffy 1, had been hitting Kurita.

Planes from Taffy 3 scored the first effective punch, a hit on
heavy cruiser *Suzuya* during the early moments of the fight. The
damage was not crippling, but it slowed the big ship and forced
it out of action astern. After that, Taffys 2 and 3 alternated in
sending in air strikes against the Japanese, so that almost continuously from the start of the battle until its end planes from the
escort carriers were nipping, clawing, and chewing at Kurita's
heels. The heaviest attacks came after about 8:30, and by a few
minutes after nine two more heavy cruisers, *Chikuma* and
Chokai, caught by surprise in sudden strikes, were crippled and
out of the fight. Eventually both had to be sunk by Japanese destroyers when it became clear that they could not be saved.
Suzuya also, battered severely in a later air attack, eventually
suffered the same fate.

The sinking of these three cruisers constituted the sum of
Kurita's major losses to the air strikes. Several other ships were
damaged. But, perhaps even more important, the air attacks, like
the actions of the destroyers and destroyer escorts, forced the
Japanese to take evasive action, lose contact, change course, and
otherwise shift about frantically to avoid being hit. And these
maneuvers made it all but impossible to press home a coordinated attack on the fleeing escort carriers.

"To a surface fleet," wrote Kurita's chief of staff, Admiral
Koyanagi, after the war, "there is no engagement so disadvan-
tageous and ineffective as an antiaircraft action. It does not pay
off. We had no air cover to repel the enemy, for whom it was
pure offensive."

And "pure offensive" it was indeed. Every torpedo plane,
bomber, and fighter that could get aloft was over the Japanese
warships, hitting them, in Clifton Sprague's words, "with every-

thing in the armory—including the doorknobs." The planes took off, delivered their attacks, landed, reloaded, and took off again for the fight. Deck crews worked frantically to refuel, rearm, and relaunch each aircraft, and the planes probably set some sort of record for least time on deck. When the supply of torpedoes gave out, torpedo planes were loaded with bombs, and when the bombs had been exhausted, the pilots made dummy runs to force the Japanese ships to continue their evasive maneuvers. The fighters strafed their targets at will, killing any Japanese foolish enough to remain exposed, knocking out automatic weapons, and distracting and confusing command and control aboard each ship. When out of ammunition, they too made dummy passes, sometimes teaming up with the torpedo bombers. One fighter pilot, Lieutenant Paul B. Garrison, made a total of twenty attacks, half of them without any ammunition, while Lieutenant Commander Edward J. Huxtable continued dummy runs for nearly two hours. Dive bombers remained high in the sky and struck from out of the blinding sun when opportunity presented itself. Many of the American planes were lost to heavy Japanese antiaircraft fire. But Kurita's vessels took more and more hits. And, maneuvering frantically to escape, they became increasingly disorganized and less able to press their attacks on the escort carriers.

In Taffy 3 the violent zigzag maneuvers of the CVE's, the heavy Japanese shelling, and, when Sprague turned southwest, the direction of the wind made it impossible for the planes to land on their carriers. Some of them refueled and rearmed on the nearby decks of Taffy 2, but many, on orders from Sprague, headed for the Tacloban airstrip on Leyte. The airfield had been captured by the 1st Cavalry Division on A-day, but had turned out to be extremely short and badly in need of resurfacing. Engineer troops had immediately begun the job of repairing and lengthening the strip, laying down a coral base on which to place steel matting. Yet the job was a difficult one, which included filling in part of a swamp. Despite all the engineers' efforts, the work went slowly. On October 24, one observer reported, trucks were still pouring loads of crushed coral "into a sea of black mud," where they "disappeared like chunks of vanilla ice cream into a sarsaparilla soda." The situation was not much better on the morning of the 25th when the field was hit by Japanese planes in a renewal of the Fourth Air Army's *Sho* offensive. Between Japanese raids the first planes from the escort carriers appeared overhead and began setting down.

From the air the field looked good. But, unknown to the pilots, one end was still soft, and even the hard portion of the runway had loose spots on it. The first plane touched down, sped along the strip, then hit a soft area and promptly turned over, blocking the runway. Seeing this, the remaining pilots zoomed helplessly about over the field. How could they land on an uncertain field with a wrecked fighter across the runway? But the alternative was a desperate attempt, on fast-emptying fuel tanks, to find Taffy 2—or else a landing in the water.

Just then a voice cut in on the pilots' radio wavelength. Lieutenant Edward Worrad, an Army Air Corps ground-control officer, was calling the planes overhead, telling them about the condition of the field and offering advice and instructions on the best place to land. At the same time impromptu engineer ground crews had formed to rescue the pilot of the wrecked fighter and drag his plane from the strip. A naval officer who happened to be present, Lieutenant Russell Forrester, and an army sergeant, Sam Halpern, joined Worrad, and the three formed a team to guide the remaining planes down. Major General Ralph J. Mitchell, a Marine air officer who had landed as an observer on A-day, also lent a hand. Seizing two signal flags, he ran to the end of the strip and wigwagged the landing planes onto the firm area of the field.

Elsewhere volunteer crews stood by to extricate pilots from planes that cracked up and to service and rearm aircraft that landed safely. Crash trucks raced up and down the strip on rescue missions. Planes that could not be salvaged were bulldozed out of the way, while everything flyable was refueled, loaded with whatever ammunition was available, and sent off to attack Kurita again. When there was a break in the landings, engineers made frantic efforts to grade and roll the particularly bad spots on the field. From time to time Fourth Air Army planes struck Tacloban, but these were shot down or driven off by antiaircraft fire.

Throughout the day the carrier planes continued to land despite Japanese strafing, American antiaircraft fire, and the poor

condition of the field. Dozens and dozens made successful landings and take-offs, only about twenty were lost in crack-ups, and
not one pilot was killed. A similar operation took place at the
Dulag strip, twenty miles south, although Tacloban got most of
the traffic.

The bold and aggressive American air strikes on top of the
courageous and selfless sacrifice of Taffy 3's light screen completely confused and frustrated the attacking Japanese surface
forces. For more than two hours a small group of six escort carriers, three destroyers, and four destroyer escorts, vigorously
supported by aircraft, had fought off a major enemy force of four
battleships, six heavy and two light cruisers, and eleven destroyers. What is more, the defenders had exacted a heavier toll in
ships sunk or badly damaged than they themselves had suffered.
It was an incredible performance, aided not a little—at least according to Clifton Sprague—by "the definite partiality of the Almighty God."

At a few minutes after nine on the morning of October 25 the
commander who knew least about the exact battle situation may
well have been Admiral Kurita. *Yamato's* evasive maneuvers had
placed the flagship well astern of the main action, and rain
squalls, heavy smoke screens, and inadequate Japanese radar prevented Kurita from observing the course of the fight. Nor were
his communications with subordinate units sufficient to provide
him with anything more than fragmentary messages. And despite
his earlier pleas to Admiral Fukudome for air support, Kurita had
not received a single reconnaissance report from shore-based
Japanese aircraft. Blinded and frustrated, he had launched his
remaining two scout planes from *Yamato,* but both had fallen to
American fighters before they could tell him anything. Thus
Kurita had no way of knowing that, despite the crazy-quilt pattern of the battle and the disproportionate Japanese losses, his
lead ships were rapidly closing in on Taffy 3 and on the verge of
destroying the almost helpless American force.

With no definite knowledge to the contrary, Kurita still believed he was facing a powerful element of Halsey's fast carrier
force. Japanese spotters, unfamiliar with American ship types,
centrated on two ships hit in the first strike. Most of the planes
ships, and escort carriers for fleet carries. And Kurita's staff, un-

able to make proper observations, estimated that the American ships were doing thirty knots, nearly twice their actual speed. On the basis of exaggerated claims by his subordinates, Kurita felt that he had seriously hurt the American force. But, after a two-hour running fight, he now concluded that any American ships not yet destroyed had probably outrun his pursuit.

To add to his difficulties, the increasing tempo of American air attacks seemed a sure portent of heavier strikes to come. Also, running at top speed, his ships were consuming fuel at an alarming rate, and this threatened to frustrate execution of his primary mission of breaking into Leyte Gulf. Still determined to carry out this mission, Kurita decided to break off the pursuit, re-form his disorganized units, and check and patch up his damage before pressing on toward Leyte Gulf. At 9:11 A.M. he began issuing orders to his scattered ships to close on *Yamato* and reassemble on a northerly course in an area clear of smoke and squalls and away from any possible American counterattack. It took nearly twenty minutes for these orders to reach all units, spread as they were over twenty-five miles of ocean, and for the ships to begin re-forming. And the actual reassembly, carried out under continuing American air strikes, was not completed until nearly eleven o'clock.

Kurita's decision came just in time to save the rest of Taffy 3. Just as it seemed to the fleeing American force that the end had come, the pursuing Japanese warships turned away. "I could not believe my eyes," recalled Admiral Sprague. "It took a whole series of reports from circling planes to convince me." Incredibly enough, Kurita had let his prey slip from his grasp.

But Kurita's decision did not completely ease the pressure on the three Taffys. For, unknown even to Kurita, the Japanese navy that morning had unveiled a new weapon, desperate in origin, macabre in concept, and fearsome in execution. This was the "kamikaze," the "divine wind," or, in plain language, the suicide bomber.

Many centuries earlier a powerful Mongol fleet had set out to invade Japan but was scattered and destroyed by a sudden typhoon. This timely storm, obviously the weapon of friendly gods, was called kamikaze and ever afterwards revered in Japanese history. In the fall of 1944, when once again a mighty enemy threatened Japan, a new kamikaze sprang up to save the Empire.

The tactic of purposely smashing a hopelessly damaged plane against its target was not new. Japanese pilots, about to crash anyway, had been doing this since Pearl Harbor, and American flyers as well as pilots from other countries had made this desperate sacrifice when there appeared to be no chance of survival. But the idea of a flyer's seeking a target with a definite intent of destroying both it and himself in a deliberate smash-up was solely Japanese in origin and was not seriously considered until late 1944. That fall, however, Japanese naval flyers, frustrated by their inability to strike American fleet units with any reasonable chance of success, began to discuss the possibilities of suicide tactics.

The man primarily responsible for initating the kamikaze tactics was Vice Admiral Takajiro Onishi, commanding the Fifth Base Air Force at Manila. With the activation of *Sho*-1 he had announced his conclusion that the only way to knock out American carriers was to crash-dive bomb-carrying Zero fighter planes onto their flight decks. On October 20 he established the first kamikaze "Special Attack Corps" with the specific mission of supporting Admiral Kurita's penetration into Leyte Gulf.

For four days the kamikaze pilots sortied forth from Philippine bases. And for four days they failed to sight even a single American warship. Then, on the 25th, they drew first blood. At 6:30 that morning, half a dozen Special Attack planes and four escorting aircraft took off from southern Mindanao, flew almost due north, and about an hour later came upon Admiral Thomas Sprague's Taffy 1, the nearest of the three Taffys. Sprague's escort carriers were in the midst of recovering the planes that had gone to assist Taffy 3 against Kurita. Some of these aircraft were landing, some were on deck being refueled and rearmed, and some were in the process of launching when the six kamikaze planes discovered them. At once the first Japanese pilot put his Zero into a dive on the escort carrier *Santee*. Machine guns blazing, he swept down on his target, crashed into the flight deck and penetrated to the hangar deck before his bomb exploded. A fire started but was quickly brought under control. Forty-three men were injured, however, a third of them fatally, and a huge hole had been smashed in the forward deck. A few minutes later the submarine *I-56*, one of several Japanese undersea craft operating in the area, put a torpedo into *Santee's* starboard side. This might have been fatal to most of the other CVE's, but *Santee* was somewhat larger and more sturdily built. She survived the torpedo as she had the kamikaze and continued in action.

Meanwhile, barely a moment after the kamikaze struck *Santee*, the escort carriers *Suwanee* and *Petrof Bay* each downed an attacking suicide plane. Still another fell to *Suwanee's* gunners before a final Japanese plane, hit and smoking, plunged into the carrier and exploded between the flight and hangar decks. Damage was extensive and casualties numerous. But *Suwanee* was back in action in another two hours.

The attack on Taffy 1 thus limited somewhat Thomas Sprague's ability to support Taffy 3. And to this extent it provided some support to Admiral Kurita. But, generally speaking, the first kamikaze strike of the war was in effect more of a warning of things to come than any sort of tactical victory.

The second kamikaze attack launched on October 25, five suicide planes and four escorts from Luzon, was more successful. These planes approached Taffy 3 shortly before eleven, as Clifton Sprague's ships were beginning to relax after their escape from Kurita. The Japanese came in just over the wavetops, too low to be picked up by radar, then shot up into the air at close range and dove swiftly down on their surprised victims.

In the first plane was Lieutenant Yukio Seki, a young officer only recently married, who had been specially chosen to lead the attack. The choice was an excellent one. Despite heavy antiaircraft fire, Seki smashed his Zero into the flight deck of the *St. Lo*. The plane penetrated the deck and burst into flames below. Torpedoes and bombs on the *St. Lo's* hangar deck exploded violently, hurling planes and parts of the flight deck and elevator hundreds of feet into the air. Fire swept the shattered carrier, and a returning Japanese pilot later reported seeing a pillar of smoke nearly 3,500 feet high. Half an hour later the *St. Lo* went down.

Meanwhile another kamikaze bounced off the port side of *Kitkun Bay*, two planes attacked *Fanshaw Bay* but were shot down, and two dove on *White Plains* but were driven off. One of them, already smoking, then plunged into the burning *St. Lo*. The other circled around and came in on *White Plains* again. Hit by almost every gun on the ship, the plane missed its mark but

exploded in mid-air to port and threw a punishing burst of fragments and pieces of the pilot at the men on the flight deck.
Twenty minutes later a second kamikaze force hit Taffy 3, inflicting considerable damage and casualties, but sinking no ships.

The attacks on Taffy 3 had thus been relatively successful. Indeed, when compared with Japanese conventional air assaults,
the kamikaze strikes of October 25 had done remarkably well.
Meanwhile, according to plan, General Tominaga's Fourth Air
Army planes were over the invasion beaches in great number that
day, but could not do much damage. Scores of land-based naval
planes of the First Combined Base Air Force, following up their
attacks of the 24th, were out in strength, searching for American
fleet units. But because of either bad weather or lack of skill on
the part of the inexperienced pilots, they were unable even to
find their targets. Thus, as two survivors of the kamikaze corps
later put it: "The superiority of special attacks was manifest.
. . . Hundreds of planes making orthodox attacks could not in-
flict as much damage on the enemy as a mere handful of
kamikazes."

At approximately the same time that the kamikazes were hitting Taffy 3, Admiral Kurita had finally regrouped his forces and
turned them southwest, heading once again for Leyte Gulf.
Thanks to the lack of coordination and effective communication
between land-based naval air units and the fleet, Kurita was completely unaware of the damage wrought to Taffy 3 by the suicide
planes. And if he noticed the huge column of smoke rising from
the crippled *St. Lo* he probably assumed that it had been caused
by his own shellfire. Indeed, he fully believed that he had sunk
three or four large carriers, two heavy cruisers, and several destroyers. Nor was he concerned by the fact that American action
and the necessity of detaching destroyer escorts with damaged
vessels had reduced his once-mighty force to four battleships, two
heavy and two light cruisers, and seven destroyers. Despite some
damage to these warships, also, he still commanded a powerful
unit. And he still meant to use it in Leyte Gulf.

But as Kurita steamed toward his objective he and his staff
began to reconsider. For the first time since the unexpected encounter with Taffy 3 some five hours earlier there was an opportunity for careful analysis and discussion of the situation. Seen

more calmly, it did not look good.

In the absence of aerial reconnaissance reports, Kurita had no definite means of determining the disposition of the various American fleet units operating in the area. But he had numerous disturbing indications. He was unaware that Admiral Ozawa had succeeded in decoying Halsey north, and his own misjudgment of the strength of Taffy 3 led him to conclude that a major portion of the Third Fleet was still before him. Ironically enough, his belief in Halsey's presence was reinforced by a message from Japanese land-based naval air units that an American carrier task force had been spotted off the northeast tip of Samar—the only hard intelligence he received all day from this source, but in fact completely erroneous. Kurita was still under attack by planes from Taffy 2, and earlier visual sightings of that force had identified it as another fast carrier group. Moreover, radio intercepts seemed to indicate that other aircraft were concentrating on Tacloban airfield in anticipation of his arrival in Leyte Gulf. Still other intercepts of American plain-language radio transmissions strengthened his fears that powerful enemy fleet units were converging on him. He had also received word of the destruction of Japanese forces in Surigao Strait. So he now firmly believed that he would have to face the full power of an aroused enemy completely on his own.

Despite these odds, it was not fear of being destroyed that influenced Kurita's next decision. "It wasn't a question of destruction," he said after the war. "That was neither here nor there. It was a question of what good I could do in the Gulf." Taking a hard look at his objective, he soon concluded that he might be shooting at a worthless target. By now, he felt, most of the American transports had probably withdrawn—and the rest could certainly escape by the time he fought his way in. Anything remaining would hardly be worth shooting at. The same questions that had arisen at Brunei Bay now arose again to torture him. Was it worth while to risk the loss of Japan's last naval striking force in a hopeless fight against powerful fleet units backed up by carrier and land-based planes for the chance of destroying a few empty transports? "We were prepared to fight to the last man," wrote Admiral Koyanagi, "but we wanted to die gloriously." Under the circumstances, to press ahead seemed more foolish than glorious.

At approximately 12:30, then, with the entrance to Leyte Gulf only forty-five miles away, Kurita abandoned his effort. He ordered his forces to put about to the north. Forty minutes earlier he had requested Philippine-based naval air units to attack the American task force reported off northeastern Samar. Now he hoped to crush that enemy force in conjunction with the air attack and then make good his escape through San Bernardino Strait. The Japanese attempt to penetrate Leyte Gulf was ended.

That afternoon, for the first time since he left Brunei Bay, Kurita's request for land-based air support was actually met. But the nearly 100 Japanese planes that searched the waters off northern Samar were unable to find any sign of the reported American task force. Nor was Kurita. Hounded by planes from Taffy 2 and from Admiral McCain's carrier group which had just returned from refueling, Kurita steamed north and entered San Bernardino Strait just as the sun was setting. He suffered little damage from the air strikes, although *Yamato* underwent an extremely annoying attack by two Japanese planes. One destroyer that lagged behind, however, was destroyed by Halsey's surface ships.

A message from Admiral Toyoda urged Kurita to "attack and destroy" American forces if he had the chance, but he had not yet sighted these forces, his destroyers were running low on fuel, and he saw no hope of making any sort of successful attack. He passed through San Bernardino Strait, lost a light cruiser and suffered other damage from Halsey's air strikes the next day, and finally made his way back to Brunei Bay after losing another destroyer. He had failed to crush the American invasion fleet and he himself had suffered heavy losses. But he had kept a powerful Japanese naval force alive, and this, at least, would remain a threat until the end of the war.

Admiral Kurita's decision to turn back will probably be discussed for as long as the Battle of Leyte Gulf is remembered. It was a decision made under the extremes of exhaustion and despair, by a commander who had been in action under the most trying circumstances for three days without rest. Given Kurita's mishandling of his approach through Palawan Passage and the Sibuyan Sea and his ridiculous inability to destroy the much weaker Taffy 3, his decision in the situation he faced and with the knowledge he had at 12:30 on October 25 appears to have been a sound one. For by then it was too late to undo his previous mistakes. His earlier decision to fall back and regroup—perhaps unavoidable under the circumstances—had given Admiral Kinkaid time to deploy Oldendorf's force across the entrance to Leyte Gulf. And that battleline supported by aircraft from the three Taffys probably had a very good chance of thwarting Kurita's entry.

Once Kurita had given up the attack on Leyte Gulf, however, he might have continued after the wounded Taffy 3 and then proceeded to run down Taffys 2 and 1. Heavy losses among the valuable escort carriers could have seriously hampered future American amphibious plans. But Kurita thought he was facing much faster ships and that he had no chance of catching them. He also believed he had already destroyed a substantial portion of this force. And, finally, by going after the carrier task force supposedly off northeastern Samar he thought he was striking a new and more important target—a target which lay in the direction he wanted to go anyway. If he found this northern task force, he did not really expect to survive the encounter. But he might be successful. And "even if we were destroyed in such a battle," wrote Admiral Koyanagi, "death would be glorious."

Kurita's defeat was due to a combination of his own mistakes and the superiority of the American forces opposed to him. But the outstanding feature of this defeat and the most important factor in it was the glorious two-hour fight against lopsided odds by the brave ships of Taffy 3. It delayed, punished, and confused Kurita—and kept him out of Leyte Gulf.

October 25, 1944, will long be venerated in the history of the American navy as a day of magnificent victory. By coincidence, October 25 is also St. Crispin's Day, the anniversary of a battle five centuries earlier when a small force of English bowmen defeated the cream of French knighthood on the field of Agincourt even as Clifton Sprague's puny ships thwarted the massed striking power of the Japanese navy.

William Shakespeare has written about the English at Agincourt in lines which suit as well the men of Taffy 3 at Leyte Gulf. In *Henry the Fifth* Shakespeare presents the English king addressing his troops before the battle. "This day is called the Feast of Crispian," says Henry.

He that outlives this day, and comes safe home,
Will stand a tip-toe when this day is named,
And rouse him at the name of Crispian.
He that shall live this day, and see old age,
Will yearly on the vigil feast his neighbours,
And . . . strip his sleeve, and show his scars,
And say, "These wounds I had on Crispin's day."

.   .   .   .

And gentlemen in England now a-bed
Shall think themselves accursed they were not here,
And hold their manhoods cheap whiles any speaks
That fought with us upon Saint Crispin's day.

And so might Clifton Sprague have spoken to his men with equal justification on another St. Crispin's Day more than five hundred years later.

xiv The End of the Battle

WHILE Clifton Sprague had been commemorating St. Crispin's Day, Admiral Halsey, far to the north, was enjoying a somewhat frustrating victory over Ozawa's decoy force. This force still consisted of the same vessels with which Ozawa had left the Inland Sea on October 20: fleet carrier *Zuikaku*, flying the admiral's flag, three light carriers, the two converted battleships or semicarriers, three light cruisers, and eight destroyers. But the aircraft they carried, relatively few to begin with, now numbered less than thirty.

On the afternoon of the 24th Ozawa had dispatched Admiral Matsuda with an advance striking force to seek night combat with Halsey's northern elements. Confused, however, by Kurita's reversal of course in the Sibuyan Sea—which he learned about through radio intercepts—and believing that the *Sho* attack had been canceled, Ozawa recalled Matsuda that evening and began to retire from the area. When it became clear that there had been no cancellation and that Kurita was headed once more for San Bernardino Strait, Ozawa turned south again. He would pick up Matsuda and, as he wrote later, "carry out diversionary operations at all cost." The rendezvous took place at about 6 A.M. on the 25th, some 280 miles east of Cape Engaño, the northeast tip of Luzon. Fittingly enough, *engaño* is the Spanish word for "deceit" or "lure."

Halsey, meanwhile, had been steaming north with the three carrier task groups commanded by Admirals Bogan, Davison, and Sherman, leaving McCain's group to join them later after refueling to the east. When search pilots spotted Matsuda and Ozawa on their radarscopes a few hours after midnight, Halsey at last formed Task Force 34 under Admiral Lee and sent it ahead of the carriers to smash Ozawa with gunfire and torpedoes. As now organized, Lee's command included all six battleships and seven cruisers still with Halsey, along with eighteen destroyers. This left ten carriers and a screen of twenty-two destroyers in Task Force 38, which Halsey had just returned to Admiral Mitscher's tactical control for the air attack on Ozawa. Altogether, not counting McCain's group, Halsey had committed more than sixty warships and several hundred planes against seventeen enemy vessels and a handful of aircraft. The Japanese decoy plan had worked to perfection although, ironically enough, communication difficulties would prevent Kurita from knowing this until after the battle.

Mitscher's night flyers had their last contact with Ozawa's ships at about 2:30 A.M. on the 25th. Two hours later, still without knowing the exact location of the Japanese force but believing it was approaching fast, Mitscher ordered his strike aircraft armed and made ready for a dawn attack. Shortly before six o'clock, the planes took off, still ignorant of just where Ozawa was. Search aircraft flew ahead, covering every possible square mile of ocean where the Japanese might be. The attack planes, 180 dive bombers, fighters, and torpedo planes, sped north for about fifty miles and then orbited to await contact reports from the scouts.

Admiral Ozawa, meanwhile, sensed that the moment for which he had been waiting for nearly a week was finally about to arrive. He knew from radio intercepts that Halsey's flyers had spotted him and, while he could not be certain that the American admiral would rise to the bait, he expected to be attacked and acted accordingly. To save his own remaining attack planes and their inexperienced crews, he ordered them to launch and make for an air base on Luzon. The ten bombers and torpedo planes took off, dipped their wings in final salute to their brave commander, and headed west. Ozawa then reversed course to the north, sent four search planes to look for Halsey, and formed his ships in their daytime antiaircraft disposition to await the inevitable attack. He still had fifteen fighters on his flight decks for his final, desperate defense and sacrifice.

Ozawa did not have long to wait. At about ten minutes after seven lookouts on the converted battleship *Hyuga* and on the flagship spotted three American carrier planes, just as the Ameri-

can pilots noticed Ozawa's force and flashed their contact reports
to the waiting strike planes and the expectant Mitscher. The three
reconnaissance aircraft remained in sight of the Japanese, continuing to report Ozawa's disposition, course, and speed. On board
Zuikaku, Ozawa reasoned fairly accurately that the American carriers were still more than 100 miles away. But he had not heard
from his own search pilots and did not reckon on Mitscher's strike
planes being already airborne. So he was surprised when at 7:40
his radar picked up large flights of approaching aircraft. He
began launching his fighters, but not all were aloft when the first
attack planes struck him at about 8:15.

Those Japanese planes that managed to take off fell quickly
before the American fighters. Ozawa now had only his antiaircraft fire for defense. This fire, heavy and rapid, could not, however, blunt the attack. With Commander David McCampbell,
group leader from the carrier *Essex,* acting as target coordinator,
the attackers bore down relentlessly on their prey. The Japanese
were steaming north in two groups, Ozawa with the first and
Matsuda leading the second, or southern, group. It was Matsuda
therefore who came under attack first. Light carrier *Chitose* was
still attempting to launch planes when dive bombers made several hits and a number of near misses on her. She stopped, listing
heavily to port, and began to settle slowly in the water. An hour
later *Chitose* was gone. Other dive bombers went after light
carrier *Chiyoda* in the same group. She took a hit, but continued
on and managed to escape the torpedo planes that followed up
the dive-bombing attack on her. Meanwhile Commander Mc-
Campbell, seeing the fatal damage to *Chitose,* had directed the
torpedo planes headed for the carrier to attack converted battleship *Hyuga,* Matsuda's flagship, which had been throwing up a
heavy volume of antiaircraft fire. These planes missed *Hyuga,* but
seriously damaged light cruiser *Tama.* Fighter aircraft meanwhile
were having a field day strafing every ship in the formation.

The attack on Ozawa's group went equally well. Light carrier
Zuiho, attempting to launch planes, took a bomb amidships, but
avoided torpedoes, so was not seriously damaged. Destroyer
Akitsuki, also bombed amidships, blew up and went down
rapidly in a burst of flame and smoke. And finally the large carrier *Zuikaku,* the prize target of the whole force, took a torpedo

aft, which seriously damaged her steering gear and made her list. Ozawa radioed Admiral Kurita that he was under heavy attack and that his decoy maneuver had worked perfectly. But this message, like those he had sent the previous day, never reached Kurita.

Maneuvering frantically to escape the American air strikes, Ozawa's ships quickly fell out of formation and became widely scattered. It was in this condition that the second air attack found them at about ten o'clock. By this time Commander McCampbell had been relieved over his helpless targets by the *Lexington*'s group leader, Commander Hugh Winters, who concentrated on two ships hit in the first shrike. Most of the planes went after *Chiyoda*. Several bombs crashed into the carrier, which burst into flames, began flooding, and showed a decided list. Her crew continued to throw up antiaircraft fire and then, when the American planes left the ship for dead, turned desperately to fire fighting and pumping. When it looked as if the damage-control parties were going to save the ship, Admiral Matsuda attempted to take *Chiyoda* in tow. By this time, however, the third American strike was approaching. Matsuda reluctantly ordered the crew taken off and the carrier sunk. But even this proved impossible. The stricken ship and its hapless passengers were left to be sunk finally by American gunfire late in the afternoon.

Meanwhile the second air strike had also hit *Tama* again, slowing the cruiser further but not putting her under. Matsuda ordered her to head for Okinawa on her own. She never made it. Late that night an American submarine sank *Tama* with three well-placed torpedoes.

In Ozawa's group the second air strike did little damage, although *Zuikaku* may have been hit again. In any event, not only was the carrier's steering control now gone, but all communications were out. *Zuikaku*'s value as a command ship was obviously at an end, and Ozawa's staff urged him to transfer his flag to another vessel. But the admiral refused. He had succeeded in his mission, his fleet was dying, and he wished to go down with his ship. No entreaties would shake him from this determination. Finally, Captain Toshikazu Ohmae, his chief of staff, ordered Ozawa carried from the bridge. At around eleven o'clock, after the planes in the second strike had left the area, Ozawa and his staff transferred to light cruiser *Oyodo,* where the admiral now raised his flag.

While Halsey's flyers were pounding Ozawa, the Third Fleet commander was receiving a series of increasingly desperate reports and pleas for aid from Admiral Kinkaid. At 6:48 A.M. he had received Kinkaid's delayed message reporting the start of the action in Surigao Strait and asking if Task Force 34 was guarding San Bernardino Strait. The puzzled Halsey had replied in the negative, but whatever concern he may have felt was relieved at 8:02 by a brief report from Kinkaid that the Japanese were withdrawing. Presumably Admiral Oldendorf's battleships could now swing over to cover Leyte Gulf against the already weakened Center Force if it chose to attack. Twenty minutes later, however, Halsey received Kinkaid's third message, also delayed, but its urgency underlined by the fact that it had been sent in the clear. This stated that Taffy 3 was under attack by a major Japanese surface force. The news arrived just as the second air strike was preparing to take off against Ozawa. Intent on bringing his battleships to bear against the same target, Halsey was still not alarmed. "I figured," he wrote later, "that the sixteen little carriers had enough planes to protect themselves until Oldendorf could bring up his heavy ships."

But only eight minutes later, at 8:30, a fourth dispatch, also in plain language and also delayed, urgently requested Halsey's fast battleships at Leyte Gulf "at once." Halsey was concerned. But he was also annoyed. After all, he felt, it was not his responsibility to protect Kinkaid. His mission was offensive and, even then, he was "rushing to intercept a force which gravely threatened not only Kinkaid and myself, but the whole Pacific strategy." Nevertheless, he ordered Admiral McCain's carrier task group, still refueling several hundred miles to the east, to hit Kurita as soon as possible. But it would be two hours before McCain could even get his carriers close enough and in position to launch planes and these would not be able to reach the battle area until noon. Meanwhile, Kinkaid's frantic messages continued to reach Halsey on *New Jersey,* the majority of them delayed in the strange slowdown that seems to have affected most communications during the battle.

Hardly had Halsey dispatched his order to McCain when, at nine o'clock, he received a fifth message from Kinkaid. This provided details of Kurita's attack and urgently requested that Admiral Lee and Task Force 34 cover Leyte at "top speed" and that Halsey's carriers make an "immediate strike." Twenty minutes later another message, actually sent before this one, came in. And this carried the startling news that Oldendorf's battlewagons were low on ammunition, "a new factor," wrote Halsey, "so astonishing that I could hardly accept it."

Actually Oldendorf, while short of armor-piercing rounds, still had enough left to defend Leyte Gulf. But he was too distant to reach Taffy 3 to provide immediate aid. Nor could he rush to the rescue with his whole force, thus leaving Leyte Gulf wide open to a possible return by those ships still afloat in Admiral Shima's 2nd Striking Force. What Oldendorf could do, however, was to get into position at the eastern entrance of the gulf to block Kurita's advance—which is exactly what Kinkaid finally told him to do. A subsequent order, directing him to go to Sprague's assistance with part of his force, was canceled when Kurita decided to withdraw.

But back on the *New Jersey*, at 9:20, Halsey was trying to figure out why Kinkaid had delayed so long in telling him of Oldendorf's ammunition shortage. Perplexed, exasperated, torn by doubts, Halsey checked the dispatch time on Kinkaid's messages. He was shocked to learn that most of them had taken an hour and a half to reach him. They thus described situations which, in the intervening delay, might have changed drastically. Nevertheless, Halsey was now too far away for his battleships to do Kinkaid any immediate good. And he still believed that the major threat came from Ozawa. Informing Kinkaid of his position and of his orders to McCain, Halsey continued to press north after Ozawa with every ship and plane he had. From Kinkaid came only continued pleas for help.

Halsey was not the only one receiving these pleas. At Pacific Fleet headquarters at Pearl Harbor, Admiral Nimitz had been monitoring all this radio traffic. He was becoming increasingly concerned over the fate of Taffy 3 and, under the impression that Task Force 34 had been guarding San Bernardino Strait, could not understand what was happening. So he dictated a brief message to Halsey, asking him where Task Force 34 was.

The Battle of Leyte Gulf was one in which communications, both American and Japanese, were mysteriously delayed, garbled, or otherwise fouled up. This may have been due to atmospheric conditions, human error, or gremlins. Whatever the cause, Admiral Nimitz's message was no exception to the general rule. It reached Halsey in a form that Nimitz had not intended and produced an explosion he could not have foreseen.

What happened was this: It was standard procedure for all coded navy messages to begin and end with some meaningless phrase or word group, referred to as "padding," to make it harder for Japanese cryptoanalysts to break the code. The padding was to be set off from the text by double letters and was not to be so worded that the recipient might mistake it for part of the actual message. Nimitz's query about Task Force 34 was sent to his communications room where a young ensign added padding at the beginning and end and inserted the proper designations for sender and addressees. As radioed to Halsey, the dispatch read:

TURKEY TROTS TO WATER GG FROM CINCPAC . . .

[addressees] . . . X WHERE IS RPT [repeat] WHERE

IS TASK FORCE THIRTY FOUR RR THE WORLD WONDERS

And it was the final padding, THE WORLD WONDERS, that caused all the difficulty.

This phrase was a clear violation of the rule against using padding that might appear related to the basic text of the message. Although clearly set off by the double letters RR, to a casual or hasty reader it appeared to be part of the question about Task Force 34, emphasizing with sarcasm the urgency of the query. The young officer responsible for the phrase had certainly not meant it that way. "It just popped into my head," he explained later, and he had written it down without realizing how inappropriate it was as padding. Perhaps on this anniversary of the "Charge of the Light Brigade" some poetic gremlin had placed in the ensign's mind a phrase reminiscent of the Tennysonian "All the world wondered." Perhaps not. In any event, few of those involved in these events on October 25, 1944, would ever forget it.

Still, it might have done no harm. Standard procedure on Halsey's flagship was to omit all padding from messages when they were typed for delivery to the admiral. Important operational dispatches would not be typed, but the message tape would be rushed to the bridge as soon as it came out of the decoding machine. The operators, however, would tear off the padding before forwarding the tape. Nimitz's message reached the *New Jersey* at 10 A.M., amidst the confusion of pursuit and expectation of imminent battle. The sailor who would have typed it out, Burton J. Goldstein, saw immediately that it should go to the bridge without delay. He ripped off the opening padding, TURKEY TROTS TO WATER, but then was stymied when he reached THE WORLD WONDERS. Clearly this seemed to be padding, for the double letters RR set it off from the rest of the message. But, as Halsey wrote much later, it "sounded so infernally plausible" that Goldstein thought it just might be part of the text. His superior, Lieutenant Charles Fox, Jr., also was puzzled and decided to forward the message with the questionable phrase still attached. If it was padding, as marked, it would be recognized as such on the bridge. But if the words were part of the text, he did not want to delete them

On the bridge the communications officer removed the message from the pneumatic tube and handed it to Halsey. Whether or not he pointed out the padding designation to the admiral is a mystery, but Halsey was not used to receiving messages with the padding still attached. So he naturally took the phrase in question to be part of the text, a sarcastic suggestion that Task Force 34 was not doing what it should. "I was stunned as if I had been struck in the face," he recalled later. "The paper rattled in my hands. I snatched off my cap, threw it on the deck, and shouted something that I am ashamed to remember." Rear Admiral Robert B. ("Mick") Carney, Halsey's chief of staff, rushed over and seized his arm. "Stop it!" he snapped. "What the hell's the matter with you? Pull yourself together!" Speechless now, Halsey handed him the message and turned his back.

For nearly an hour the Third Fleet continued north. Nimitz's words gnawed deeper and deeper into Halsey's mind. Angered, frustrated, and, to use his own words, "in a rage," at 10:55 Halsey at last ordered most of Task Force 34 and Bogan's carrier group to swing about and head south. "At that moment," he wrote later, "the Northern Force . . . was exactly 42 miles from the muzzles

of my 16-inch guns. . . . I turned my back on the opportunity I
had dreamed of since my days as a cadet. For me, one of the biggest battles of the war was off." In the years to come Halsey
would insist that "bowing to pressure and turning south" at this
moment was the only action in the whole battle that he regretted.
"I consider this the gravest error I committed." At 11:15, as he
sped south, he notified Kinkaid that he was coming but that he
would be unable to arrive before eight o'clock the next morning.

Admiral Mitscher's Task Force 38 now consisted of two carrier groups (those of Davison and Sherman) supported by four
cruisers and ten destroyers detached from Task Force 34 and
commanded by Rear Admiral Laurance T. DuBose. Mitscher
continued to pursue Ozawa and, shortly before noon, launched
his third air strike of the day. This included more than 200 planes.
Shunning the nearest targets, Admiral Matsuda's force grouped
around the dying *Chiyoda*, they went after the two remaining
carriers, farther north with Ozawa. By about 1 P.M., the attackers
were over their prey. Half of them struck the crippled *Zuikaku*,
the rest concentrated on the lightly damaged *Zuiho*. *Zuikaku*
went first. The big carrier caught fire and began to settle. An hour
later, at 2:14, the game veteran of Pearl Harbor and of almost
every Pacific carrier fight since that time, rolled over and sank.
Zuiho, meanwhile, had been hit and set aflame, but managed to
extinguish the fires, only to be hit again and again. A few planes
flew back to Matsuda's group, but did no damage.

Three more air strikes battered the wounded decoy force before darkness called a halt to the attacks. The fourth strike of the
day finally sank *Zuiho*, which went to the bottom just before 3:30.
After that, everyone went after the two converted battleships, *Ise*
and *Hyuga*, concentrating especially on the former, in Ozawa's
group. The two warships maneuvered sharply, put up a heavy
curtain of antiaircraft fire, and managed to avoid most of what
was thrown at them. Although rocked by scores of near misses
and frequently swept by bomb fragments, the only real damage
they sustained was a single hit on *Ise*'s port catapult. On board
Oyodo, Admiral Ozawa watched approvingly as the captain of
the *Ise* took the big ship smartly through her evasive turns while
his antiaircraft gunners maintained their rapid fire. "I thought,"
recalled Ozawa a year later, "that the bombing of the afternoon

wasn't so efficient. . . . Over one hundred planes bombed these ships; every time they missed. I . . . thought the American pilot is not so good." But Mitscher's flyers were pretty tired by now, after two days of concentrated action following a month of sustained operations. And their score for the 25th—four carriers and one destroyer sunk, a cruiser seriously damaged, and several others lightly hurt—was not too bad when you came right down to it.

While the afternoon air strikes were taking place, Mitscher had shifted course to the east, lest his carriers find themselves suddenly within gunfire or torpedo range of Ozawa. At the same time, just after two o'clock, he directed Admiral DuBose's group, with a few additional destroyers, to continue north and sink any crippled Japanese warships they could catch up with. There was a risk that Ozawa, who still had considerable punch, might turn on DuBose, but this seemed unlikely before nightfall. At about 4:30 DuBose came upon the helpless *Chiyoda* and took nearly half an hour to sink the already dying carrier. This delay ruled out any chance of catching up with the fleeing Ozawa.

Earlier, however, Ozawa had sent three destroyers back to rescue survivors and, just before darkness, DuBose encountered them. Two of the destroyers escaped at high speed but the third, *Hatsuzuki*, exploded after a two-hour running fight. Well before she went down, however, her skipper got off an urgent message to Ozawa on *Oyodo*. After a considerable delay, while Ozawa tried unsuccessfully to get *Hatsuzuki* to tell him her position— again communications failed him—the admiral took his flagship, the two converted battleships, and a destroyer and headed back to the rescue. But it was now too late. After a fruitless search until nearly midnight, Ozawa finally turned north and headed for home with his remaining force. DuBose, meanwhile, had reversed course after sinking *Hatsuzuki*. His destroyers were beginning to need fuel and, in any event, continued pursuit to the north would bring him within range of Formosa-based air attack in the morning. Task Force 38, including DuBose, now moved south to rejoin Halsey, leaving any final mop-up of Ozawa to American submarines.

Two days later Admiral Ozawa was safe in port in the Ryukyus. He had lost four carriers, a cruiser, and two destroyers.

But, as he said later, he had "expected complete destruction," so
the ten ships still afloat represented something of a victory. Even
more important was the fact that he had succeeded remarkably
well in his mission. His assignment had been a difficult, unappeal-
ing, and perhaps even hopeless one. But he had carried it out
with skill and courage. He had lured Halsey north and thus saved
Kurita from complete destruction. Yet the breakdown in Japanese
communications had kept Ozawa's great success a secret from
Kurita, who had failed to take advantage of it and turned back at
the critical moment.

Ironically enough, had Ozawa not intercepted Kurita's message late on the 24th reporting the retirement of the 1st Striking
Force in the Sibuyan Sea, he would not have recalled Admiral
Matsuda's advance force and would not himself have reversed
course that evening. Matsuda would thus have encountered and
been completely destroyed by the powerful Task Force 34 before
dawn. And Ozawa, the carriers, and the rest of the decoy fleet—
seeking a rendezvous with Matsuda 120 miles farther south than
where they actually met as a result of the delay—would have
been wiped out just as thoroughly as soon as the sun came up.
Then Mitscher's carriers, that much closer to Leyte Gulf, would
have been free to go to the aid of Taffy 3. And, finally, Task
Force 34 could easily have cut off Kurita on his way back to San
Bernardino Strait, in which case the 1st Striking Force would also
have been annihilated.

All these events did not take place. Yet, even then, Kurita's escape was a close one. Had Halsey detached Task Force 34 at 8:22
A.M., when he first learned of Clifton Sprague's predicament, and
sent it racing south, he still could have reached San Bernardino
Strait ahead of Kurita. To do this would have meant leaving most
of the destroyers behind, since they were running low on fuel, but
a battleline of six powerful battleships, supported by two heavy
and five light cruisers and at least a few destroyers, should have
been strong enough to defeat Kurita's remaining force, already
badly mauled, of four battleships, two heavy and two light
cruisers, and seven destroyers. And any attempt at interference
by the Japanese land-based aircraft operating off northern Samar
during the afternoon could probably have been handled by
American planes launched from the three Taffys, McCain's task

group, and Tacloban airfield.

But this, too, did not occur. Indeed, it was not until 11:15 that Task Force 34 and Bogan's carrier group turned away from the pursuit of Ozawa and headed south. By now it was too late to prevent Kurita's escape, unless, of course, Kurita continued toward Leyte Gulf and made no attempt to retire through San Bernardino Strait—and this, at the time, was what he appeared to be doing. Task Force 34 steamed south for some two and a half hours before it was forced to slow down in order to refuel destroyers. As it proceeded at half speed, Halsey heard from Kinkaid that Kurita had broken off his action against Taffy 3 and was headed north. In a final attempt to prevent Kurita's escape through San Bernardino Strait, Halsey took his two fastest battleships, *Iowa* and his flagship *New Jersey*, along with three light cruisers and eight destroyers, formed them into a task group under Rear Admiral Oscar C. Badger, and sent this force racing south at top speed as soon as it had fueled. But even this was a futile gesture, for Badger by now could not possibly outrace Kurita. All his task group could do was catch a single straggler, destroyer *Nowaki*, which his cruisers and destroyers quickly blasted out of the water. Perhaps it was just as well for Badger. Had he met Kurita, he would have been badly outgunned. Bogan's carrier planes would have helped considerably, although not in a night action, and it is difficult to say who would have won.

Of all the scenes evoked by memory of the Battle of Leyte Gulf—Kurita's painful approach, the reckless sacrifice of Surigao Strait, the embattled Taffy 3, and Admiral Ozawa's elaborate hoax—perhaps the most frustrating is the dash of Halsey's powerful battleships north after Ozawa and then south again after Kurita, racing frantically in both directions without firing a single shot. Exasperating as this was for the Third Fleet commander, perhaps even more annoying was the way it was described in the press. Halsey's first name was William, and his friends naturally called him Bill. But his tough, pugnacious nature had led newspapermen to dub him "Bull," and it was as Bull Halsey, an aggressive, determined sea dog, that he was known to the public. It was perhaps inevitable, then, that the fruitless course of his battleships back and forth on October 25th should have been referred to as "Bull's Run" by the somewhat insensitive gentlemen of the press. This was, of course, less than fair. But it was typical of the tendency to make Halsey the goat of Leyte Gulf—despite the fact that the battle was a great American victory.

An evaluation of Halsey at Leyte Gulf must revolve around two decisions: the first, on the evening of the 24th, to uncover San Bernardino Strait and go north after Ozawa; the second, late the next morning, to send Task Force 34 south after Kurita. The decision to go north grew out of Halsey's belief that Kurita had been so badly damaged that Kinkaid could handle him and that Ozawa's carriers represented the greater threat, not only at the moment but for the remainder of the war as a whole. Examining this in detail, it is clear that Kurita was nowhere near so badly hurt as Halsey imagined. Yet it is not at all evident that the Seventh Fleet was incapable of defeating Kurita. Despite somewhat reduced ammunition stores on Kinkaid's heavy ships, there was still an adequate supply for one more fight. Most of Admiral Oldendorf's destroyers had expended their torpedoes in Surigao Strait, but nine more destroyers, fully armed, joined him that morning. Kurita, on the other hand, was getting low on fuel, only four of his remaining seven destroyers had any torpedoes left, his fire control gear was inferior, and he and his men were dog-tired after two days of almost continuous action. Under these circumstances Oldendorf, well supported by planes from the escort carriers, might well have formed battleline at the entrance to Leyte Gulf and capped Kurita's T just as he had Nishimura's. Even if Kurita had not botched his fight with Taffy 3 and had swept down unhindered on Leyte Gulf, he himself was without air support or cover, and his ability to hold an effective attack formation may well be questioned. Certainly his vulnerability to air attack was a significant cause of his failure against Taffy 3.

The fact that Kinkaid could probably have defended Leyte Gulf by himself on the 25th does not in itself justify Halsey's decision to go north after Ozawa—unless it was clear that Ozawa represented a more important target than Kurita. Halsey thought so. And his reasoning appears to have been sound. While Kurita had four battleships in his force, Ozawa had two semibattleships and *four carriers*. There was no way of knowing whether or not these carriers were loaded with planes, but it was highly unlikely that the Japanese would risk such important units without their aircraft and incredible that they should deliberately sacrifice them as bait. In any event, Halsey could not afford to assume the carriers were harmless. If Ozawa had carried planes and Halsey ignored him, who can say what might have happened? The fact that destroying the carriers was more important in the long run than sinking Kurita's battleships is perhaps irrelevant. What mattered was the immediate threat—and here the alternatives were clear.

In balancing the risk of Kurita's battleships reaching Leyte Gulf against the chance of being caught between those battleships and Ozawa's carriers, Halsey chose to ignore the former in order to prevent the latter. Under the circumstances his choice was correct. Unless he could have absolute knowledge that Ozawa had no planes, his decision to go north was a proper one. And as a matter of fact, if Ozawa had not hesitated on the night of the 24th, Halsey would have met and destroyed him much farther south and returned in ample time to crush Kurita.

Admiral Kinkaid has argued that, even if Halsey was right in chasing Ozawa, he did not need the whole Third Fleet to do it. According to Kinkaid, two of Halsey's battleships and no more than two carrier groups could have taken care of Ozawa's two semibattleships and four carriers. This would have left Halsey four battleships and a carrier group to handle Kurita. Perhaps this argument has some merit. But Halsey feared that splitting his fleet into two portions incapable of supporting each other would allow Japanese surface units backed by land- and carrier-based airpower to destroy each portion in turn. Since he believed that Kinkaid was strong enough to face Kurita, he saw no reason to depart from the time-honored principle of naval warfare that a fleet should be concentrated at the point of decison and never so weakened by diversion that it can be beaten in detail. Axiomatically, the principal objective of naval tactics is the complete annihilation of the opposing fleet. This is accomplished by concentrating masses against the enemy's fractions, which is exactly what Halsey proposed to do. In the light of hindsight, Kinkaid's solution would probably have been the better one. But on October 25, 1944, Halsey would not have been justified in taking the risk.

He may, however, be fairly criticized for his complete neglect of San Bernardino Strait. Prudence should have dictated leaving a destroyer patrol to watch the strait and report on the strength and timing of any Japanese force that came through. He should not have automatically assumed that Kinkaid would cover the area with search planes or that these planes would necessarily spot Kurita. As it was, Halsey might have got away with this error had it not been for a few pieces of bad luck: Kinkaid's misreading of Halsey's preparatory order about Task Force 34, the failure of the PBY search, and the delay in transmission of Kinkaid's message asking if Task Force 34 was guarding San Bernardino Strait. Kinkaid, it is true, might have ordered more air searches—but he, after all, had no reason to doubt that Halsey's night flyers were checking the strait.

Halsey himself has criticized and regretted his second major decision, detaching Task Force 34 just when he was about to close with Ozawa. By so doing he lost his opportunity to wipe out the Japanese Northern Force. This was a mistake. If he was correct in going after Ozawa, then he was wrong in letting him escape. In any event, the time to have detached Task Force 34 was when he first learned of Kurita's attack, not nearly three hours later when he was that much farther north. By this delay he allowed both his adversaries to escape and gained nothing for his pains. The dispatch of Admiral Badger's force in a last-minute attempt to head off Kurita was equally too late. And it was also unwise. Kurita had the stronger force, and, had the interception succeeded, neither Badger nor Halsey, who was sailing with him, might have survived.

The Battle of Leyte Gulf was a great American victory. And for this Halsey must be given much of the credit. Yet there were others no less responsible: Commanders McClintock and Claggett, who skillfully intercepted Kurita's force; Mitscher's pilots, who followed up effectively and then did the same against Ozawa; Admiral Oldendorf, who fought a classic action in Surigao Strait; and, above all, the officers and men of Taffy 3, whose magnificent defense and sacrifice was a glorious event in American naval history. In playing their roles, all these actors were hampered by chance, faulty communications, and inadequate information. Equally so were the Japanese who opposed them, who were also brave and skillful men. Both sides made mistakes, but the primary difference was that the Japanese made more and costlier ones.

The first Japanese mistake was the *Sho* plan itself, a highly complicated scheme requiring accurate intelligence, precise timing, reliable communications, and the utmost cooperation and coordination between air and naval forces. Difficult of accomplishment in any event, it became even more so when the shortage of fuel forced a division of the Combined Fleet into two elements incapable of supporting each other. Admiral Kurita's decision to split his command and the careless commitment of Shima's element further divided the fleet into four parts, only two of which, Shima and Nishimura's, were capable of mutual support, which Admiral Toyoda declined to allow.

Compounding this poor coordination was the complete inability of the Japanese to integrate their air and naval attacks. Part of this was the fault of Toyoda, who prematurely committed his air strength—and lost most of it—in the Formosa air battle, and part can be traced to the Japanese system of divided command, which hampered them throughout the war.

There was also the question of timing. Having committed his air force too early, Toyoda got his fleet to the Philippines too late. The *Sho* plan had called for an attack while the Americans were landing or immediately thereafter. Circumstances and mistakes prevented this, yet the inflexibility of the plan once set in motion doomed the Combined Fleet to helpless battle even though the optimum moment was past. Having missed their chance, the Japanese might well have saved the fleet for another day. By sacrificing it uselessly at Leyte they simply eased the way for further American advances up the island chain toward Japan. More important, they made the Pacific an American lake. Six months later the Emperor asked the chief of the Navy General Staff, "Was not the use of our warships inappropriate at Leyte Gulf?" The form of his question implied the answer.

In addition to the Japanese strategic errors at Leyte Gulf, there was a series of lesser blunders, primarily by Kurita. Victim of a nightmarish plan and assigned an unenviable role in executing it, hampered by bad communications, inadequate intelligence, poor radar, and miserable gunnery, Kurita was probably doomed to failure from the start. But he seemed intent on making things worse. His choice of an approach route was poor, his vacillation in the Sibuyan Sea was worse, and his failure to destroy Taffy 3 was inexcusable. He made the proper decision when he finally decided to retire, but his timing left something to be desired.

Nishimura and Shima did the best they could under the circumstances and, despite what has been written about these two unfortunate commanders, only their ship handling may be fairly criticized.

Admiral Ozawa made no mistakes. And perhaps because he was skillful he was also lucky. He carried out his mission successfully, saved much of his fleet, and emerged with his reputation untarnished. Ironically, poor communications made his sacrifice a useless one.

The Japanese losses in the Battle of Leyte Gulf were staggering: one large and three light carriers, three battleships, six heavy and three light cruisers, and ten destroyers, plus widespread damage to other vessels. Sunk were approximately 300,000 tons of combat shipping, well over a third of the total surface tonnage of the fleet before the battle, and more than 25 percent of the aggregate losses suffered by the Japanese navy in the entire war. The fleet was destroyed as an effective combat force and the Japanese were no longer any threat to American naval control of the Pacific. The losses in Japanese aircraft made this even more of a certainty.

For this great victory American losses were surprisingly light. Damage in Taffys 2 and 3 was widespread, but actual sinkings in both Third and Seventh Fleets amounted to less than 40,000 tons: one light carrier, two escort carriers, two destroyers, a destroyer escort, and one PT boat. The number of planes that failed to return was disproportionately low in comparison with the Japanese losses. And, most important of all, the Japanese never did manage to get into Leyte Gulf or do any damage to the amphibious shipping there.

But what if the *Sho* plan had worked? Suppose that Kurita had overcome all the handicaps of a difficult plan, bad luck, and his own ineptitude and managed to reach Leyte Gulf. Suppose, then, that he had fought his way through Admiral Oldendorf's battleline and burst into the gulf to do his worst. What could he have accomplished?

The answer usually given is that Kurita could have wreaked tremendous havoc. The view in MacArthur's headquarters, according to Major General Courtney Whitney, a top aide, was that if Kurita's force had penetrated Leyte Gulf "the American invasion would in all probability have experienced a setback of incalculable proportions. The enemy's heavy guns would have experienced little trouble in pounding the remaining transports and landing craft. Shore positions and troop installations could have been bombarded almost at leisure." MacArthur himself has written that the whole invasion would have been "placed in jeopardy." And General Krueger, the Sixth Army commander, has stated that Kurita "could have leisurely and effectively carried out the destruction of shipping, aircraft, and supplies that were so vital to Allied operations on Leyte."

Admiral Halsey, not surprisingly, had a different opinion:

> That Kurita's force could have leisurely and effectively carried out the destruction of shipping, aircraft, and supplies in Leyte Gulf was not in the realm of possibilities. . . . Kurita would have been limited to a hit-and-run attack in the restricted waters of Leyte Gulf. He would further have been subjected to the attack of the cruisers present in Leyte Gulf. He would have been limited to minor damage. . . . The statement that an enemy naval victory would have an effect of incalculable proportions . . . can only be premised on the thought that our naval forces would be almost totally destroyed. The prognostication of such a condition could be reasoned on none of the facts existing. . . .

The fact of the matter is that by October 25 most of the supplies carried with the invasion force and with two additional supply echelons— enough for a month of operations—had already been unloaded. The greater number of the ships carrying these supplies had discharged their cargoes and departed Leyte Gulf. On the morning of Kurita's abortive advance there were in the gulf: one attack cargo ship, twenty-three tank landing ships, two medium landing ships, twenty-eight Liberty ships, and three amphibious force flagships. This was still a considerable amount of shipping, but by no means the hundreds of cargo and landing ships that had been in and out of the assault area in the preceding days.

Yet on board this vulnerable shipping were most of the pierced steel landing mats essential to the completion of the Tacloban and Dulag airstrips, and finishing these fields was vital if the invaders were to maintain local air superiority. The escort carriers providing air support could not remain in the area too long, especially after the mauling they had taken from Kurita and the kamikazes. A large amount of engineer construction material also was still afloat, and its loss would not only have affected airfield construction but in addition would have seriously delayed the building of roads and installations. Finally, a naval bombardment could have caused much damage ashore. Many of the supplies were still exposed in the beach area and troops and equipment also would have suffered.

The crucial factor, then, was the number and condition of Kurita's warships that would have survived the fight with Oldendorf's defending battleline and the gantlet of American air strikes they would have had to run. Undoubtedly they would have been badly hurt on their way into the gulf and, in the confined waters inside, would have been attractive targets for both carrier planes and those of Oldendorf's ships still afloat, as well as for heavy artillery on shore already turned to meet them. Maneuvering with difficulty under continuing attack, their strength reduced, with inadequate fire-control radar and shrinking fuel levels, their effectiveness would have been seriously limited. Kurita's own estimate that in this situation "I could not be effective" was the key to his decision to turn back.

Weighing all these factors, a careful guess would have to be that Kurita's presence inside Leyte Gulf would have caused trouble—more than Halsey thought but far less than MacArthur and Krueger believed. Kurita would undoubtedly have sunk shipping carrying important supplies, destroyed some of the stores ashore, and inflicted casualties on troops. But he could not have delayed Sixth Army operations more than a few days or, at most, weeks. And, once he himself had been destroyed on Halsey's return, he could not have prevented the continued and stepped-up resupply of the Sixth Army that General MacArthur was ready to provide.

The American victory at Leyte Gulf was a decisive one, achieved at relatively light cost. It destroyed Japanese naval power and sealed the fate of Leyte, on which Imperial General Headquarters had placed its hopes for a decisive battle. In such a situation a nation other than Japan might well have sued for peace. But the Japanese were a long way from giving up. Even as the remnants of the once-powerful Combined Fleet were being hunted down in their flight from Leyte, Japanese combat reinforcements were pouring ashore on the island. The bitter struggle for Leyte was not yet over. It would not be ended for some time to come.

Part Five

WESTWARD FROM THE BEACHHEAD

<<<<<<<<<<<<<<<<<<<<<<<<<<<<<<<<<<<<<<<<<<<<<<<<<<

>>>

xv *The Race to Reinforce*

FOR THE next few weeks the battle for Leyte became a race. For the Japanese it was a race to bring in sufficient ground combat troops to crush the Sixth Army before the invaders could drive inland from their beachhead. To win this race it would be necessary to flood the area with enough new air strength to protect the movement of ground reinforcements and at the same time block any American attempt to reinforce. For the Americans it was a question of moving in land-based air support strong enough to protect the beachhead, cover the advance inland, and halt the flow of Japanese reinforcements. Additional ground troops were available to throw into the fight, yet only if American airpower failed to halt Japanese reinforcements would these troops be necessary. The invaders already outnumbered the defenders on Leyte by about five to one. This ratio would be sufficient for victory if it could be maintained. But it could be maintained only by establishing overwhelming air superiority over the island—and this in turn depended on how soon General Kenney's air units could be established on the Leyte airstrips.

Kenney was charged with relieving Kinkaid's escort carriers of their mission of providing direct support over Leyte "at the earliest practicable date." This date was keyed to how soon army planes—specifically fighters and light bombers of Major General Ennis C. Whitehead's Fifth Air Force—could be based on Leyte.

And this, in turn, depended on how quickly the engineers could convert the short muddy landing areas of the captured Japanese airstrips into solid ground capable of supporting heavy and sustained operations by hundreds of American planes. The first of Kenney's fighter groups were scheduled to come in on A plus 5, October 25, but by that date neither Tacloban nor Dulag airstrip, the only ones then in American hands, was in any shape to receive them. Indeed, it was all these strips could do to handle their unexpected visitors from Taffy 3. The Japanese had done little or nothing to surface the runways and the engineers were learning at first hand about Leyte's "unstable" soil, poor drainage, and thick mud.

So the end of the Battle of Leyte Gulf found Kinkaid's escort carriers, battered and exhausted as they were, still faced with the necessity of protecting the Sixth Army. With the three Taffys barely able to defend themselves, much less in condition to fly support missions over Leyte, Kinkaid asked Halsey to provide cover until Kenney's planes could be based ashore. Halsey's carriers, while in much better shape than Kinkaid's, were low on food, fuel, and ammunition. A number of them, however, along with several of the escort carriers, managed to stay in the area and to fly cover and support missions. Yet this was at best a temporary solution. Land-based airpower was needed—and quickly.

Unloading of the steel matting for the two captured airfields —the same matting that Kurita might have destroyed had he fought his way into Leyte Gulf—continued at a stepped-up pace on the night of the 25th. Engineers and Air Force ground crews rushed to complete the coral base necessary before the landing mats could be laid on the muddy strips. Other service crews were busy hauling off wrecked carrier planes left over from the day's engagement and patching up others that were still able to fly. Interruptions were frequent, as planes from Tominaga's Fourth Air Army struck at the airstrips, sending everyone except the antiaircraft gunners headlong into gullies and hastily dug slit trenches. But as soon as the "all clear" signal was given floodlights flashed on again and everyone went back to work.

Japanese planes returned on the 26th. And so did the rain. Which was more annoying, is hard to say. The Japanese were more dangerous, but the heavy downpour, which turned roads into bogs and fields into sticky mud, washed out gravel beds, and generally made life miserable, was the more frustrating. Yet the work went on despite interruptions, and soon after dawn on the 27th the weary engineers laid the last section of more than 2,500 feet of steel matting on the Tacloban strip. Conditions at Dulag were far worse and deteriorated even more as the monsoon season continued in earnest. It would be another three weeks before work there could be completed. But at Tacloban, at least, the field was ready.

A few minutes after noon on October 27, thirty-four P-38's of the Fifth Air Force swept low over the strip and then made a hasty landing. One cracked up when it overshot the short runway, but the others made it down without difficulty. Among the newly arrived fighter pilots was Major Richard I. Bong, the army's leading ace with thirty Japanese planes to his credit. The reception committee was no less illustrious. These were the first American planes to be based in the Philippines in two and a half years, and both MacArthur and Kenney were on hand to greet them. As luck would have it, General Tominaga's representatives failed to put in an appearance all afternoon. The P-38's refueled quickly and soon several of them were up in the air hunting Japanese. Ground crews meanwhile added another 1,000 feet to the runway as insurance against further accidents. And that evening responsibility for air support of Sixth Army passed from the navy to General Kenney.

For the next few days, while kamikazes and other planes from Admiral Fukudome's command struck at American shipping in Leyte Gulf, Tominaga sent everything he had against the Tacloban airstrip. Opposing him were only the thirty-three P-38's that had landed safely on the 27th. Tacloban was too small and crowded to take any more planes, so the entire burden fell on less than three dozen fighters—and they were so outnumbered they could do little more than defend the airstrip.

This they did well. On the first day they knocked down six attackers and before a week had passed they had raised the score to fifty. No Americans were shot down, but Japanese bombs and operational accidents in the increasingly bad weather took their toll. By the 30th only twenty fighters were able to get off the ground. Additional P-38's flew in that afternoon and the next day, but the steady rains delayed further airfield construction and made it impossible to bring up light and medium bombers to support Krueger's troops.

Hundreds of planes were ready to move forward from rear areas, but without air bases on Leyte they had no place to go. And as long as the heavy rains, and occasional typhoons, continued, building air bases was agonizingly slow work. This meant that the few fighter planes on the island would have to fly support missions that should have been flown by bombers. And, in the face of the enemy aerial buildup on nearby Japanese-held islands, Kenney's fighters were almost too busy defending themselves and their airfield to do much in the way of attacking Japanese ground forces. As a result, General MacArthur was forced to request continued naval air support of operations. The battered escort carriers, harried by kamikazes and a few Japanese submarines, were mostly out of the fight by the 30th. But Admiral Halsey, grumbling and complaining at being tied down, remained to support MacArthur for nearly a month.

And all through this period the rain continued. It rained all day and all night. Or it rained in intermittent showers. It rained in gusty blows or in a steady drenching downpour. It rained thirty-five inches in the first forty days. The wind blew down tents and drove the rain under lashed-down tarpaulins, soaking men and supplies and equipment. The water sat in puddles, at first, and then in small lakes on the low, poorly drained ground. Roads were streams of mud, and everywhere the earth was soft and boggy. The engineers rebuilt the roads and struggled to maintain the fields at Tacloban and Dulag. The infantry captured the rest of the east Leyte airstrips. The engineers put them into shape and the bad weather knocked them out again. Finally, in December, a new strip was built on firmer ground at Tanauan, in time to support the final stages of the campaign.

But until then Halsey's carrier flyers and Kenney's long-range planes operating from rear areas had to carry the bulk of the load. Planes based on Leyte itself, including a group of Marine night fighters, were in the air every day that the airstrips could be kept operational. But the first direct support mission of the ground troops could not be flown from a Leyte field until late November, and no more than a dozen such strikes by land-based aircraft were possible before the end of the year. Most of the time, whatever American planes could get into the air over the Leyte area were busy fighting off Japanese attacks or seeking desperately to halt the flow of enemy ground reinforcements. In the latter effort they were something less than successful.

The first Japanese reinforcements to reach Leyte, the so-called "Tempei ("Heaven Sent") battalion of the 57th Independent Brigade, landed at the west coast port of Ormoc on October 23. Moving in barges and small boats, the troops had crossed the narrow waters from Cebu without incident. A second convoy arrived on the 25th, bringing more than twice as many men. After the convoy left Ormoc, planes from Sprague's escort carriers hit it twice. A cruiser, two destroyers, and two transports were sunk—too late, since their precious cargo of reinforcements was already safe ashore on Leyte. Meanwhile barges and transports continued to reach Ormoc each day through October 30, raising the total number of reinforcements to over 6,000 troops, mainly of the 30th and 102nd Divisions. By morning of November 1, General Suzuki and Thirty-fifth Army headquarters also had landed.

Suzuki now had on Leyte all the Thirty-fifth Army units that he had ordered forward earlier. But this was only the beginning. Late that day, an additional 13,000 troops arrived, the first of the reinforcements promised by General Yamashita on October 22.

Yamashita had released these only reluctantly, despite his promise. For neither he nor the staff of the Fourteenth Area Army had been reconciled to the decision to fight an all-out battle on Leyte. Even as he had informed Suzuki that reinforcements were on their way, Yamashita and his top staff officers continued to argue that these reinforcements should be limited. To strip Luzon of troops for Leyte, he explained to Southern Army and Imperial General Headquarters representatives, would so weaken defenses on Luzon that the island would fall like a ripe plum to the Americans. Better to send only a few units and hold the rest in hand to meet the inevitable invasion of Luzon. General Muto, Yamashita's tough and outspoken chief of staff, even went so far as to assert that if major reinforcements had to be sent to Leyte, the Fourteenth Area Army could not be held responsible for the defense of Luzon.

But Yamashita really had no choice. A personal call on Marshal Terauchi failed to shake the Southern Army commander in his determination to back General Suzuki all the way. The only concession Yamashita could obtain was the promise of additional divisions to replace the troops he sent to Leyte. The dangers involved in pulling units out of the already shaky Luzon defenses and replacing them with new ones unfamiliar with the area and the plans to defend it made no difference. Major reinforcements would be dispatched to Leyte—and without any further delay.

First to go would be the 26th Division, elements of which were ready to embark from Manila within a few days. Next was the 1st Division, a crack unit originally held in reserve for the *Sho* operation but now sailing from Shanghai to Manila and already assigned to the Fourteenth Area Army. It would be easier all around, Yamashita felt, simply to let the division go right on to Leyte, much as he hated to give it up. The same applied to the 68th Independent Brigade, then on Formosa but also newly assigned to Yamashita.

In midafternoon of November 1 three naval transports anchored off Ormoc and swiftly disembarked a regiment of the 26th Division. These ships were the advance element of a convoy transporting the bulk of Lieutenant General Tadasu Kataoka's 1st Division. The 1st Division had reached Manila on October 27, where it was personally reviewed by Yamashita and then combat-loaded for Leyte. In order not to expose the entire division to possible loss at one time, a battalion of each regiment was put ashore, to follow on a later convoy. The main force of General Kataoka's troops sailed on the 31st aboard four transports, shepherded by six destroyers, four smaller escorts, and occasionally by about a dozen navy fighter planes. Rain provided additional cover, and the convoy reached Ormoc unscathed late on November 1.

Not until the next day, after all the troops and most of the supplies and equipment were ashore, were American planes able to do any damage. Some thirty P-38's from Tacloban strafed and dropped small bombs on the anchorage, and two dozen B-24's from Morotai struck the convoy. These attacks killed a number of men in the deck crews and wrecked guns and equipment still on board. The heavy bombers also sank one of the transports. But the blow had come too late to prevent the 1st Division's arrival. And it was "this unit, more than any other," according to General Krueger, that "was responsible for the extension of the Leyte operation."

Small shipments of men and equipment continued to reach Ormoc by barge from nearby islands during the next week. As fast as they arrived they were unloaded and moved safely inland by General Suzuki's efficient transportation service. "The enemy," noted Krueger's intelligence officer, Colonel Horton V. White, "is operating over short, protected internal lines of communication, as yet free from serious interdiction by our air and naval forces." He might have added that the heavy weather provided numerous cloud fronts to screen the passage of Japanese convoys moving south from Manila, and that the same clouds, blanketing Leyte's central mountain range, were an additional barrier to American planes flying over these mountains to attack Ormoc. Japanese pilots covering the Ormoc convoys from bases in the Visayas were spared this problem. They also flew from drier fields, since Leyte's heavy rains were not fully shared at this time of year by the islands farther west. Both geography and weather, in short, favored the Japanese. As long as this situation lasted, warned Colonel White, the Japanese would "continue bringing in reinforcements and supplies to Leyte."

The next major convoy from Manila, carrying the rest of the 1st Division and the major part of the 26th Division, reached Ormoc in two sections on November 9. The advance section, with the 1st Division troops, anchored, unloaded, and departed again without incident. The second echelon was less fortunate. Just as it made its turn into Ormoc Bay, four medium bombers and nearly a score of fighters from Tacloban swooped in at low level to strafe and skip-bomb the transports and their escorts. Several of the ships took hits and, although none went down, there was considerable damage to decks and equipment and several casualties among the soldiers and sailors. "The waters of the sea around us were tinted with blood," recalled one Japanese officer, "and a few wounded men were floating."

Once in port, the convoy disembarked its troops during the night, but a breakdown in the Thirty-fifth Army's hitherto smooth transportation service frustrated unloading of the cargoes. The barges previously used to bring heavy equipment ashore had either been destroyed in air attacks or were engaged elsewhere, and it was extremely difficult to unload the vitally needed guns, heavy equipment, ammunition, and other supplies still aboard the transports. Shortly after daylight, fearing another air attack, the convoy commander halted unloading operations and put to sea as fast as he could. In vain. A heavy force of medium bombers and fighters caught the ships at about the same point where the first attack had come. Despite the loss of several planes to antiaircraft fire, the Americans sank two badly needed transports and an escort ship and chased the rest back to Manila heavily damaged. Survivors from the sinking vessels, floating on boards, casks, and other debris, were soon engulfed in a mass of flaming oil that covered the surface of the water. A tremendous explosion on board one of the dying ships extinguished the blaze, and a few men were picked up by the next convoy from Manila.

This convoy, carrying the rest of the 26th Division and a considerable amount of ammunition and other supplies, reached Ormoc on the 11th. Before unloading could begin, well over 300 planes from Task Force 38 struck the ships. Bombing and strafing, they sank all five transports in the convoy and five of seven escort vessels. They also shot down more than a dozen Japanese fighters that tried to intercept. Nine American planes, however, fell before the fighters and antiaircraft fire. Of the convoy's valuable cargo, everything was lost to the Japanese except those soldiers who managed to swim ashore. The cost of reinforcing Leyte had gone up.

It continued to rise throughout the remainder of the campaign. As the American air effort improved, the Japanese lost more and more of their resupply and escort ships. And fewer and fewer troops and, no less important, supplies managed to survive the hazardous journey to Leyte. Yet as far as the Americans were concerned, the damage had been done. For by mid-November the Japanese 1st and 26th Divisions, elements of the 30th and 102nd Divisions, and several other units, for a total of more than 35,000 troops, had landed at Ormoc. And even after this period, despite rising losses, the Japanese managed to bring to Leyte at least another 10,000 men, including the bulk of the 68th Independent Brigade, part of a regiment of the 8th Division, and additional elements of the 30th and 102nd Divisions. Many of these men had to swim ashore, and the supplies and equipment that littered the bottom of the sea were of little use to General Suzuki. Yet the fact remained that Japanese ground forces on Leyte during most of the campaign were far stronger, far more capable of both offensive and defensive action, than they had been before A-day.

Japanese aerial reinforcements to the Leyte area also were heavy. Both Tominaga's Fourth Air Army and Fukudome's First Combined Base Air Force continued to move aircraft into the central Philippines. In line with this, an increasing number of planes and air units reached the islands in November and December. Tominaga's pilots concentrated on attacking American airstrips in eastern Leyte and on trying to protect Japanese convoys against American aerial attack. Toward the end of the fight for Leyte more and more Fourth Air Army planes undertook kamikaze attacks on American shipping. Most of the navy planes were already engaged in kamikaze operations, and this horrifying tactic inflicted widespread damage on the Third and Seventh Fleets. Gradually it became the most important and effective Japanese aerial weapon.

The effort to build up Japanese air strength around Leyte never really succeeded. A failure of aircraft production at home, mounting losses to American airpower in the Philippines, and the frittering away of Japanese planes in kamikaze attacks all combined to bring a gradual decline in the number of Japanese aircraft over Leyte. Nevertheless, for most of the campaign, Tominaga and Fukudome in the air, like Suzuki on the ground, were much stronger and more dangerous than they had been at the start of the operation. If they never gained control of the air over Leyte themselves, they at least prevented the Americans from winning it until the battle neared its end.

The unbelievably bad weather that thwarted American efforts to establish land-based air strength on Leyte thus enabled the Japanese to greatly increase their defensive capabilities on the island and to carry on the fight for longer than would otherwise have been possible. In November, then, General Krueger was forced to commit two additional divisions, the 11th Airborne and the 32nd, as well as the 112th Cavalry Regimental Combat Team.

In December the 77th Division joined the fight. Air strength also built up slowly, including additional Marine air units, but it was necessary to maintain carrier support in the area far longer than had been contemplated. Admiral Halsey, indeed, had to call off a long-anticipated carrier raid on Tokyo in order to continue his support of MacArthur.

The Battle of Leyte Gulf had been a great American victory, which should have ended the fight on Leyte. With MacArthur's line of supply and communications secure, he should have had no difficulty in polishing off the small Japanese force defending the island. Yet defeat of the Japanese fleet did not seal off Leyte. And with the weather as their powerful ally the Japanese were able to bring in enough reinforcements through the island's back door to prolong the battle for many long and bitter weeks.

By running in so many additional troops and aircraft before the Americans could either isolate or capture Leyte, the Japanese had won the race to reinforce. And by winning they made it all the harder for Krueger's men to finish the battle.

xvi X Corps to Carigara

IF American success in the Battle of Leyte Gulf failed to halt the flow of Japanese reinforcements to the island, it nevertheless achieved the highly important goal of securing the seaward flank of the Sixth Army beachhead. With his rear and supply line thus protected, General Krueger was free to press forward in the drive to occupy the rest of Leyte.

Once the beachhead was well established, Krueger's main objective was the town of Carigara, across the northern Leyte Valley on the island's north coast. From here the Sixth Army could push south through the mountains into the Ormoc Valley, drive down that corridor to seize Ormoc itself, and bring the campaign to a close. But Carigara was a two-way street. For even as Krueger viewed it as a major steppingstone for American victory, Generals Yamashita and Suzuki had just the opposite idea. To them Carigara was an important assembly area for the Japanese reinforcements rushing toward Leyte. If the 16th Division could hold long enough for these reinforcements to be brought forward from Ormoc to Carigara, then Suzuki would be in excellent shape to launch a major offensive across the Leyte Valley and throw the Americans back into the sea. Control of Carigara, therefore, would determine the future direction of the battle.

Unfortunately for Japanese ambitions, General Makino's decision on the night of October 26 to withdraw west of the Burauen-Dagami road, and his earlier inability to hold high ground farther north, gave the Americans an edge in the race for Carigara. Within a week of A-day the Sixth Army beachhead was all but secured. The northern Leyte Valley lay open to General Sibert's X Corps, while in the south little remained to frustrate the advance of Hodge's XXIV Corps.

The last Japanese stronghold in Hodge's area was the town of Dagami, where the road coming north from Burauen met the road leading inland from Leyte Gulf. An important junction and the last enemy-held town of any significance in the corps beachhead area, Dagami on October 28 was defended by several hundred weary but determined troops of the 20th Infantry Regiment.

The Japanese defenses were securely established in depth for about a mile south of the town, plugging the road from Burauen against the advance of the American 7th Division. A heavy swamp on either side of the road would funnel any attack into a relatively narrow corridor. A waist-deep marsh and muddy stream blocked the center of the corridor. Along the north side of this natural obstacle, dominating it from high ground, numerous log and sandbag pillboxes, foxholes, and spiderholes lay concealed in the heavy timber and deep cogon grass. A long causeway and ruined stone bridge provided the only avenue of advance across the marsh and stream, a fact that the Japanese gunners well appreciated.

Early on the morning of October 28 advance elements of the 17th Infantry Regiment attacked the Japanese positions. Medium tanks moved up the road, while the infantry sloshed through belt-high muck and water on either side. Heavy Japanese fire slowed the advance, but three of the tanks were able to get across the causeway and bridge before the ancient span collapsed from their weight. The infantry managed to ford the stream, but then could go no farther in the face of Japanese machine guns, mortars, and rifles. The three tanks nevertheless continued on alone—a dangerous mistake, as they soon discovered. After advancing about 250 yards into the Japanese positions, they were halted by mines and antitank fire and surrounded by enemy soldiers. The Japanese rushed at the tanks, threw explosives beneath their treads, and quickly knocked out two of them. One exploded in a burst of flames, incinerating the crew. The other did not burn, so the men inside were able to escape through the floor hatch and take cover behind the remaining tank. Thus protected, they retreated slowly to the stream, where three companies of the 17th Infantry maintained a precarious bridgehead.

Now it was the turn of the infantry. One company, on the left, began a slow, difficult advance into the line of pillboxes and foxholes. Punishing Japanese fire took a heavy toll of the attackers, but failed to halt them. In the many separate actions that characterized the fight, squads and individual soldiers were pitted against isolated pillboxes and foxholes hidden in the grass or covered with palm fronds. Private Leonard C. Brostram earned a Congressional Medal of Honor by singlehandedly knocking out a pillbox with grenades despite the fact that he was hit three times in the stomach before he reached his target. While this was taking place, two other companies managed to slip around the other Japanese flank and launched a strong attack on the defenders from this angle. The pressure of this assault, combined with a renewed frontal attack, was too much for the Japanese. As the Americans moved through the 20th Infantry positions, destroying pillboxes with grenades and cleaning out foxholes and trenches with rifle and machine-gun fire, the Japanese began to wilt under the attack. Still fighting back effectively, they started to withdraw from their exposed forward positions. By nightfall the attacking 17th Infantry had occupied most of the Japanese defenses. The cost in American casualties had been heavy, but the worst part of the fighting was over.

The next morning the Americans attacked again. Advancing swiftly into the remaining Japanese positions, they moved from pillbox to pillbox, destroying each in turn with concentrated fire from small arms and self-propelled artillery. When necessary, individual soldiers closed in to hurl grenades through firing apertures or stuff them down ventilating shafts. By afternoon the area seemed secure and the road into Dagami apparently lay open.

Just south of the town, however, some of the troops found their way blocked by an old cemetery. Weeds and cogon grass filled the graveyard, standing well over the men's heads and partially concealing the old-fashioned Spanish stone crypts built above the ground. As the men passed through the cemetery, headstones suddenly tilted back from the crypts and Japanese riflemen opened fire on the surprised Americans. The Japanese quickly ducked back into their improvised pillboxes but continued to shoot through holes drilled in the headstones and sides of the crypts. Several Americans were hit, one officer falling dead beneath a statue of the Virgin Mary, before the 17th Infantry troops could take cover. Then they began the grim task of knocking out each crypt that contained a live inhabitant. Relying primarily on flame throwers, they soon cremated or otherwise disposed of all Japanese in the cemetery.

With the last obstacle before Dagami cleared, and with General Makino unwilling to expend any more troops of his shattered 16th Division to hold the area, the 17th Infantry entered the town and secured it on October 30. The regiment quickly made contact with X Corps elements to the north and with 96th Division troops along the road to Leyte Gulf. The corps beachhead line was now secured.

Other 7th Division elements had meanwhile pushed down the shores of Leyte Gulf to Abuyog, about fifteen miles south of the original division beachhead at Dulag. From Abuyog a zigzag mountain trail corkscrewed west across the mountains to Baybay on the opposite coast. With too few troops to hold even the beachhead area against the Sixth Army, General Makino had been unable to maintain any sort of defense of this trail. So he blew some bridges, destroyed portions of the trail, threw up some roadblocks, and notified Thirty-fifth Army headquarters that the trail was impassable. His report proved somewhat exaggerated, for a small force of 7th Division troops pushed unopposed and with only minor difficulty over the trail, reaching Baybay late on November 2. This force was too weak and the distance up the coast to Ormoc too great to allow for any attempt at seizing that port immediately. Had the capture of Ormoc been possible at this early date, the bulk of the Japanese reinforcements might have been blocked. But this was not to be. The 7th Division elements in Baybay were but a hint of things to come, and a sign that southern Leyte was clear of Japanese.

General Suzuki, secure in the thought that Makino had effectively blocked the trail, had no idea there were any Americans in Baybay. Only with the announcement of the 7th Division advance by the San Francisco radio did he realize what had happened. Alarmed, but correctly guessing the small size of the force in Baybay, he dispatched a company of reserve troops down the coast from Ormoc to hold the approaches to that city against an American advance from the south. For a while this would be sufficient.

To the north, meanwhile, Sibert's X Corps had won the race to Carigara. On the Sixth Army right General Mudge's 1st Cavalry Division had secured Tacloban, the heights west and north of the town, and both shores of narrow San Juanico Strait within a week of A-day. A small force that had sailed through San Juanico, a squadron of the 7th Cavalry Regiment, continued its amphibious advance along the north Leyte coast in a series of unopposed landings on the shores of Carigara Bay. Advance elements landed at the town of Barugo on October 28 and quickly pushed forward the last three miles to Carigara. Here they met their first opposition.

Since the 25th Japanese reinforcements from Ormoc had been moving up the Ormoc Valley toward Carigara, on their way to join the 16th Division in the Dagami-Burauen area. By the 28th the bulk of the 41st Infantry Regiment of the 30th Division, the Tempei battalion, and two battalions of the 102nd Division had reached Carigara. Completely unaware of the amphibious advance of the 7th Cavalry—Japanese intelligence estimates had indicated that San Juanico Strait was unnavigable even for landing craft—the lead Japanese elements were surprised to encounter a troop of American cavalry in the eastern portion of Carigara.

The two forces deployed rapidly. A brisk skirmish began as they exchanged small-arms fire from buildings, ditches, and whatever other cover was handy. But the cavalrymen were clearly outnumbered and soon fell back to Barugo, leaving Carigara in Japanese hands. At Barugo they were joined by other divisional elements, which had advanced overland from Tacloban almost unopposed through difficult mountain terrain.

Although strong elements of the 1st Cavalry Division were now concentrated within a few miles of Carigara, General Sibert hesitated to make an immediate attack with these forces. Intelligence reports indicated that as many as 5,000 Japanese might be in Carigara—a fairly good estimate, actually—and the enemy seemed bent on defending the important little town. Rather than risk a repulse, Sibert decided to wait until the 24th Division and X Corps heavy artillery units were in position to join in the assult. This combined force, he reasoned, should be sufficient to assure success.

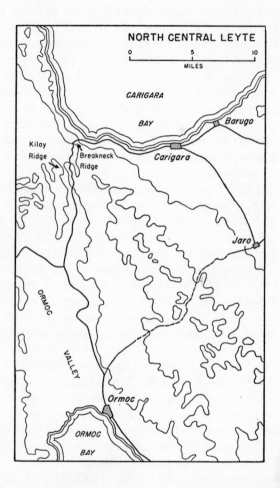

But the 24th Division, advancing on the left of the 1st Cavalry, was still encountering considerable opposition. After securing the Palo area on the 25th, General Irving's men had attacked overland toward Carigara. Crushing small Japanese detachments and rebuilding destroyed bridges, the division made good progress against the crumbling but sometimes bitter defenses of the battered Japanese 33rd Infantry Regiment.

Resistance stiffened as the troops pushed ahead, however. The 19th Infantry bloodied its nose on a particularly stubborn Japanese trailblock several miles west of Palo. The heart of the position was a small fort, disguised as a cluster of grass-covered native huts and flanked by trenches and log bunkers. Attacking late in the afternoon, two companies attempted to storm the fort, got within 100 yards of it, and then were thrown back by intense, searing machine-gun fire. Again and again the men tried to get close enough to use flame throwers or to plant demolitions, but the Japanese machine guns were too deadly. Even artillery seemed to do little good. Finally, heavy mortars, moved forward under cover of darkness to almost point-blank range, did the trick. At daylight their crushing shells stilled the Japanese guns and gave the riflemen the chance to close in and overrun the position. Then the advance continued.

In the 34th Infantry sector, Japanese defenses at an important river crossing held things up for most of the day on October 28. A single-lane steel bridge spanned the 150-foot gorge through which the river flowed, but Japanese rifles, machine guns, and grenade launchers effectively covered the approaches to the still intact bridge. A frontal assault was unsuccessful. Patrols, however, soon discovered a ford several hundred yards downstream, its approaches concealed from Japanese eyes by thick vegetation. Under cover of a second frontal attack, and hidden by the drenching showers of a heavy rain, two companies waded across undetected and scaled the opposite wall of the gorge. Then they struck at the Japanese flank.

The charge, in the words of one observer, "was almost pure Hollywood." The men ran forward quickly, firing continuously and shouting Rebel yells, leapfrogging light machine guns to cover each advance, and pausing only when the opposition was too strong to overrun. So swiftly did this advance roll up the Japanese line that the defenders were wiped out or dispersed before they could set off demolition charges placed earlier on the bridge.

Pushing ahead rapidly from this victory, on the 29th elements of the 24th Division entered Jaro, where the roads from Palo and Dagami meet and turn toward Carigara, just ten miles to the northwest. The Japanese 33rd Infantry, the main defensive force in the area, had been badly mauled. Little appeared to stand in the way of a swift advance to Carigara.

At Thirty-fifth Army headquarters General Suzuki and his staff were still unaware of the speed of the American drive. They neither expected such rapid success nor, as yet, had any means of learning about it. But other Japanese were finding out at first hand. The inland drive of the 24th Division had cut Japanese supply and communications routes. Japanese couriers and supply columns, moving over trails and mountain paths unaware of the extent of the American advance, discovered this too late when they were cut down by sudden gunfire. One 24th Division platoon received an unexpected gift of rice and tuna fish when a Japanese supply party stumbled unknowingly into the American perimeter. Other Japanese went to sleep beside a path without leaving any guard—the last mistake most of them ever made.

On the night of the 28th the 2nd Battalion, 19th Infantry, had formed a perimeter across a mountain trail. Out of the dark appeared a group of Japanese soldiers transporting a load of ammunition on horse-drawn carts. Evidently they were lost, for one of them strolled up to an American outpost guard and asked him a question in Japanese. The guard, not hearing well and thinking his questioner was someone from the 2nd Battalion, started to answer. Suddenly both men realized their error and leaped for cover. But, for the Japanese, it was too late. American machine gunners and antitank men, the latter firing canister, opened up on the supply train. Most of the Japanese were killed in a few moments. The horses died more slowly, and finally a sergeant took pity on them and walked along the trail to shoot each moaning, agonized animal in the head.

Later that night another group of unsuspecting Japanese walked into the 3rd Battalion perimeter, some distance away, and met the same fate. One wounded man was captured. He said that he and the others were truck mechanics, sent to repair vehicles in an area the 19th Infantry had in fact seized thirty-six hours earlier. Clearly, Japanese information about American dispositions was out of touch with events, and 16th Division communications along the front had broken down. It would be several days before Japanese commanders could straighten out their situation maps.

The Japanese in Carigara, however, were slightly better informed than most. To them, the presence of American troops in that town on the 28th—however easily these small elements were driven back—indicated that Sixth Army forces had already infiltrated the coastal area northeast of Carigara. This was contrary to earlier Japanese estimates, which had assumed that MacArthur would first have to secure the beachhead area and airstrips before striking inland from Tacloban. Under that assumption moving Japanese reinforcements through Carigara would be relatively safe. But the rapid drive across the north Leyte Valley by Sibert's X Corps now threatened to block this avenue.

Despite the obvious danger to his flank, the commander of the Japanese 41st Infantry Regiment decided to continue his advance from Carigara. He still had received no direct word from the 16th Division but, in accordance with his orders, was determined to locate and join General Makino's forces. Late on the 29th, then, leaving the other Japanese units in Carigara to protect his rear, he set out with his regiment for Dagami via Jaro.

At Jaro, Colonel "Red" Newman's 34th Infantry Regiment secured the town that afternoon but then spent an uncomfortable night. A few survivors of the Japanese 33rd Infantry attempted to infiltrate the American positions, and heavy firing continued in the darkness. Three Japanese made it to within twenty-five feet of a battalion command post before the startled troops there could shoot them. Through all of this the rain fell heavily, drenching the tired men, despite their ponchos, and turning the ground to soft, slippery mud. At first light on the 30th, nevertheless, Newman ordered the advance on Carigara to continue.

Almost exactly at eight o'clock the regiment moved out. As the plank houses of Jaro gave way to nipa huts on the town's outskirts, machine-gun fire suddenly struck the lead company. Several men fell in the mud before the Americans could take cover and return the fire. The Japanese—apparently whatever was left of the 33rd Infantry—were dug in under the huts and in the grassy hills beside the road. When these positions proved too strong for Newman's men to crack, a column of Sherman tanks rolled up, sending shells crashing into the huts and sweeping the hills with their machine guns. But heavy Japanese fire continued to dominate the road. The infantrymen were unable to move forward and support the tanks, and the column prudently withdrew. A call went back for artillery, but no one knew for sure just where the Japanese were. So tanks and infantry cautiously moved forward again to try to establish the enemy positions. Fifty yards they went—but no farther. Intense, crippling fire drove the infantry to cover. The tanks, without support, halted.

By now Colonel Newman was getting concerned about the delay. Running forward to the lead platoon, he asked first Lieutenant Lewis F. Stearns what was holding things up. "I told him he had better get down in the ditch," Stearns wrote later, "but he replied: 'I'll get the men going okay!'" Newman began to walk ahead and Stearns yelled to his platoon, "Let's go! The colonel is here!" Just as Newman's example had inspired his troops on A-day, his courage again was infectious. The men rose from their cover and started to follow him.

The Japanese mortars began firing. A shell hit the soldier closest to Newman, blowing the man to pieces. The colonel himself clutched his middle and crumpled to the ground. Lieutenant Stearns and an aidman ran to him, cut away his shirt and trousers, and tried to stop the blood flowing from the great tear in Newman's stomach. The wounded regimental commander, recalled Stearns, "was in complete command of his faculties. He asked if we could remain in position and drop mortar fire on the enemy. I told him men were being killed every minute and we would have to do something and do it fast." Newman thought for a moment, trying to ignore his pain and make the right decision. Finally he told Stearns to send word back for artillery support and in the meantime to put mortar fire on the Japanese position. "Leave me here," he ordered. Stearns refused to abandon the colonel and with the help of the aidman dragged him back to safety on a poncho. The rest of the platoon fell back with them. Newman, evacuated to the rear, lived to fight another day. For his courage he was awarded the Distinguished Service Cross.

While Stearns' platoon was disengaging, one of the tanks took a freak hit. A Japanese antitank gunner put a round right down the barrel of the American Sherman. As it happened, the tank gunner had just pulled open the breech block to reload and the Japanese shell crashed through the open breech, passed through the gunner's compartment, and struck the tank radio behind it. The explosion wounded three men in the tank and put it out of action.

Now the supporting American artillery opened up, pounding away for twenty minutes. On the heels of this barrage 34th Infantry troops pushed off again, this time with somewhat more success. Driving back the remnants of the 33rd Infantry, they drove forward some 200 yards before they again ran into a stone wall of Japanese resistance. Machine-gun and rifle fire, mortars, and even some light artillery lashed the Americans. The 41st Infantry had apparently arrived from Carigara just in time to halt the 24th Division advance. The 34th Infantry attempted to flank the Japanese defenses from the west. When this failed, the troops formed defensive positions and dug in for the night. They were still on the northern outskirts of Jaro, with little to show for the day's efforts.

Darkness brought with it the usual Japanese attempts to infiltrate the American positions, repulsed with not too much difficulty. Then the American artillery went into action. The engineers had slaved all day over the muddy road to Jaro, sweating to make it passable for the big guns and ammunition trains. Thanks to them, division artillery was in place by dark and pounded steadily away at the Japanese positions north of the town. The heavier guns of X Corps artillery, with their longer range, dropped shells at will up and down the road from Jaro all the way back to Carigara. The firing rocked the ground and even shook dust into General Sibert's dinner at the nearby X Corps command post. On the receiving end of this bombardment, the Japanese sought shelter in foxholes and caves. They lacked their own heavy artillery to return the fire, and suffered heavily from the shelling.

With morning, the 34th Infantry resumed the attack. Slowly, yard by bloody yard, they forced their way forward along the road and over the hills and ridges that flanked it. The 41st Infantry had taken considerable punishment from the night's artillery fire, yet it held out stubbornly against the American attack. Each hill had its share of Japanese mortars and machine guns, each section of the road seemed to be covered by small-arms and light artillery fire. But the heavy pressure was too much for the defenders. The American attack overpowered them, clearing the road and scattering battered remnants of the 41st Infantry into the hills to the northwest.

Behind the 41st Infantry a battalion of the Japanese 102nd

Division had set up defenses across the road. The advancing
Americans struck these, smashed the forward positions, and then
ground to a halt. Gains on October 31 had been only about three
miles, and there had been many casualties. But Japanese losses
were far heavier. And the 41st Infantry, the main enemy force
blocking the road, had been badly cut up. Another day's effort
against the reeling Japanese might do the trick.

That night there was no Japanese attempt to infiltrate 24th
Division positions. Indeed, under cover of darkness, Japanese
troops in front of the 34th Infantry began to pull out, some falling
back toward Carigara, others moving off the road into the hills to
the west. So when the American regiment moved out on the
morning of November 1 nothing was there to oppose it.

In a steady drizzle that faded as the morning wore on, the
34th Infantry advanced quickly but cautiously. Japanese dead,
victims of American artillery fire, lay scattered along the road and
in positions on the hillsides. Blackened cremation pits gave grim
indication of how many others had died. And the little boxes of
ashes, wrapped in white cloth, that stood in neat piles in one
abandoned position testified to the hasty withdrawal of the Japanese. Elsewhere, discarded weapons, equipment, and ammunition
littered the area. Personal belongings—packs, clothing, letters,
pictures—lay strewn about former bivouac areas. Everything
pointed to an almost frantic retreat. By evening lead elements of
the 34th Infantry were little more than two miles from Carigara.
Only twice had the regiment encountered any Japanese. In both
instances these rearguard positions fell quickly to the American
attack. For the first time in many days 24th Division casualties
could be counted on the fingers of one hand.

What had happened to the Japanese? Late on the evening of
October 30 Major General Yoshiharu Tomochika, chief of staff of
the Thirty-fifth Army, had reached Ormoc with the advance
echelon of General Suzuki's headquarters. Unable to get a clear
picture of the situation in eastern Leyte, Tomochika felt that the
plan to launch a counterattack from Carigara was still feasible.
Yet, since the 16th Division was apparently unable to exercise
effective command over the units in Carigara, he decided to re-
tain control of them himself. On the morning of the 31st Tomochika dispatched Major Chuji Kaneko, a 102nd Division staff

officer, to represent him in Carigara. Kaneko carried orders for the 41st Infantry to advance to Dagami while the other units formed a defensive line east of Carigara to cover the assembly of additional reinforcements there. These instructions in effect confirmed the course of action that the 41st Infantry commander had adopted two days earlier.

Major Kaneko reached Carigara on the morning of November 1. "Contrary to expectations," as he put it later, he met elements of the 41st Infantry and other units "retreating from the front." The situation had obviously deteriorated beyond the point where General Tomochika's instructions could be followed. Not only had the American advance blocked any possible move of the 41st Infantry to Dagami but the proposed defensive line east of Carigara had already been outflanked.

An immediate decision was clearly necessary, and Kaneko did not shrink from it. If Carigara could not be held as an assembly area, it still might be possible to mass reinforcements in the hills to the west and southwest and eventually mount an attack from there. In General Tomochika's name, Major Kaneko ordered Carigara to be abandoned and all units in the area to set up defensive positions on the high ground a few miles outside the town.

General Sibert, meanwhile, felt he was now ready to launch a full-scale attack with X Corps on Carigara. Filipino guerrilla scouts reported that the number of Japanese in that town had diminished somewhat but that there were still two to three thousand enemy troops there. On November 1 this figure was probably not excessive, although apparently no American reconnaissance parties attempted to check it. And by the next morning there were probably only a few hundred Japanese left in town— all of them hastening to get out.

Throughout the day on the 1st, the 1st Cavalry had made preparations to spearhead the corps attack on Carigara. A heavy artillery barrage greeted the dawn on the 2nd, and the artillery continued to fire concentrations against supposed Japanese positions for over an hour. Then the 1st Cavalry attacked from Barugo and the 24th Division resumed its advance up the road from Jaro. Unopposed, the two forces closed in on Carigara. Just at the edge of town 34th Infantry troops stopped to wipe out a suicide squad of Japanese soldiers. Both divisions quickly entered the abandoned town, stalked cautiously through the deserted streets, and secured the area by midafternoon. Advance elements pushed west along the coastal road against small groups of Japanese fighting delaying actions. By evening American troops were dug in nearly three miles beyond Carigara.

At Ormoc, meanwhile, General Suzuki had arrived and drawn up final plans for an early counterattack from Carigara toward Tacloban. Not until the next morning would he learn from a messenger dispatched by Major Kaneko just how futile these plans were.

xvii The Best-Laid Plans

WITH Carigara firmly in his possession, General Krueger planned a swift move to eliminate Japanese resistance on Leyte. While Hodge's XXIV Corps cleared the southern portion of the island, Sibert's X Corps would push west along the shores of Carigara Bay, then pivot left through the mountains to the Ormoc Valley. Then, directed Krueger, Sibert would "advance vigorously to the south, destroy enemy forces encountered, and seize Ormoc." The Japanese would either be crushed between the two American corps or driven into the mountains west of Ormoc, cut off from any base of supply and unable to function effectively.

But Krueger reckoned without the heavy Japanese reinforcements pouring into Leyte. Nor, apparently, did he anticipate his own continued lack of ground-based air support. And he was unaware that his opponent, too, planned an offensive.

General Suzuki's plan also had its weaknesses—the primary one being that it was based on a good deal of misinformation. First of all, reports reaching the Thirty-fifth Army commander after the Battle of Leyte Gulf spoke of a great victory, and indicated that the Japanese now controlled both air and sea around Leyte. The Americans would clearly be unable to continue operations on the island. Next, Suzuki had yet to learn that the Sixth Army had reached Carigara in force. And, finally, at this time he still believed that the rugged cross-island road from Abuyog to Baybay had been effectively blocked by bomb craters and the destruction of bridges, and he was unconcerned about Ormoc's southern flank.

On the basis of these assumptions, Suzuki ordered the bulk of the Japanese troops at Ormoc to advance north through the open Ormoc Valley to Carigara. From here the 1st Division would spearhead a drive toward Tacloban aimed at rolling up the American beachhead. Other elements would join the offensive as quickly as they could land at Ormoc and move forward. And, as the attack progressed, reinforcements could come ashore directly at Carigara, eliminating the tiring and time-consuming overland march from Ormoc. Like Krueger's plan, Suzuki's scheme was a good one—provided the assumptions behind it were correct. But since they were not—in either case—then both plans were doomed to failure.

Execution of Suzuki's plan got under way first. On the afternoon of November 2, as X Corps elements were securing Carigara, the 1st Reconnaissance Regiment, advance guard of the 1st Division, left Ormoc and hastened north through the valley. That evening the division commander, General Kataoka, followed with the rest of his troops. Several hours later—the next morning, in fact—Major Kaneko's messenger reached Ormoc with news of the situation at Carigara. By then it was too late for Suzuki to warn Kataoka. Quickly approving Kaneko's emergency dispositions, the Thirty-fifth Army commander issued orders placing all troops around Carigara under Kataoka's temporary command. Then he could only hope that the 1st Division was as good as its reputation.

Meanwhile, early on the morning of November 3, the 34th Infantry, 24th Division, began the X Corps advance west from Carigara. The regiment pushed rapidly along the coastal road, the morning sun warming the men's backs in a welcome change from the incessant rain. Just at about nine o'clock the 1st Battalion, in the lead, ran headlong into forward elements of the 1st Reconnaissance Regiment. Although the Japanese were completely surprised, they managed to organize a defensive position along a stream and force the 1st Battalion to deploy. Artillery fire and a flanking maneuver finally cleared the way, but even then the stream crossing proved expensive. Sergeant Charles E. Mower, leading his men across, was badly hit just as he reached midstream. Unable to move forward, he remained exposed to Japanese fire while continuing to supervise the attack. So effectively did he locate and direct fire on Japanese positions that almost every enemy gun in the vicinity was soon turned upon him. Hit again and again, he sank into the water. But the attack succeeded. A posthumous Medal of Honor testified to Mower's bravery.

General Kataoka arrived on the scene early in the afternoon. He had come on ahead of the division main body with just a small detachment of riflemen and was startled to discover troops from the 1st Reconnaissance Regiment withdrawing into the hills south of the coastal road. He immediately ordered them back onto the road, to make another attempt at halting the American advance. Then he sent back word for the rest of his division to close up as quickly as possible.

Reconnoitering a few miles farther to the west along the coastal road, Kataoka was again surprised—this time by what appeared to be a full American battalion landing on the practically undefended beach. What he saw was actually only a company—K Company, 34th Infantry—that had embarked on amphibious tractors in an attempt to outflank the Japanese defenses. As 24th Division artillery at Carigara pounded the beach, the big amphibians crawled ashore, their heavy machine guns sweeping the way before them. Only rifle fire from about 100 Japanese escapees from Carigara opposed the landing. As K Company moved quickly inland, two light Japanese field pieces opened fire, but American mortars knocked them out before they could do any harm.

General Kataoka ordered an immediate attack on the beachhead by the 57th Infantry, the lead regiment of the 1st Division main body. Soon an American spotter plane saw truckloads of Japanese soldiers approaching the landing area. Despite heavy fire from 24th Division artillery, the Japanese began to build up in force around K Company. As they did so, the pilot in the spotter plane continued to call down artillery fire, the bursts coming so close to K Company's position that some of the shell fragments fell among the Americans. Nevertheless, by late afternoon, with ammunition running low and Japanese pressure increasing, it was clear that the tiny beachhead could not be held. Back came the amphibious tractors, the weary men climbed back aboard, and, with artillery providing a covering curtain, the small force escaped into Carigara Bay.

That night 24th Division guns pounded every inch of the coastal road not in American hands. Kataoka pulled his troops in-

244 _Decision at Leyte_

land into the hills. The next morning the 34th Infantry advanced unopposed along the coast to the point where the road turned south toward Ormoc, some twenty miles or so away. But the route south was blocked by a series of steep ridges and rough, rocky hills that guarded the northern entrance to the Ormoc Valley.

To support the drive through this rugged barrier, 24th Division artillery began displacing forward. Trucks brought up supplies for the infantry and the tired men of the 34th cleaned their weapons, checked their ammunition, and cursed the soaking rain that now fell steadily again. But support and supply constituted a real problem. The Japanese had destroyed bridges along the coastal road and the road itself was rapidly deteriorating. Laid mainly on marshy ground, it consisted primarily of rock fill that the heavy trucks, artillery, and tanks quickly chewed up. Rain flooded across the broken surface and mixed with muddy swamp water that oozed up through the widening cracks in the roadbed. Soon long stretches were impassable, even to tracked vehicles.

Working steadily, sweating engineer troops labored to restore the road. Pontoon and wooden bridges replaced the destroyed spans, and bulldozers pushed earth and rock fill into the torn-up, marshy roadbed. Engineers cut countless palm trees with portable power saws to corduroy the surface and Filipino laborers swung picks and shovels to support these efforts. But it seemed to do little good. The rain continued to fall and the road, in the words of one engineer officer, "became an absolute bog." Only emergency traffic traveled along it. Everything else moved by landing craft through Carigara Bay to 24th Division supply dumps further along the beach. General Irving, the division commander, warned Sibert and Krueger that the coastal road could not support a major drive to the south.

Krueger was worried—not only by this situation but even more by his fear that the Japanese might attempt an amphibious landing on Carigara Bay. They seemed to be bringing reinforcements into Ormoc at will. If Sibert moved south, what could prevent a Japanese landing to his rear that would cut off all X Corps forces committed to the push toward Ormoc? Clearly the coast of Carigara Bay would have to be readied to repulse an amphibious attack. But preparing beach defenses would leave no troops available for the drive south.

Krueger checked his forces. Hodge's XXIV Corps was fully committed against stubborn 16th Division defenses in the foothills west of Dagami and in clearing and patrolling all of southern Leyte. Borrowing troops from Hodge would only slow this effort and postpone his later operations in the west coast. In Sibert's corps, the 1st Cavalry Division had all it could do to defend northeast Leyte and the southern corner of Samar. The 24th Division was still operating with only two regiments, although the 21st Infantry, which had landed at Sogod Bay in southern Leyte, was on its way to rejoin the division. The other two regiments had been in heavy action almost continuously since A-day. And the 19th Infantry was still fully occupied securing the high ground west of the Jaro-Carigara road against the Japanese forces that Major Kaneko had pulled out of Carigara. Indeed, the only unit immediately available for the drive into the Ormoc Valley was the 34th Infantry—and, after leading the 24th Division drive to Carigara, that regiment, in fact, was weary and in need of relief. If it had to defend the beach in its area, it could send nothing but patrols into the heights to the south.

These heights, Krueger realized, were the key to the Ormoc Valley. If he could seize them while they were still lightly defended, as his orders to Sibert had originally directed, then the valley would be open for an early drive south. But if Japanese forces—which Krueger's aerial spotters could see rushing up from Ormoc—once occupied this high ground in strength, then the advance into the Ormoc Valley would be slow and costly.

A more aggressive general might have ignored the seaward threat to Carigara, shifted some of Hodge's forces north, and thrown everything into seizing the crucial ridges and hills before the Japanese could secure them. But Krueger was not by nature inclined to take such a gamble. A careful, deliberate commander, he was not averse to taking risks when necessary. Yet he was more cautious than others might have been, and in this situation his instinct prescribed the conservative course. On the afternoon of November 4 he ordered Sibert to delay his drive south until the X Corps could secure Carigara Bay against a Japanese landing. Meanwhile aerial reconnaissance had discovered a trail from Jaro southwest across the mountains to Ormoc. Sibert would send what elements he could to block this trail and to support his advance, when he resumed it, into the Ormoc Valley.

After the end of the campaign, General Krueger argued that additional troops—even a single regimental combat team—would have permitted an immediate attack on the heights guarding the northern Ormoc Valley. He had, in fact, during planning for the Leyte operation, requested an extra regiment for the assault phase, but this force had not been available. And it would be mid-November before Sixth Army reserves could reach Leyte—since a shortage of amphibious shipping dictated that these units would have to use the same transports that carried the A-Day assault forces. So, thanks to this combination of circumstances, General Suzuki had a small but important gift of time in which to improve his defenses guarding the northern Ormoc Valley.

Throughout the day on the 5th the 1st Cavalry and 24th Divisions organized positions to defend the shores of Carigara Bay. Patrols probed the areas southwest of Carigara and pushed down the Jaro-Ormoc trail. Divisional artillery units moved into position to cover the coast while the heavy corps artillery prepared to either defend the shoreline or support the drive to the south. The 21st Infantry regiment relieved the weary 34th Infantry at the northern terminus of the road to Ormoc. Sixth Army staff officers, meanwhile, conferred with Seventh Fleet commanders who pointed out that Japanese shortages of assault shipping and the powerful American artillery would probably rule out any attempt to storm the shores of Carigara Bay. Krueger directed Sibert to begin the push south. This attack was now scheduled for the morning of the 7th.

The brief delay in the X Corps offensive was all the Japanese needed. Hampered themselves by the heavy rain which made mudholes of trails and slowed or blocked the movement of artillery and other heavy equipment, hurt by two American air strikes that killed men and destroyed vehicles, General Kataoka's troops were still able to occupy the heights south of Carigara Bay and prepare a hasty but effective defense.

The key to this defense was a long, steep ridgeline, broken by sharp spurs branching off irregularly and topped by a series of rocky knobs commanding almost every approach. Along the open slopes, coarse, tall cogon grass stood shoulder high and thick woods clogged the valleys. The terrain reminded veteran 24th Division officers of the jungled heights of Guadalcanal, and they sensed that another grueling, bloody fight lay ahead. They called the ridgeline Breakneck Ridge in deference to its ugly, precipitous sides. It lay astride the road to the Ormoc Valley, blocking any approach from the north.

On the morning of the 5th elements of the Japanese 57th Infantry surprised a 34th Infantry patrol attempting to probe the western edge of Breakneck Ridge. Two companies of the 21st Infantry rushed forward to the rescue and easily occupied a hill and nearby spur. As Japanese strength built up during the afternoon, however, the 21st Infantry units found themselves cut off and hard pressed to defend themselves. They spent the night beating off 57th Infantry attacks and infiltration attempts. By morning the Japanese had managed to bring heavy mortars and field pieces forward, making the American position increasingly uncomfortable. Under cover of their own artillery, then, the two companies withdrew to the coastal road. Breakneck Ridge remained in Japanese hands.

By now, November 6, General Kataoka had the equivalent of two regiments supported by light artillery dug in along this ridge. The equally rugged heights extending to the east were as yet unoccupied—by either Americans or Japanese—but the rest of the 1st Division was moving up to plug this gap. Farther along on Kataoka's eastern flank, below Carigara, stood the 41st Infantry and other units that had held that town a week earlier. When the remainder of his troops came up, Kataoka would have, in effect, four reinforced infantry regiments, and with these he planned an all-out attack on Carigara.

Until he had completed his deployment, Kataoka perforce would have to remain on the defensive. Working frantically, then, the Japanese on Breakneck Ridge had constructed an amazing series of defenses along the steep heights. With skill and imagination they had prepared a complicated system of trenches, spiderholes, and firing pits that took advantage of every favorable terrain feature. Each wooded ground pocket was turned into a fort, each rocky outcropping a semipillbox. Machine guns and light field pieces covered major avenues of approach, and the thick cogon grass was carefully cropped to provide broad fields of fire.

Reverse slopes were honeycombed with concealed, mutually supporting positions. Since the number of troops General Sibert
could spare to attack Breakneck Ridge was at this time no greater
than the number of Japanese defending it, the advantage appeared to lie with the defense. Only their more powerful artillery
gave the Americans an edge.

For the next ten days Breakneck Ridge saw some of the bit-
terest fighting of the campaign. It was grim, savage combat, often
hand to hand, up and down the slick, muddy, rainswept heights
and valleys. Sometimes the Americans attacked, sometimes the
Japanese, with the struggle sweeping back and forth and in and
around the spurs and ridges until it was hard to tell front line
from rear, Japanese position from American. There was courage
and determination and fortitude on both sides. And there was
pain and dying.

Death came in many ways. The clean, sudden death of a bullet in a vital organ. The slow, painful mortal bleeding when a
burst of fire cut across the belly. The choking impact of a bayonet, the sharp slash of a saber. The jagged death from a bursting grenade or exploding shells. The searing agony inflicted by a
flamethrower or a white phosphorous shell that spewed its liquid
fire unchecked across the ground. And always there was the cry
of "Medic! Medic!" and the rushing, dodging, crawling figure of
the aidman, himself a target for the sniper's bullet.

The Americans usually attacked with artillery and mortar support when possible. Frequently the Japanese would then fire a
few rounds into the forward American positions. This sometimes
caused American units, believing their own supporting fire was
falling short, to send back word to cease firing.

Tanks were impossible to use on the steep, slippery heights,
and even on more level terrain the going was often too muddy for
the heavy vehicles. Riflemen had to guard the tanks on all sides.
Otherwise the Japanese would rush from concealment to slap
magnetic mines, grenades, or other demolitions against the vulnerable tracks of the tanks.

More often than not, small teams of American infantrymen
had to clear each trench and spiderhole methodically with grenades, submachine guns, and flamethrowers. When they did,
hidden Japanese riflemen on the flanks of these positions took a

heavy toll of the attackers, often forcing them back, their target still untouched. Concealed spiderholes, dug flush with the ground, would remain undiscovered after troops had searched an area time and time again. Then the Japanese would crawl from hiding to snipe at unsuspecting targets, hurl grenades, or seize American machine guns and turn them on other American positions. Sometimes scores of Japanese riflemen, supported by machine guns and mortars, would remain silently under cover and permit American scouts and forward elements to pass unchallenged. Then, when more compact American formations appeared, the Japanese would open up a devastating fire. Individual Japanese snipers, often using telescopic sights, fired constantly at troops moving along the trails or, it seemed, at aidmen and litter-bearers wherever they were.

Japanese counterattacks usually came in the late afternoon and evening, when the 21st Infantry troops were tired and low on ammunition. These attacks made proper consolidation of American front-line positions before dark all but impossible. Frequently Japanese assault troops, their helmets concealed by crowns of grass or weeds, crawled along the ground in silence until they were almost into the American positions. The sight of clumps of grass moving amidst the tall cogon would be the first indication of a Japanese attack. Even then, 21st Infantry outposts might hesitate to fire, since American troops sometimes tied grass to their helmets.

The Japanese supported more obvious attacks with well-placed mortar and machine-gun fire. Short on artillery, they used it only occasionally and on particularly important targets, shooting just one or two pieces at a time and making no effort to mass their fire. The Japanese infantry assaults were rarely the wild, hysterical *Banzai* charges Americans had come to expect. More often than not they were careful, well-planned maneuvers, resembling standard American tactics. Only occasionally would a small group mass in a disorganized, savage rush, shrieking wildly, officers swinging sabers, until American heavy weapons fire cut the attackers down in bloody clumps on the wet ground.

At night the Japanese attacked by stealthy infiltration, singly or in small groups. To cover their approach they sometimes pretended to be Americans, talking loudly in English. Once within

21st Infantry lines, they bayoneted men in their foxholes, threw grenades into the middle of defensive positions, and cut communication lines and then waited silently in ambush for linemen coming to make repairs. Larger night attacks rarely succeeded in penetrating 21st Infantry perimeters. Artillery, flame, and white phosphorus usually managed to break up any mass assaults.

Artillery sometimes had an unexpected effect. An entry in a captured Japanese diary describes how on November 7 five soldiers were about to stab an American prisoner to death on orders of their battalion commander. "At that instant," the diary continues, "an enemy artillery shell fell five yards in front, killing the prisoner of war" and wounding four of the five Japanese.

For both sides supply was a nightmare. Trails were quagmires and carrying parties lurched and stumbled through the mud, skidding and sliding up and down the slippery heights, often too exhausted or blinded by heavy rain to see where they were going. To avoid being spotted by American artillery observers, the Japanese moved most supplies at night, dragging heavier loads in handcarts into even the most forward positions. Maps were jokes, little more than rough guesses of what lay ahead. Supply teams became lost and plodded miles out of their way. Little wonder that food, water, and ammunition were seldom delivered on time.

Inch by bloody inch the 21st Infantry fought its way across Breakneck Ridge. Each hill or spur captured had to be searched again and again for hidden Japanese, each yard gained to be defended against determined counterattacks. By mid-November the regiment had won control of the entire ridge. As the crow flies, however, it had advanced barely more than a mile. But nearly 2,000 of General Kataoka's troops had died in the gallant effort to halt this advance. And casualties in the 21st Infantry, while considerably lighter, were hardly negligible. The average line company was down to a single officer and eighty-five enlisted men. The regiment was exhausted, and clearly in need of relief.

But if the 21st Infantry had done the bulk of the fighting in the preceding week and a half, it had not done it all. A battalion of the 19th Infantry had moved into the unoccupied high ground east of Breakneck Ridge, defeated advance 1st Division elements attempting to seize this area, and, cutting southwest, by mid-November had set up a block across the Ormoc Road some two and one half miles south of Breakneck Ridge. At the same time a battalion of the 34th Infantry, embarked on amphibious tractors, had landed on the far shore of Carigara Bay and advanced south unopposed well to the west of Breakneck Ridge. Supplied by airdrop and by Filipino guerrilla carriers, the battalion reached an area known as Kilay Ridge, overlooking the Ormoc Road and just west of the 19th Infantry block. The ridge had apparently been prepared as a fall-back position by General Kataoka's troops, for it was covered with trenches and dugouts. But not a Japanese was on it. The Americans quickly moved into the empty defenses, pleased at being spared the arduous work of digging in themselves. By these maneuvers General Irving's 24th Division had effectively blocked the Ormoc Road, forcing Japanese supplies and communications to make a wide detour through the mountains.

Another result of these actions had been the capture on November 8 of a 1st Division field order outlining Kataoka's plan for an attack on Carigara. The best way to forestall this attack, General Krueger decided, was to maintain the initiative himself, keeping as much pressure as possible on the Japanese. Accordingly, while urging Sibert to continue attacking in the Breakneck Ridge area, he also directed the X Corps commander to push elements into the mountains southwest of Carigara, between the Leyte and Ormoc Valleys, as another means of gaining access to the latter corridor.

This job Sibert assigned to the 1st Cavalry. The division's 1st Brigade struck southwest from Carigara against scattered and uneven resistance, primarily by the 41st Infantry Regiment. Even more difficult than the Japanese was the rugged mountain terrain, heavily forested and constantly drenched by rain. Supply was difficult, grueling, at times impossible. The men sometimes had only one meal a day. Only the lack of steady resistance prevented an ammunition shortage. Evacuation of the wounded was no less difficult and the trip to the rear over slippery mountain trails was a painful experience. By mid-November, 1st Cavalry patrols were covering most of the high ground between the northern Leyte and Ormoc Valleys and forward units had occupied heights eight miles southwest of Carigara, within sight of, although still some distance from, the Ormoc Road.

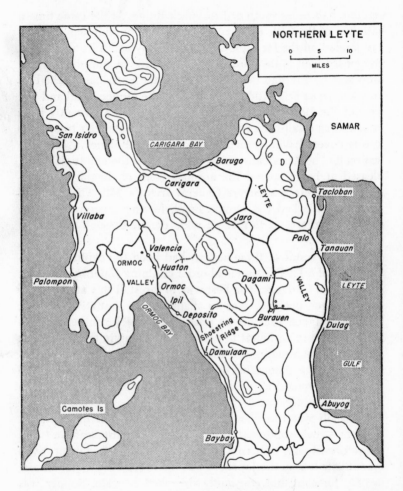

Hodge's XXIV Corps meanwhile took over responsibility for all of Leyte south of the line Palo-Jaro-Ormoc. Troops were shifted over a wide area to fill this broader mission and in the process the 96th Division was involved in bitter fighting against 16th Division remnants dug in on the rising ground west of Dagami. General Makino's forces grimly contested every inch of the American advance.

After the campaign was over, one of Yamashita's senior staff officers bitterly accused Makino of "lack of initiative," poor judgment, and other weaknesses for his failure to hold out longer in the beachhead area. Yet in early November the 16th Division commander fought an able and imaginative delaying action. Perhaps he had been inspired by a message dispatched at the end of October by Field Marshal Terauchi to Generals Yamashita and Suzuki—and presumably forwarded to Makino. The Japanese, Terauchi had declared, were now "faced with a decisive battle, chiefly on the ground," the results of which would "determine the fate of our Empire." The failure of the 16th Division to hold the beach area and the airfields had "caused great concern." With "another decisive counteroffensive . . . in the offing," Makino's division should "do everything possible . . . to turn the tide." Above all, "every effort should be made to prevent the enemy from establishing a base on Leyte and obtaining control of the air." In this endeavor the operations of the 16th Division were "of such importance" that they would "determine the fate of the armed forces of the nation."

In the action west of Dagami, Makino's troops met this challenge. Taking skillful advantage of the rough, hilly ground, they resisted stubbornly from deep entrenchments, coconut-log pillboxes, and the many natural defensive positions they found on the jungled ridges. At night they hurled counterattacks against the American perimeters, sometimes halted only by artillery concentrations, or incinerated by flamethrowers, or thrown back finally in ugly hand-to-hand combat. They tried to infiltrate and shoot up American artillery positions, synchronizing their fire with that of the big guns in order to avoid detection. Marine artillery units assigned to XXIV Corps sometimes found it safer to load their pieces and then let the gunners take cover before firing.

The Japanese themselves rarely withdrew from a key position, preferring to die in place. To reduce one particularly stubborn pillbox, the Americans poured gasoline down the ventilation pipes and set it afire. Still, not a single Japanese left his position. In the end, though, the pressure was too much. Most of Makino's officers were dead, practically no heavy weapons remained, food and ammunition were low, and the 16th Division was only a shell of its former self. "Bloody Ridge," "Suicide Ridge," and other aptly named terrain features fell one by one to the Americans. By mid-November the 96th Division had eliminated major Japanese defensive positions in the heights west of Dagami.

Farther south the 7th Division had pushed most of its 32nd Infantry across the island from Baybay. And from here the regiment was beginning to move up the west coast toward Ormoc. Yet the division was too widely dispersed elsewhere in southern Leyte to make any major effort at this time. General Krueger hoped to attack north from Baybay with the whole 7th Division while Japanese attention was still fixed on the north, but this would have to await the arrival of more American troops. Indeed, the 32nd Infantry was already encountering resistance from a Japanese battalion sent south from Ormoc to block its advance. Operations here would obviously require a much greater effort.

As part of this effort Krueger proposed to make another amphibious landing with a fresh division—when it was available—near Ormoc. This was fine with MacArthur, who had utilized this sort of "end run" maneuver with great success on a number of occasions. But Admiral Kinkaid's staff raised certain practical objections. With command of the air still very much in doubt, there was no guarantee that Japanese kamikaze attacks could be prevented. And heavy shipping losses to the suicide planes would mean the postponement if not cancellation of amphibious operations planned for elsewhere in the Philippines. There was also the annoying fact that assault shipping was still in short supply. "My disappointment was naturally very great," recalled Krueger, "but instead of dropping the project, I laid it aside for the time being and awaited a more propitious moment for putting it into effect."

While Krueger consoled himself with the thought that such a moment would soon arrive, his adversaries were facing up to their own disappointment. Still shaking their heads over the unexpectedly rapid Sixth Army sweep across northern Leyte to Carigara, the Japanese were becoming increasingly concerned about the slow but potentially dangerous buildup of American airpower on the eastern Leyte airstrips. In Manila, especially, General Yamashita's staff was fast losing confidence in the Thirty-fifth Army plan to mount an attack through Carigara. Recapturing that town would be a time-consuming operation, during which the 16th Division would have to continue fighting alone and unsupported in eastern Leyte. Eventual success would be so delayed, if not actually prevented, that the Americans would be able to rebuild the east Leyte airfields, stock them with enough planes to guarantee local air supremacy, and cut off all reinforcement and supply of the Thirty-fifth Army. General Suzuki's forces would be doomed.

Obviously, a change in plan was in order. In early November the 16th Division had still occupied strong positions within striking distance of several of the American-held airstrips. On the 5th, then, Yamashita directed Suzuki to shift the main weight of his attack from Carigara to the 16th Division front. Only a holding action should be attempted below Carigara, while everything else should be thrown into a major effort through central Leyte aimed at quickly recapturing the airfields. But Yamashita's order, seriously delayed in transmission, did not reach Suzuki until the 12th. By then the Thirty-fifth Army had already taken serious losses in attempting to regain Carigara. And the 16th Division had been pushed back from its forward positions.

By then, also, Yamashita had made another unsuccessful attempt to write off the Leyte campaign. More than ever he and his staff were convinced that the island could not be recaptured and that committing additional reinforcements, throwing good money after bad, would only jeopardize still further the already weakened defenses of Luzon.

On November 7 Yamashita's chief of staff, Muto, had called on Lieutenant General Jo Iimura, his counterpart at Southern Army headquarters. "I . . . explained the situation," Muto recalled, "and argued that the time had come to admit to ourselves the failure of the decisive naval and air battle and to consider subsequent operations." Muto urged an immediate halt in reinforcements and the abandonment of Leyte to the Americans. But Iimura was unbending. The decision to risk all on Leyte had been made in Tokyo and could not be changed. At this point Muto lost his temper. Southern Army and Imperial General Headquarters, he shouted, had "lost all signs of flexibility" and "countless lives . . . were being needlessly lost as a result." Iimura remained unconvinced.

Two nights later the senior Japanese officers in the Philippines held one of their regular dinners at Field Marshal Terauchi's official residence. Afterwards, when they had left the table and were talking casually, Yamashita took Iimura aside to press the case for breaking off operations on Leyte. The Fourteenth Area Army commander had no more success than his chief of staff, but he did persuade Iimura to carry his views to Terauchi. The next morning, November 10, the field marshal called a Southern Army staff conference. Present were two of Yamashita's key officers, who explained in detail the arguments against continuing the fight for Leyte. For two hours, while Terauchi and Iimura listened in silence, the Southern Army officers heard out the presentation, asked questions, and offered opinions. Not one of them thought Leyte should be abandoned. Nor, of course, did Terauchi and Iimura.

Then, on the 11th, they summoned Yamashita and Muto. Terauchi wasted no time. "We have heard the opinions of the Fourteenth Area Army," he said, "but the Leyte operation will be continued." The Fourteenth Area Army would "do its utmost" to support them. Then, as he had done on a similar occasion less than three weeks earlier, he handed Yamashita a brief formal order. "The Leyte battle," it began, "will be carried out as before." Yamashita could expect to receive additional reinforcements to strengthen Luzon, "but this must in no way interfere with the execution of the Leyte battle." Once more Yamashita had no choice. The time for argument was past. He bowed stiffly. "I fully understand your intention," he said. "I will carry it out to a successful end."

On November 15 he sent Suzuki an order reiterating the approved strategy. "The Thirty-fifth Army will endeavor to accomplish the destruction of the enemy on Leyte, setting as its minimum objective the disruption of the enemy's use of air bases." Suzuki could expect still further reinforcements if it were at all possible to get them to Leyte. But Yamashita could not resist one final qualification. "In the event that further troop shipments cannot be accomplished," he concluded, "Luzon will become the main theater of future operations in the Philippines."

With the matter apparently settled, Marshal Terauchi and his staff left Manila two days later for Saigon, French Indo-China. Terauchi had never agreed with Tokyo's decision to move Southern Army headquarters from Singapore to Manila. He had consistently held that he could best exercise control over his entire command only from some central location, preferably on mainland Asia. It was not until October, however, that he could convince Imperial General Headquarters of this. And then the invasion of Leyte and his desire to be present during the initial stages of the decisive battle postponed his departure from Manila.

Now, he finally felt able to leave. Like MacArthur, nearly three years earlier, he was going before the fight was over. But, unlike MacArthur, he did not publicly vow to return.

xviii A Desperate Struggle and a Shoestring

ON NOVEMBER 8 MacArthur had visited Krueger's headquarters at Tanauan. The two men discussed the progress of the battle, the frustrating effect of the continuous rain, and the disappointing condition of the Leyte airstrips. Another major problem, Krueger told MacArthur, was the lack of sufficient trained replacements to meet Sixth Army needs.

By now Krueger's troops had been in action continuously for almost three weeks. Fighting over rugged terrain in unbelievably bad weather, against a tenacious and resolute enemy, the Americans were tired and beginning to lose their edge. Casualties—injuries and sickness as well as combat losses—had cut into effective strength, especially in the rifle companies, since the infantry, as usual, was paying close to 80 percent of the price. While the Sixth Army still had a 2-to-1 numerical superiority over Japanese forces on Leyte, the terrain favored the defense and, in the absence of adequate air support, Krueger was seriously concerned about the future.

During the planning for Leyte he had argued unsuccessfully that Sixth Army units should start the invasion with an overstrength of 10 percent, in effect carrying their own replacements. He had then asked that a total of 19,000 trained replacements be scheduled to reach Leyte in the first month of the campaign. This, too, was denied him. Finally, on the eve of embarkation, Krueger received 5,000 additional troops. But these replacements, while welcome, were untrained and had to learn their trade on the job—a difficult process when the job involved killing and being killed. Their presence was an important factor in the rapid X Corps advance across northern Leyte, but they were far fewer than Krueger needed.

By the time he saw MacArthur on the 8th, then, Krueger was faced with a serious troop shortage. Despite the fact that additional units were on the way to Leyte, the Sixth Army commander needed individual trained replacements to fill the ranks of units already on the island. This situation he outlined to MacArthur in no uncertain terms, and, as he wrote later, asked for "adequate replacements . . . without delay."

MacArthur was sympathetic. He immediately ordered that all replacements available in the Southwest Pacific be rushed forward to Leyte. Yet these were actually few in number. Some, already en route, landed that day, but the total that reached Krueger during the entire campaign was just over 5,000. For the remainder of the operation, units were consistently understrength. And as Krueger's personnel officer, Colonel George S. Price, complained afterwards, at no time did Sixth Army staff officers know definitely just how many replacements were available, when they would arrive, and what type they would be: infantry, quartermaster, engineer, artillery, ordnance, or other brand of soldier. Such uncertainties made planning difficult—to say the least. Fortunately for the American effort on Leyte, reinforcements in the form of additional units did reach the island. But the individual replacement picture was always dark.

On November 14 Major General William H. Gill's 32nd Infantry Division disembarked on Leyte. A part of Sixth Army Reserve, rather than an additional reinforcement, its arrival had been delayed by the general shortage of assault shipping. Krueger had originally planned to use the division on Samar, where a regiment of the 1st Cavalry was already committed, but the absence of large Japanese forces on that island along with the lack of sufficient American replacements on Leyte led him to throw Gill's troops into the main battle. On November 15 the 32nd Division began relieving the weakened 24th. Fresh troops replaced the weary 21st Infantry on Breakneck Ridge and took over for other 24th Division elements in supporting positions. Farther south, the battalion of the 19th Infantry blocking the Ormoc Road and the battalion of the 34th Infantry on Kilay

Ridge remained in place. On Sibert's orders they were attached to
Gill's division and held their important positions until the fight for
the area south of Breakneck Ridge was over.

This struggle continued for over two weeks—weeks of grim,
bloody, bitter, and confused combat. Most of the Japanese 1st
Division was now committed to the fight, and General Kataoka
ordered an immediate attack toward Carigara. This the 32nd Division, also attacking, met head on. Along the high, broken
ground and wooded crests between Breakneck Ridge and the
Ormoc Valley, the battle raged. Gradually American pressure
began to dominate, forcing the Japanese almost entirely on the
defensive. Repeated infantry attacks backed by pulverizing artillery fire proved too much. Kataoka's troops fought stubbornly but
lost position after position.

To the east, the remnants of the Japanese units that had
fought around Carigara were still holding out against the 1st
Cavalry Division. Indeed, these units had even been somewhat
reinforced. But Krueger had also thrown in reinforcements here,
specifically the 112th Cavalry Regimental Combat Team—
another dismounted cavalry unit and actually just passing
through Leyte in preparation for other operations when Mac-
Arthur made it available for Krueger's immediate use. Thus
strengthened, the 1st Cavalry moved slowly ahead over the difficult mountainous terrain, pushing the Japanese back in a series of
small but hard-fought actions.

General Suzuki, meanwhile, bound by Yamashita's order to
shift his efforts toward a drive across central Leyte, could spare
no more troops for the fight in the north. He would have preferred to pursue his original plan to recapture Carigara. But he
had his orders and all he could do was obey them. Nevertheless,
it was imperative that the line in the north be held. Indeed,
Suzuki felt hopefully, the combined strength of all Thirty-fifth
Army units here might even destroy the American forces opposing them. At the very least, if the 1st Division could mount another assault, this might divert American attention from the projected Japanese offensive to the east. So Suzuki ordered Kataoka
to continue his attacks. Kataoka, with a more realistic apprecia-
tion of the situation, protested that he could barely hold his position, much less attack. He received little sympathy. What had to

be done had to be done, and neither Suzuki nor his harried staff were in any mood to listen to excuses. "It was difficult to understand . . . complaints," wrote the Thirty-fifth Army chief of staff, "when certain measures had to be carried out."

By late November, nevertheless, the 32nd Division had all but turned Kataoka's western flank. When the 1st Division commander shifted forces to meet this threat, he left a gap on his eastern flank and Gill's troops drove forward to fill it. Now the entire Japanese position was in danger of collapse. Not only had Kataoka failed to hold the 32nd Division in front of him, but his flanks were caving in and he had been completely unable to dislodge the small American forces at the roadblock behind him on nearby Kilay Ridge. "This period," recalled Colonel Junkichi Okabayashi, Kataoka's chief of staff, "proved to be one of the most disastrous for the 1st Division." American infantry attacks increased in strength and frequency; punishing artillery fire sought out the Japanese wherever they hid. Units were decimated, supply lines cut by the shelling, everything disorganized. Under this steady pressure the continued stubborn Japanese defense was a tribute to the skill, courage, and determination of Kataoka's men.

Early December found the 32nd Division in possession of most of the area between Breakneck Ridge and the roadblock two and one half miles south, tied in with Kilay Ridge to the immediate west. Although the distance actually gained was small, the territory won was important. From here the Americans could look down into the Ormoc Valley. The 1st Cavalry troops had made similar progress to the east. Ormoc still lay some sixteen miles south, but the rugged mountain approaches to the valley were now for the most part in X Corps hands.

Suzuki ordered Kataoka to continue all efforts to check the American advance—the Thirty-fifth Army commander was no longer speaking in terms of attacking—but there were still no reinforcements available. Indeed, as American pressure increased elsewhere, Suzuki began withdrawing small detachments from Kataoka's command for other emergency missions. The 1st Division—its regiments reduced to battalion size or less, its food and ammunition low, its supply and communications lines all but broken by American artillery fire—was now in critical shape. The troops, wrote Colonel Okabayashi, "were resigned to die on the field of battle." Shortly thereafter Kataoka received orders from Suzuki to "defend the positions to the end." The planned Japanese offensive to retake Carigara, in the words of one Japanese writer, "had become a desperate struggle to hold the enemy away from Ormoc."

Meanwhile the focus of the battle for Leyte had shifted south, where both Krueger and Suzuki were planning major actions. On November 12 the Thirty-fifth Army commander had ordered the newly arrived 26th Division to move overland from the Ormoc area toward Burauen in preparation for the projected central Leyte offensive. Yet hardly had the division commander, Lieutenant General Tsuyuo Yamagata, started his troops on the road than word reached him of the American advance up the west coast from Baybay. Yamagata immediately ordered a battalion south to reconnoiter this threat and protect his right flank. The remainder of the 26th Division pushed slowly east over steep, jungle-covered heights, repairing or more often building roads and trails as it struggled forward.

The detached battalion moved down the coast, harassed occasionally by Filipino guerrillas. Then, on November 14, it ran into forward patrols of the American 32nd Infantry Regiment above the town of Damulaan, midway between Ormoc and Baybay. This initial encounter was brief and indecisive and both sides recoiled from the contact. The Americans fell back to build defensive positions, pending the arrival of the rest of the 7th Division. The Japanese also dug in, but made ready to attack.

The fight that soon began was to be known as the "Battle of Shoestring Ridge." This was not a reference to the terrain, although the fight was indeed a struggle for a ridgeline. Rather, the battle took its name from the fact that both sides fought it on a shoestring. And in the end the American shoestring, in the words of 32nd Infantry commander John M. Finn, proved to be "just a trifle longer."

When General Yamagata reported the encounter at Damulaan, Suzuki ordered him to continue his advance toward Burauen but to send whatever additional force was necessary to help contain the 32nd Infantry. Yamagata immediately dispatched additional strength to support his lone battalion at Damulaan, but the problem was one of supplies rather than men.

The 26th Division had lost most of its heavy weapons, ammunition, and equipment to American air strikes while unloading at Ormoc. Unless it could be resupplied, its operations would be severely limited.

To meet this need, as well as to prepare for the projected offensive to the east, several Japanese convoys attempted to run supplies from Manila to Ormoc. But despite stepped-up cover by the Fourth Air Army, few ships managed to get through. P-40's from Tacloban and carrier planes from the Third Fleet sank most of these vessels. And, to add insult to injury, a few of the ships that did manage to reach Ormoc Bay fell victim to a sneak attack by American PT boats prowling those waters in search of trouble. There would be no resupply for the 26th Division.

On the American side the situation was only slightly better. Just one regiment, the 32nd Infantry of Arnold's 7th Division, was at Damulaan, and while it had been reinforced with artillery and a few tanks, it was operating with but two of its three battalions. It also had fifteen miles of coast from Damulaan south to Baybay to defend against possible Japanese landing attempts. Supply across the jungle mountains and swollen streams between the east coast and Baybay was a major problem. From Baybay north it was even worse. The engineers built or repaired bridges, rigged makeshift ferries, and hauled tons of gravel to save the main road—in many places hardly more than a trail—from turning into a bottomless stream of mud. Amphibious vehicles and native bancas helped move supplies along the coast, but foul weather constantly disrupted these operations. Colonel Finn's troops at Damulaan were thus at the end of a tenuous supply line, better equipped than the Japanese facing them but only slightly more fortunate when it came to resupply.

By November 23 Japanese strength above Damulaan amounted to four battalions, enough for the local commander, Colonel Jiro Saito, to launch an attack with. Toward evening Japanese light artillery and mortars opened up on 32nd Infantry positions along Shoestring Ridge, a steep crest perpendicular to the coast just north of Damulaan. After several hours of intermittent bombardment that cut communications wires and kept heads down, Colonel Saito's infantry moved to the attack. This was no wild *Banzai* charge but a carefully coordinated combination of fire and movement that would have done credit to the best American infantry unit. The Japanese advanced skillfully, taking advantage of natural avenues of approach through the tall cogon grass and bamboo thickets. Probing efficiently, they soon discovered gaps in the thinly held American line, isolated some of the defenders, and seized positions along the ridge and began to dig in. By dawn the 32nd Infantry line had been cracked and penetrated in several places.

November 24 saw a feverish effort on both sides to move supplies, especially ammunition, forward. The Japanese made ready to attack again and the Americans prepared to receive them. Each tried to disrupt the other's efforts with artillery, while small groups of infantry hunted each other along the slopes and draws of Shoestring Ridge. By afternoon 32nd Infantry counterattacks had regained some of the lost ground, but Saito's troops still held large areas within the right of the American position, threatening to turn the defenders' exposed flank. That night, with a full moon to light the way, they struck again.

The Japanese pre-assault artillery fire was much heavier than on the preceding night, smashing not only at the dug-in American infantry but also at defending artillery positions to the rear. The American gunners stuck to their posts through the hail of explosives, trying valiantly to locate and destroy the Japanese artillery. They had little success, however, and Colonel Saito's guns did not cease firing until his infantry began advancing. Then the American artillery started to take its toll of the attackers. All night the gunners fired at concentrations of Japanese infantry, at enemy machine-gun positions, and at any other target that seemed profitable. A machine gunner from a battery of Marine artillery supporting the 32nd Infantry knocked out several Japanese machine guns that had cut off one of the defending platoons.

The fight between Japanese and American infantry was vicious, bloody, and often at close quarters. Automatic weapons and mortars raked the area and there were frequent exchanges of hand grenades. Just before dawn the Japanese gave up the attack. Gathering up their dead and wounded, they slipped back to their original positions. The 32nd Infantry had held, but Colonel Saito still posed a major threat to the American right flank.

For several days the attacks continued in the same pattern. The Japanese struck, penetrated, were thrown back, struck again, and were again pushed back. Casualties mounted on both sides, although Japanese losses were far heavier. A particularly desperate Japanese attack, involving most of Saito's troops, threatened to split the 32nd Infantry line in several places before it was finally and bloodily repulsed. The assault followed an extremely heavy artillery and mortar barrage, as Japanese infantry struck in force against the key section of the American line, held by G Company. So fierce was the Japanese supporting fire that Saito's troops were caught in a punishing cross fire of their own and American machine guns. Still, recalled Colonel Finn, "they came on like a tide." Thrown back, finally, they attacked again over the dead and dying bodies of their comrades. This time the Japanese did not withdraw when they were stopped. They dug in and from their advanced positions attempted to infiltrate G Company's defenses. The company commander, his executive officer, and all his rifle platoon officers had been hit. Technical Sergeant Marvin H. Raabe took over the company, changed dispositions, directed fire, called up more ammunition, and finally threw the Japanese back.

Saito's men tried again, sliding off G Company and making similar penetrations into the American position on either side. In the confusion a defending platoon misunderstood orders and began to withdraw. Before it could be sent back, Japanese troops spilled into the gap and quickly dug in amidst a heavy bamboo thicket. Caught in their advance was an American artillery observer, First Lieutenant Desmond M. Murphy, high in a tree in the occupied area. In whispers over his telephone line, he described the activity of the Japanese around him and continued to direct artillery fire. But he begged the Fire Direction Center not to ring his phone lest the Japanese should hear. Don't call me, he said in effect; I'll call you.

Back and forth the struggle shifted. The Americans repulsed one penetration only to discover another elsewhere along the thin line. Finally, as night gave way to gray dawn, a 32nd Infantry counterattack drove back most of Saito's troops, rescuing Lieutenant Murphy in the process. But it was afternoon before the last of the Japanese were ousted from Colonel Finn's position. It had been a costly effort for Saito: perhaps 200 or more Japanese lay dead in and around the American foxholes. Casualties in the 32nd Infantry were considerably lighter, but the men were exhausted.

Other nights were not so bad. Yet still the Japanese kept trying. They made particular efforts to knock out the American artillery with their own batteries and, when this failed, by attempting to infiltrate the American firing positions—for it was the big guns supporting the defenders that time and time again broke up attacking troop concentrations or threw back Colonel Saito's assaults. The artillery was particularly vulnerable to infiltration since, in the absence of extra infantry for its defense, it had to be fairly close to whatever units were available and therefore practically in the front lines. Japanese infantry was thus a constant threat. The American gunners frequently came under machine-gun and rifle fire, and supply parties moved only with great caution. A group of Japanese managed to slip unnoticed to within a few yards of one American artillery battery, so close in fact that the defenders could not fire their individual weapons for fear of hitting each other. A battle of grenades followed, ending only with the death of all the attackers. One Japanese succeeded in exploding a satchel charge behind the breechblock of a howitzer, knocking out the weapon even as he himself was killed. Other attempts were less successful, although the weary American gunners were never in doubt about being in the thick of the fight.

The 32nd Infantry developed a number of tricks to use at night against infiltrating Japanese. The Americans would shoot off a mortar flare and then, as the light died down, fire a round of high explosive. When the flare went up, any Japanese in the open would hit the ground. When the flare went out, they would get up and run—right into the bursting high-explosive shell. Another tactic was to set booby traps just outside the perimeter, attaching trip wires to grenades. A Japanese brushing against the wire would detonate the grenade. Even if the Japanese heard the grenade handle fly off and was able to take cover before the explosion, it still did him little good. As soon as the grenade exploded the nearby Americans would spray the area with automatic rifle fire, catching the Japanese just as he started to run or crawl away. Both tricks worked well in theory and frequently in practice. And, if nothing else, they were excellent morale boosters for the Americans.

By November 27 two more battalions of the 7th Division had reached Damulaan and, with this additional strength, Colonel Finn had no more trouble holding Saito's attacks. The Japanese, weakened by the cost of their fruitless assaults, were indeed no longer in condition to mount any further major blows. They contented themselves with small probing attacks aimed at keeping the Americans off balance and preventing a 7th Division offensive.

But an American offensive was not far off. On November 18 Major General Joseph M. Swing's 11th Airborne Division had reached Leyte, prepared to stage there for subsequent operations. MacArthur had immediately made it available to Krueger, who attached it to the XXIV Corps, thus freeing the remainder of the 7th Division to move to the west coast. By the beginning of December General Arnold's entire division was concentrated for the first time in western Leyte and Colonal Finn had finally cleared all Japanese from Shoestring Ridge. General Yamagata, meanwhile, had been forced to commit almost all of the 26th Division to the Damulaan area to counter the American threat. He still lacked resupply of weapons and equipment, and the four battalions he had originally committed had been fairly well chewed up. But he had the usual Japanese advantage of favorable defensive terrain.

Yet the very fact that Yamagata was now on the defensive at Damulaan, instead of advancing aggressively toward Burauen, was a serious blow to General Suzuki's plans. For it meant that practically one whole division was removed from his projected offensive to recapture the eastern Leyte airfields. It also left undefended a relatively large area between the remnants of the 16th Division, west of Dagami, and the bulk of the 26th Division, above Damulaan. The only organized Japanese force between these units was a single battalion of the 26th Division, still pushing gamely but slowly toward Burauen, almost a week's march away over the difficult mountain terrain.

To make matters worse from the Japanese viewpoint, Krueger was planning a concerted push with the XXIV Corps into this weakly held area. The 96th Division, on the right of Hodge's corps, was consolidating its gains west of Dagami and readying to move strong elements into the heights to the southwest. Immediately to the south the 11th Airborne had taken over most of the area formerly held by the 7th Division, in preparation for a drive west from Burauen. The 7th Division, below Damulaan, would attack up the coast toward Ormoc, where it seemed that conditions were at last right for an amphibious assault by still another division. To support the XXIV Corps offensive, Krueger directed Sibert to launch a simultaneous push with the X Corps. Sibert's objective was to break into the Ormoc Valley and, so doing, tie down any Japanese forces that Suzuki might want to send against Hodge. The two corps, attacking at once, would crush the thirty-fifth Army between them.

Mounting an offensive by the entire Sixth Army obviously involved a major supply effort. And supply, over the weather-soaked swamps and mountains of Leyte, continued to be Krueger's biggest problem. It was now the height of the rainy season. Each day wind and water tore at supply dumps, inundated roads, and soaked men and equipment. Just as airfield construction was almost impossible under these conditions, so the movement of supplies was a wet, sloppy, slippery nightmare. In the first place, the invaders had captured intact only a single dock in the whole beachhead area, and even here it took six weeks to dredge out a channel deep enough to admit fully loaded transports. So most cargo came ashore across the beaches, where wind, weather, tides, and the Fourth Air Army combined to slow and sometimes halt operations. The same enemies nearly crippled the construction of additional docks. Once ashore, supplies had to be sorted, tabulated, loaded on trucks or jeeps, and then moved inland over flooded roads and trails. Many of these routes were completely under water a good deal of the time. Even the streets of large towns like Tacloban were no more than mudholes after a steady rain. The heavy traffic along main supply routes would have quickly disintegrated the primitive roads even in good weather. In the torrential rains, the churning wheels of the big trucks spun in soft, thick, grasping mud while the drivers cursed the war, the Japanese, and most of all, the weather.

In a valiant attempt to keep the roads open, the engineers worked endlessly under the most difficult conditions. It was not at all uncommon to see large groups of engineer troops, soaked to the skin, struggling in mud and driving rain to dig drainage ditches, build up road surfaces and shoulders, repair or erect bridges, or cut new roads where none had been before. A week's work for a platoon in good weather became on Leyte the labor of an entire battalion for a month. And with the available engineer troops spread thin across the island—many of them assigned to work on airstrips, hospitals, and other high-priority installations —battalions normally responsible for five miles of roadbuilding were now told to build thirty. There were more engineer troops on Leyte than had served in any other operation previously commanded by MacArthur. And there was more friendly native labor available than ever before. But demand still far exceeded supply.

The island seemed to be one huge marsh. The engineers hauled loads of rock or gravel for miles and then watched it disappear into bottomless holes. Or, if they managed to lay a decent roadbed, they found that two feet of heavy gravel was necessary for the surface instead of the four inches of light gravel that had been sufficient elsewhere. When there was no handy gravel supply, they used sand if it was available or cut trees to corduroy the road. They dug drainage ditches, but the flooded streams were so full that there was no place for the water to run off to, and it sat in lakes on the roads. The high water in the streams drowned out fords and bridges. More than one engineer lost his life in the swift currents while trying to put in a new span.

Under these conditions it was not unusual for rain or flooding to wash out several days' work as soon as it was completed— which then had to be done all over again. Even more annoying to the engineer troops was the sight of rear-echelon GIs joyriding or making other unnecessary trips that helped to chew up the vulnerable road surfaces. Another burden for the weary engineers was what was called "immersion foot," Pacific cousin of the infamous trench foot of European fighting. Working continuously in mud and water, the engineers, like many of the combat and other supply troops, found that their shoes disintegrated and the skin peeled from their feet, leaving raw sores where tropical fungi discovered fertile breeding grounds.

In the face of these problems, the engineers performed some sort of miracle to keep as many roads open as they did. In some areas, construction or maintenance was impossible with the means at hand, and frequently there was no way that supply trucks or even jeeps could get anywhere near the forward combat units. Then other means of transportation had to be devised. The supply line to the 12th Cavalry Regiment was a good example of this. Trucks carried the load from warehouses in Tacloban as far as Carigara. Here amphibious tractors took over, pushing three miles inland through deep, sticky rice paddies to a point where the slowly rising ground grew firm. The supplies were then loaded on trailers and pulled by artillery tractors to a large base high in the foothills of the central Leyte mountain range. And from this point hundreds of barefoot Filipino porters carried 50-pound loads on their heads and shoulders up steep, slippery trails, waded swift streams, and struggled through heavy undergrowth to reach the combat troops. The whole trip, from Tacloban to the 12th Cavalry, took four days. When extremely bad weather or infiltrating Japanese interfered, it took longer. Since a single regiment in action consumed about thirty-four tons of food and ammunition each day, building up extra stocks over this tenuous supply line meant an ever greater and more arduous effort.

Small boats and amphibious tractors logged a good many hours hauling supplies and men back and forth along the coast of Leyte. They also served as river ferries or traveled up and down the island's inland water routes where no land vehicle could possibly have gone. The versatile amphibious tractors—aptly nicknamed "Buffaloes"—were built to carry a four-ton cargo afloat and two tons on land. On Leyte they carried four tons everywhere and managed to do the job.

In extreme emergencies, when all other means of transportation were unavailable or inadequate, cargo planes airdropped supplies to troops in forward, isolated positions. Beginning in mid-November, nearly 300 of these drops were made to deliver more than a million pounds of rations, ammunition, and other supplies by the end of the campaign. But these drops were limited by the weather, since rain interfered both with flights and, in the thick forests, with recovery of supplies. Nevertheless, despite monsoons, terrain, and the fact that supply parachutes occasionally landed dangerously close to Japanese positions, at least two thirds and sometimes nearly all the supplies in each drop reached the troops they were intended for.

Thanks to this sort of effort, supplies for Krueger's big push were gradually built up in the forward areas. The X and XXIV Corps were poised to close the jaws of a gigantic trap on Ormoc and the Ormoc Valley. But before they could snap them shut the Japanese would mount one last offensive on Leyte.

Part Six

DECISION AT LEYTE

<<<<<<<<<<<<<<<<<<<<<<<<<<<<<<<<<<<<<<<<<<<<<<<<

>>>

xix The Wa Operation

BY THE latter part of November Japanese plans for an offensive to recapture the Leyte airfields were well advanced. The attack was scheduled for early December, but, thanks to a combination of circumstances, it actually began somewhat sooner.

Japanese army and naval air reinforcements to the Philippines had greatly increased the striking power of both General Tominaga and Admiral Fukudome. Thus, when Yamashita asked Tominaga to provide air cover for the 26th Division resupply convoys in late November, the Fourth Air Army commander was ready to make a major effort—which, indeed, he felt was necessary to combat the rapidly growing American air strength around Leyte. Normal escort measures, Tominaga believed, would probably be inadequate. The situation clearly demanded something special: a major air offensive against American air bases and shipping coupled with an airborne raid by special troops designed to knock out the main American airfields. Tominaga's staff had long studied the possibilities of landing small forces on enemy airfields to destroy aircraft, equipment, and installations. They had developed a plan along these lines, designed solely as a "last resort" measure, to be employed "during an extremely desperate situation." The Leyte situation was now desperate enough to implement this plan.

On November 22 Tominaga directed an all-out effort to cover the movement of the resupply convoys. For the next five days Fourth Air Army planes would attack American airfields and anchorages. Admiral Fukudome agreed to make simultaneous strikes against warships and transports at sea. Then, on the 26th, twin-engine transports carrying the eighty men of the Kaoru Airborne Raiding Detachment would crash-land with their wheels up on the Buri and Bayug airstrips, two of the three fields just east of Burauen, blocking the runways. The raiders would "demolish airfield installations and then withdraw westward to join the 16th Division."

The attack on the two airfields was thus simply a hit-and-run operation designed to disrupt American air strikes on the Japanese convoys. Yet when Tominaga informed Yamashita of his plan, the Fourteenth Area Army commander was immediately struck by the potentialities for a more ambitious operation. Imperial General Headquarters had recently given Tominaga the 2nd Parachute Brigade for use on Leyte. Why not, reasoned Yamashita, incorporate a major airborne attack into the forthcoming Thirty-fifth Army offensive to recapture the Leyte airfields? A coordinated airborne and ground assault would obviously have a much greater chance of success than the unsupported land offensive already planned. Yamashita could not order Tominaga to commit his paratroopers, since the Fourth Air Army was still under Southern Army control, but the airborne brigade had been sent to the Philippines for just such an operation. Tominaga proved more than willing. Staff officers immediately drew up plans for a joint attack and orders were issued on November 23.

These orders incorporated Tominaga's original plans for air strikes and the raid on the airstrips and called, as well, for continuous army and naval air attacks during the first week in December. Between the 5th and 10th of the month—the exact date would be decided later—the 2nd Parachute Brigade would make a night drop to seize the three Burauen airfields. And the next day General Suzuki would attack with the 11th and 26th Divisions to link up with the paratroopers. The whole operation was named the *Wa* Operation after Lieutenant General Takaji Wachi, who had earlier replaced Major General Tomochika as Thirty-fifth Army chief of staff in order to give Suzuki a more senior and experienced assistant.

On the morning of November 24 nearly 100 Japanese army

and navy planes were over the Leyte area. They struck at airfields, at the Sixth Army anchorages, and at American shipping in Leyte Gulf. These raids continued for the next four days. At the same time Admiral Halsey's carrier pilots, operating over Luzon, reported increasingly heavy opposition in the air. The carriers themselves came under punishing kamikaze attacks. The Japanese pilots swept in close to the water, hoping that the American radar would be unable to distinguish them from the signals caused by high waves. Or they tried to sneak in behind American planes returning to their ships, again seeking to get within range of their targets before being discovered. Sometimes they just dove in from high in the sky, with only the bright sun and the element of surprise to blind American eyes. Antiaircraft fire and the combat air patrols took care of many of these kamikazes. Still, a few got through.

On the 25th, four carriers were hit, with serious losses in dead and wounded. The ships themselves were not too badly hurt, although the suicide planes inflicted considerable damage on the *Intrepid* and lesser injuries on the others. This attack signaled the end of Halsey's already prolonged coverage of the Leyte operation. Having stayed more than a month longer in Philippine waters than originally planned, the carrier attack forces were weary and badly in need of rest, repairs, and resupply. With no other choice before him, Halsey notified MacArthur that he would have to withdraw temporarily from the area.

Farther south, Kinkaid's Seventh Fleet also was under heavy air attack. Both kamikaze and torpedo planes struck at the vessels, inflicting considerable damage and not a few casualties. The planes flew in low, from over the Leyte and Samar shores, so that the radar echoes from the nearby hills would mask the "pips" reflected from their own approach. Most of the raids came at night, as did those on the Leyte airstrips, and General Kenney's flyers, on whom the burden of local air defense now fell, were unable to cope with all of them. MacArthur and Kenney put in a request for several squadrons of Marine flyers, one of which was equipped with more versatile night fighters. These began arriving at Tacloban on December 3, greatly increasing American air defense capabilities.

On November 24, meanwhile, Tominaga visited Lipa airfield

in southern Luzon. There he spoke personally with Lieutenant Shigeo Naka and the men of the Kaoru Airborne Raiding Detachment. Morale was high, and the Fourth Air Army commander returned to Manila with optimistic hopes for the success of Naka's mission.

Two nights later the Japanese raiders climbed aboard four small transports and took off from Lipa. After a flight of about two hours, they reported by radio that they had reached the target area. Unfortunately for Lieutenant Naka and his men, only one plane was actually over the Burauen airfields. As it attempted to land at Buri, antiaircraft fire practically tore it apart. The transport crashed into the ground. None of its occupants survived the impact to carry out their demolition mission.

The other three planes completely missed Burauen. Two of them crash-landed on the beach south of Dulag, the third in the water just offshore. Nearby American units at first assumed that the planes were friendly, but were quickly disabused of this impression when they tried to help. When bullets greeted the would-be rescuers, the Americans returned the fire and the two transports on the beach were soon aflame. Most of the Japanese managed to escape, but the majority of these were rounded up and killed within a few days, before they could do any appreciable damage.

Back at Manila, Tominaga had no further word of his raiders. But when American planes failed to put in an appearance over Ormoc Bay the next day, he assumed that Lieutenant Naka had been at least partially successful. He could not know that all that the raid had achieved was to alert Krueger to the remaining phases of the *Wa* Operation. For some inexplicable reason— certainly contrary to all Japanese security regulations—the plane that had crashed at Buri had carried documents outlining the entire *Wa* plan. Krueger alerted the Sixth Army to the probability of other airborne attacks, but few commanders, apparently, took these warnings too seriously.

In Tokyo, meanwhile, Imperial General Headquarters announced to the public that the Kaoru Detachment had "occupied key positions" of the Burauen airfields "by means of suicide tactics" and that Naka's men had "accomplished their mission." Ironically enough, not only had the mission failed but by now it

was clear to American engineer officers that the heavy rains, poor
drainage, unsatisfactory surface conditions, and washed-out access roads made it impossible to keep the Burauen fields operational. The Fifth Air Force insisted on retaining one of the strips,
but by the end of November all work had halted at Buri and San
Pablo and the two muddy fields were abandoned to the elements.
A few liaison and artillery spotter planes still used them occasionally, but unknown to the Japanese, only Bayug airstrip remained as a suitable target for the 2nd Parachute Brigade. Dulag
and Tacloban were now fully operational, however, and work
was under way on a new field at Tanauan, midway between
them. Yet the *Wa* Operation was aimed at none of these. And
only by the wildest stretch of optimism could the Japanese hope
to drive all the way to the three coastal airfields. Indeed, they
were not even aware of the work begun at Tanauan.

The orders for the *Wa* Operation reached Thirty-fifth Army
headquarters at Ormoc in the hands of Major Mitsusuke Tanaka
of Yamashita's staff. Yamashita chose this method of delivery to
avoid any possible mistakes in transmission or breaches in security and also to impress upon Suzuki the importance of the operation. Respectfully, but clearly, Tanaka explained to Suzuki that
the recapture of the airfields was necessary not only for the successful defense of Leyte but also to prevent the development of
major American air bases on the island. Heavy American air units
operating from Leyte might well be able to cut the vital line of
communications between Japan and those areas of the southwest
Pacific still in Japanese hands. This capability was to be denied
the enemy at all costs.

Just how much credence Yamashita placed in this argument it
is difficult to say. Certainly if it was true at the end of November, it had been equally valid a month or even two weeks earlier,
when Yamashita was opposing the decision to fight an all-out battle on Leyte. If it had no major importance then, its weight now
would seem to be no greater. But whatever Yamashita actually
believed, he told Major Tanaka to emphasize this argument to
Suzuki. Tanaka also informed the Thirty-fifth Army commander
that the *Wa* Operation had been specifically ordered by Imperial
General Headquarters—and this was clearly an exaggeration.

Suzuki was duly impressed. But he had problems. For nearly

two weeks, in accordance with Yamashita's earlier orders, Suzuki had been attempting to make preparations and move forces into position for an attack on the Burauen airfields. But the badly mauled 16th Division had been thrown back from its positions close to the airfields and, in any event, was in poor shape to launch an offensive. General Makino, indeed, was down to about 2,000 hungry and tired troops and was losing an average of seventy-five men each day. The 26th Division, drawn into the fight at Damulaan against the American 7th Division, had only a single battalion anywhere near Burauen. And even this battalion would need another week to reach the target area, for the mountain trail it was following was barely passable, and already it was encountering forward elements of the American 11th Airborne Division.

Suzuki therefore notified Yamashita that he would be unable to mount a coordinated attack on the airfields before December 7. This was well within the originally designated time period of December 5 to 10, but by now Tominaga's staff had chosen the night of December 4–5 as the best time to make the paradrop. Suzuki would have to attack on the 5th, and Yamashita so informed him.

The Thirty-fifth Army commander nevertheless interpreted these orders as broadly as possible, directing the 16th and 26th Divisions to launch their assaults on the night of the 5th. He did not order them to make any prior probing attacks, despite the fact that Yamashita's original instructions had specifically called for this tactic. Perhaps he wished to impose no additional problems on his already burdened division commanders. Perhaps he realized they would have difficulty making any sort of attack as early as the night of the 5th. The objective of the 16th Division would be Buri airstrip, northernmost of the three fields. That of the 26th Division would be Bayug, south of Buri and just east of Burauen, the only one of the three still in general use. San Pablo airstrip, east of Bayug, had also been indicated by Yamashita as an objective for the 26th Division, but it is not clear whether or not Suzuki passed this order on to General Yamagata.

When Suzuki's orders reached the 16th Division, General Makino hastily organized an assault force of about 1,200 men. This group included everyone still able to participate in an attack, with most of the remaining weapons. It amounted to little more than a battalion, but it assembled in the hills northwest of Burauen determined to do the work of a division.

Suzuki meanwhile had ordered Yamagata to move the bulk of the 26th Division overland from Damulaan to join his advance battalion in the attack on the Bayug airstrip. Yamagata would leave three battalions behind until December 6, when the 68th Independent Brigade was expected to land below Ormoc and take over the Damulaan front, freeing those battalions to rejoin the 26th Division. Yamagata would also be reinforced by a newly arrived battalion of the 30th Division. Suzuki himself, accompanied by General Wachi and six other staff officers, left Ormoc on December 1 to set up an advance command post on the route of the 26th Division advance to Burauen. From here, he intended to exercise close personal supervision over the attack.

On December 3 Fourth Air Army meteorologists making their final prediction for the next night came up with a forecast of stormy weather. Tominaga made an immediate decision to postpone the airdrop twenty-four hours, and Yamashita flashed word to Suzuki to delay the Thirty-fifth Army attack until the 6th. The information reached General Yamagata and his advance battalion, the latter now assembled in a defile well to the west of Burauen, in time to prevent a premature assault. But a breakdown in radio communications made it impossible to get through to General Makino and the 16th Division.

On the evening of December 5 an intelligence officer in XXIV Corps headquarters describing the situation around Burauen concluded that "reports of action in this area" might "well warrant the assumption that organized resistance has about ceased." As he wrote, the 16th Division assault force set out from its assembly area for the Buri airstrip. Some of the men were too sick or weak to proceed, and American artillery fire further reduced the size of the group. The majority of the troops, however, successfully avoided American patrols and infiltrated unseen as far as the Burauen-Dagami road. Shortly after dawn an American artillery observer caught sight of some of Makino's men crossing the road and relayed the news to corps headquarters—quite possibly just as General Hodge was reading the estimate that organized resistance had about ceased.

Buri airstrip, as well as the rest of the Burauen area, fell within the zone of General Swing's 11th Airborne Division. Most of the division was in the mountains to the west, however, and the airfields were occupied primarily by service troops. An airborne infantry company also was at Buri airstrip and a company of the 96th Division, attached to the airborne division, was dug in between the field and the Burauen-Dagami road. The first actual contact came at about 6:30 A.M., when 16th Division soldiers crept into the bivouac area of a construction battalion. Many of the men were still asleep and the Japanese bayoneted several of them on the ground. Swiftly, however, most of the Americans grabbed their weapons and, shoeless, in their underwear, attempted to fight off their attackers. One cook killed five of General Makino's hungry soldiers trying to loot his mess area. But the attack was too much for the confused engineer troops, who, in any event, were not used to combat and probably had not fired their weapons since training days. Shooting wildly in the general direction of the Japanese, they fell back quickly from the area.

Other 16th Division troops were meanwhile attacking the hastily formed defenses of an ordnance unit on the edge of Buri airstrip and chasing members of a signal company from their bivouac north of the field. Gradually resistance stiffened as word of the Japanese attack spread and the confused Americans began to organize their defenses. Soon two medium tanks from a nearby tank outfit joined the fight. Faced with this opposition, their casualties increasing, Makino's men started to dig in amidst the heavy woods north of the strip and to build up a base of fire to support their continued attack.

Now American reinforcements began to appear. More airborne infantry reached the airfield and additional companies from the 96th Division were ordered into the area. Small American combat patrols struck at the Japanese, inflicting casualties and relieving some of the service units that had been pinned down by machine-gun fire. The Japanese, in their initial attack, had managed to overrun about half the airfield. By late afternoon counterattacking American infantry had recaptured most of the field and wiped out a Japanese pocket to the east. Makino's troops still occupied areas along the north edge of the airstrip as well as stronger positions in the woods beyond.

Meanwhile, at Angeles and Lipa airdromes on Luzon, the day had been a busy one as members of the 2nd Parachute Brigade prepared for the scheduled drop. A shortage of planes meant that only one of the brigade's two regiments could participate in the initial attack, with the other to follow later. Even then, the assault regiment would have to jump in three waves, each separated from the next by the several hours it would take the transports to get back to Luzon, refuel, reload, and return to Leyte. The honor of making the assault went to Lieutenant Colonel Tsunehiro Shirai's 3rd Parachute Regiment. Shirai's 700 men were in high spirits, anxious to take off. Only three days earlier, General Tominaga had visited them and left with their commander a battle flag personally inscribed by the general with the words "Exert your utmost for your country." Shirai would carry this with him when he jumped from his plane with the initial wave.

Late in the morning of December 5, while the planes took on fuel and ammunition, the 350 paratroopers of the first wave began boarding the twenty-six small, two-engine transports that would carry them to Leyte. They wore new parachutes and most of the equipment they bore had never been used before. They were armed with automatic pistols, light machine guns, rifles and bayonets, grenades, small land mines, and other explosives. For signaling, they carried flares, panels, and a variety of musical instruments: harmonicas, bugles, whistles, wooden clappers, flutes, and gongs. And for identification they had unit flags and wore strips of luminous material on their left sleeve cuffs. They were also well supplied with rations, water, and, in some cases, small bottles of liquor.

In the early afternoon fighter planes took station over Angeles airfield. At exactly 3:38 the transports began to take off. They gained altitude, grouped in formation, and, with the fighters as escorts, headed south for Leyte. To avoid detection, the planes flew over the Japanese-held central Visayas, passed around the southern tip of Leyte, then continued north over Leyte Gulf, and finally, as the sun was setting shortly after six o'clock, turned inland below Dulag to follow the course of a river that led to the Burauen area. Other Japanese aircraft were already over eastern Leyte: about two or three dozen fighters and bombers flew over the airfields, dropped a few bombs, and attempted to strafe them.

Heavy American antiaircraft fire kept most of them high, however, and shot down several that ventured too close. Incendiary bombs set fire to a gasoline dump and a liaison plane on San Pablo airfield, but otherwise the damage was slight.

Now the transports had reached Burauen and turned north and east in a wide sweep over the three target airstrips. Four of the planes had fallen to the intense antiaircraft fire, but the others came on. The preparatory signal was given, the paratroopers fastened their jump lines, and the leader of each group opened the door of his transport. They were now flying at about 750 feet. The sun had gone down, but there was still enough light for the men to see the landing areas below. It was just 6:40 when the first paratroopers jumped.

The Japanese had intended to drop most of the first wave on Buri airstrip, with smaller groups assigned to Bayug and San Pablo. In the confusion of the attack, however, possibly because of the intensity of the antiaircraft fire, most of the paratroopers came down on or near the San Pablo strip. Only about sixty Japanese, including Colonel Shirai, landed on Buri airfield and none at all appear to have landed at Bayug. A few missed the target altogether and dropped farther east. Several were killed when they hit the ground, victims of faulty quick-release harnesses that separated them from their chutes while they were still several hundred feet in the air.

On the ground there was considerable confusion among American service and Air Force troops, although the premature attack by the 16th Division that morning had alerted most of them. With a few nearby infantry elements, they attempted to form defensive positions around the airstrips and opened fire on the Japanese. At Fifth Air Force headquarters at Burauen, General Whitehead's men also began digging in. Yet there was no over-all command for the Americans, no means of coordinating defensive measures. And most of the inexperienced men fired their weapons wildly and inaccurately. Many abandoned their bivouac areas, arms, and equipment in panic.

Fortunately for the defenders, the Japanese seemed just as confused. Some methodically went about the job of setting fire to gasoline stores, tents, ammunition dumps, and the few liaison planes still using the Buri and San Pablo airstrips. But many seemed to the watching Americans to be either drunk or drugged. In the flickering light of the fires they raced up and down the San Pablo field, screaming wildly, shooting off flares and sounding their signaling instruments indiscriminately. The bewildered and incredulous Americans later swore that some of the Japanese had shouted in English such sentences as: "Hello! Hello! Where are your machine guns?" and "Surrender! Surrender! Everything is resistless!"

Meanwhile, the second wave of Colonel Shirai's paratroopers took off from Lipa at 10 P.M. This force included two small groups scheduled to drop on Dulag and Tacloban, apparently just to make trouble there. But bad weather forced the planes to return to the field almost immediately. The third wave, also at Lipa, never got off the ground. The Japanese inability to drop the entire 2nd Parachute Brigade at one time now meant that barely half a regiment was in action—less than that after allowing for initial losses. But this force had by now managed to organize itself. The large group at San Pablo assembled at the west end of the field and at dawn of December 7 moved northwest to Buri airstrip. Here Shirai's smaller force had linked up with 16th Division troops. By midmorning Japanese paratroopers and infantry were in complete control of the strip.

During the night Krueger had asked MacArthur to release to him a regiment of the 38th Infantry Division, which had just arrived on Leyte to stage for future operations. MacArthur quickly agreed and, around noon of the 7th, a battalion of that division joined 11th Airborne troops at San Pablo. The men of the 38th Division were greeted personally by General Swing, the airborne commander, whom Krueger had placed in complete charge of the operation to drive the Japanese from the Burauen area. "We've been having a helluva time here," said Swing. But now he wanted no more nonsense. The Japanese were to be destroyed and Buri airstrip secured by nightfall.

The battalion of the 38th moved north immediately, delayed more by a deep swamp than by the negligible Japanese resistance it encountered. By evening it had reached the western end of Buri airstrip and tied in with a battalion of airborne troops and a battalion of the 96th Division. These two battalions had been fighting Japanese north and west of the field and had killed quite a few of the enemy. But, Swing's order to the contrary, the Americans were unable to gain more than a toehold on the edge of the airfield before darkness fell.

The Japanese strengthened their defenses during the night and it took three more days of hard fighting and the commitment of another battalion of the 38th Division before the combined American efforts could retake the strip. During the battle Private Ova A. Kelly won a Congressional Medal of Honor by leading a charge against a particularly stubborn position and personally killing eight Japanese before he himself was hit. His wound was not fatal, but as he lay in a foxhole awaiting evacuation, another bullet killed him.

There were Japanese heroes too. The outnumbered paratroopers and 16th Division soldiers held out stubbornly against the four American battalions. And they suffered heavy casualties in attempting night infiltration attacks on the surrounding American positions. But the odds were too great. On December 10 a coordinated American assault, with artillery and mortar support, swept the remaining Japanese off the Buri airstrip.

In one last, futile effort a group of Japanese pushed down the road toward Burauen, firing captured American machine guns into the Fifth Air Force headquarters area. An Air Force staff officer got on the phone and called one of the forward units to order a halt in "that promiscuous firing." When he learned that the Japanese were doing the shooting, he protested, more in frustration than anything else, that the bullets were "coming right through" General Whitehead's quarters. "Tell the general," came the answer, "to get down on the floor." Which the general apparently did. The Japanese kept coming, killed or wounded a few of the defenders, burned some tents, and did other damage. Then Air Force troops counterattacked and drove them off. More than a score of Japanese bodies lay scattered around the area.

By now those Japanese who had managed to survive the five-day battle might well have been wondering what had happened to the other units scheduled to participate in the attack on the airfields. Where, for example, was the 26th Division, not to mention the rest of the 2nd Parachute Brigade?

The 26th Division had done its best to carry out Suzuki's orders. But, unhappily for the Japanese, its best was far from good enough. Struggling over a rough mountain track that was never more than barely passable on foot, Yamagata's men were hampered by their lack of trail-breaking equipment and by drenching rain. Engineer troops, working practically barehanded, attempted to cut a supply trail but had little success, despite their use of forced Filipino labor. The combat elements pressed forward anyway, only to run into 11th Airborne Division troops on almost all sides. Most of General Swing's division had pushed into the mountains southwest of Burauen. The Americans advanced slowly but, thanks to air resupply, were able to send patrols over much of the trackless mountain area. Numerous small clashes took place between airborne and Japanese troops, with Yamagata's soldiers frequently blundering into ambushes set by the enterprising Americans.

By midday of December 6, only a few hours before he was scheduled to launch a full division assault on Burauen, Yamagata had barely one regiment on the eastern slope of the mountains. And only the advance battalion was anywhere near its objective. The other units, hampered by terrain and the 11th Airborne troops, were too far back to play even a supporting role. Yamagata therefore ordered the advance battalion to attack Burauen on its own, without waiting for the rest of the division. "Tonight," wrote a staff officer in his diary, "holds the key to victory or defeat." For those at 26th Division headquarters, he noted, it would be "a night of waiting and of listening to the distant thunder."

Yamagata's advance battalion pushed east that evening—only to run into a battalion of 11th Airborne artillerymen operating as infantry, which threw back the Japanese with sharp losses. A second attempt on the night of the 7th had no greater success. Subsequent efforts, culminating in an infiltration attack by forward elements on the night of the 10th, also were defeated. The remnants of the advance battalion retreated west, pursued and harassed by 11th Airborne troops. Very few survived.

Meanwhile, early on the morning of December 7, despite the bad weather, units of the Fourth Air Army took off from central Visayan bases to hit the Dulag and Tacloban airfields. Unable to penetrate the storm, however, the planes turned back. As they headed west over Ormoc Bay, the pilots suddenly noticed a large group of American ships landing troops across the beaches several miles south of Ormoc. It was ten o'clock before this news could be radioed to Tominaga's Manila headquarters. The

general made an immediate decision to postpone the remainder
of the planned paradrop on the Burauen airstrips and to concentrate instead on throwing all available air strength at the new
American landing operation.

By now Yamashita had learned of the American landing. And
word of Tominaga's decision as well as news of the 26th Division's
difficulties southwest of Burauen helped Yamashita make the obvious decision. Around noon he notified Thirty-fifth Army headquarters that the *Wa* Operation was canceled. Suzuki should
forget about Burauen and focus his attention on the beaches
south of Ormoc.

This was easier said than done. Suzuki was at his advance
command post in the mountains, out of touch with events at
Ormoc. Most of the 26th Division was scattered over this rugged
terrain, under heavy pressure by the 11th Airborne Division.
What was left of the 16th Division was still involved in the fight
for Buri airstrip, or in the hills to the west, and probably out of
contact with Suzuki. General Tomochika, who had been left in
command at Thirty-fifth Army headquarters, attempted frantically to organize some sort of attack on the American beachhead
and to get word to Suzuki of what had occurred.

Not until the following evening, December 8, did Yamashita's
orders reach Suzuki, who now faced the difficult task of extricat-
ing himself and his two divisions from the mountains of central
Leyte. The Thirty-fifth Army commander directed the 26th Division to withdraw to Ormoc Bay and attack the American beachhead. The 16th Division was to follow, prepared to join in the
fight. Suzuki himself set out the next morning for Ormoc, but
found his way blocked by 11th Airborne troops which were now
all around his advance command post. Carefully making his way
through the American units, it took him four days to rejoin his
headquarters. General Wachi, his chief of staff, did not get in for
another twenty-four hours.

Meanwhile the 26th Division, the greater part of it almost
completely cut off by the 11th Airborne, was unable to follow
Suzuki's orders. Split up into small units, low on food and ammunition, Yamagata's scattered forces concentrated on fighting off
American attacks and attempting to infiltrate to the west in disorganized groups. Few survived the experience. Those who man-

aged to work their way back to the Ormoc area took at least a month to do so. By then they were too weak and too late to affect the outcome of the campaign.

The 16th Division may never have received Suzuki's order to retreat. Tomochika, meanwhile, had directed it to a stay in the Burauen area and conduct raids unless it received contradictory instructions from Suzuki. But this order too may never have reached General Makino. In any event, no more than a few hundred starving men of the 16th Division ever made their way out of the central Leyte mountains. And it was February before they reached the Ormoc area. If any of Colonel Shirai's paratroopers survived the fight for the airstrips, they may possibly have been with them.

The *Wa* operation thus ended in failure—almost before it had begun. Planned as a coordinated offensive by two divisions and a parachute brigade, it was actually undertaken in disorganized and confused fashion by two battalions of infantry and half a regiment of paratroopers. It achieved little: the destruction of some liaison planes, ammunition, fuel, and equipment, and the temporary isolation of Fifth Air Force headquarters. Aimed unwittingly at airfields no longer in use, it failed to disrupt American air operations or to delay in any appreciable way the advance of the Sixth Army. The cost to the Japanese was high. The crippled 16th Division was completely destroyed. A small but well-trained and equipped force of paratroopers was wiped out. And, most important of all, the bulk of the 26th Division, which might have opposed the landing below Ormoc, was committed to the central mountains and so scattered and cut up that it could make no further contribution to the defense of Leyte. The disorganization of Thirty-fifth Army headquarters merely compounded these losses.

As early as November 30 Suzuki had warned Yamashita that an American landing in Ormoc Bay was possible if not "imminent," and that a "full-scale attack" here would "greatly affect" the outcome of the *Wa* Operation. As events turned out, the decision to undertake the *Wa* Operation, as much as its subsequent failure, virtually guaranteed the success of the American landing below Ormoc.

xx Two Sevens in Ormoc

GENERAL KRUEGER'S offensive had begun on December 5. Objective: "to defeat the enemy in the Ormoc area." From the north, Sibert's X Corps resumed its battering at the entrance to the Ormoc Valley. From the south and southeast, Hodge's XXIV Corps drove into the mountains all the way from Burauen to Shoestring Ridge. And in eastern Leyte, the recently arrived 77th Division was hastily assembling to re-embark for an assault landing below Ormoc. The jaws of the trap were ready to snap.

The spearhead of the X Corps attack was the 32nd Division, pushing south along the Ormoc Road and supported by a simultaneous advance by the 1st Cavalry over the mountains to the east. Both divisions had slow going, delayed as much by the rugged terrain as by the Japanese, for Thirty-fifth Army forces, while brave and tenacious in opposing Sibert's advance, were exhausted, low on supplies and ammunition, and crippled by casualties. The Japanese 1st Division, charged with the vital defense of the Ormoc Road, was in particularly bad shape. Hardly had Gill's 32nd Division begun its attack when General Kataoka sent a staff officer to Ormoc with a message that his own unit had "reached the stage of collapse." But General Tomochika, running Thirty-fifth Army headquarters in the absence of Suzuki and Wachi, offered an unsympathetic ear. He had expected a great deal of the 1st Division, and in his disappointment was inclined to be considerably more critical of Kataoka than that officer deserved. So he ordered a small force to shift out of the central mountains and bolster the division flank, and then brusquely directed Kataoka to "continue to check the enemy advance." The 1st Division commander, wrote Tomochika later, "lacked brave command ability" because he "worried about the loss of his troops."

Tomochika should have checked with Sibert. Whatever Kataoka's failings as a leader, he managed to hold the American advance to a snail's pace. Able use of the terrain, well-prepared and camouflaged defenses, and a determined resistance characterized 1st Division operations. Since Japanese troops farther east were doing almost as well against the 1st Cavalry Division, initial progress of the X Corps attack was slow and costly. If Sibert had any hopes of breaking into the Ormoc Valley in a rush, they were disappointed. But the heavy pressure he exerted did tie down a substantial portion of the Thirty-fifth Army, which is precisely what Krueger intended. The Japanese 1st Division, those portions of the 30th and 102nd Divisions that had managed to reach Leyte, and miscellaneous smaller units were all committed and deeply engaged in defending the northern and northeastern approaches to the Ormoc Valley. Badly mauled in the fighting so far, they faced heavy odds. And they were in no position to shift elsewhere to meet any new American pressure.

Farther south, meanwhile, as the 11th Airborne and 96th Divisions pushed into the mountains west of the Burauen-Dagami area, the 7th Division attacked north from Damulaan. In this attack General Arnold for the first time had his entire division available for operations on the west coast. His relative strength was further increased by the withdrawal from the area of most of the 26th Division for the abortive *Wa* Operation. On December 5, then, Arnold's troops made good gains over the sharp ridges that ran down to the sea like so many bony fingers across his route of advance. On his seaward flank, a battalion of amphibious tanks, also newly arrived on the west coast, moved offshore to deliver flanking fire on the stubborn Japanese positions. Yet so steep were the ridges and so tenaciously defended by only about a regiment of Japanese, that as the crow flies the 7th Division advance was barely a mile in some places, far less in others. It was hard, costly going—successful but slow. And it continued that way for several days. But early on the morning of the 7th, as the amphibious tanks sailed north along the coast for another flanking movement, the seagoing tankers spotted a large force of American transports and warships. The curtain was about to rise on the key act of the Sixth Army offensive. The 77th Division was in the wings.

Major General Andrew D. Bruce's 77th Infantry Division was known as the "Statue of Liberty Division," or "New York's Own," because most of its men hailed from New York City. The division had fought well on Guam that summer and then been given to Krueger as part of Sixth Army reserve. A week or so after A-day, however, in a burst of optimism, MacArthur decided that the 77th would not be needed on Leyte. Without telling Krueger in advance, he released the division to Admiral Nimitz's command and the admiral promptly ordered it to New Caledonia for rest and re-equipping. By the time Krueger found out about this it was too late to stop the transfer. He complained to MacArthur, but it did him no good. Apparently the subject came up again when the two men discussed the replacement situation on November 8, for within forty-eight hours MacArthur asked Nimitz if he could have Bruce's division back. Nimitz agreed, the convoy was turned around, and on November 23 it reached Leyte.

But the 77th had left most of its supplies and equipment on Guam, so it arrived on Leyte with only a limited amount of rations, and poorly armed for combat. Krueger was glad to see Bruce, yet he was not at all happy about the supply picture. He already had enough logistical headaches and the 77th Division's arrival, as he wrote later, "intensified a difficult supply situation and made the preparation of the Division for combat a distinct problem." Krueger solved it by taking supplies and equipment away from other units—which gave their commanders a chance to be unhappy too.

Now occurred something of a paradox. MacArthur had planned to invade the island of Mindoro, in the shadow of Luzon, in early December. Air support for the invasion was to have come from Leyte, but the inability of the engineers to make airfields out of mudholes on Leyte meant that air cover for Mindoro would be practically nonexistent. MacArthur was eager to go ahead anyway. But General Kenney, his air commander, had grave misgivings, and Admiral Kinkaid strongly protested against sending unprotected assault shipping and escorts into the narrow seas around Mindoro. Also, Halsey's fast carriers had left Philippine waters by now, and Kinkaid practically had nightmares over the thought of exposing any of his vulnerable jeep carriers to kamikaze attacks in the restricted channels off Mindoro.

MacArthur finally, but reluctantly, agreed to postpone the Mindoro invasion. And this decision, in turn, made available enough assault shipping and naval escorts for Krueger to carry out his earlier plan to land a division—the 77th—on the Japanese rear doorstep at Ormoc. Thus the lack of airfields on Leyte, which more than any other single cause had delayed American victory there, now made possible a maneuver which finally, and definitely, assured that victory. Admiral Kinkaid was still uneasy about exposing shipping to Japanese airpower, which had yet to be driven from the skies over Ormoc Bay. But, after weighing risk against potential gains, he at last went along with the plan.

The warning order for Ormoc reached General Bruce on December 1. At that time his division was dispersed on scattered missions practically all over the XXIV Corps area and it took a major effort to reassemble troops and supplies in time to sail at midday of the 6th. Frequent air alerts slowed the loading of the ships but did not delay the convoy's scheduled departure. In the meantime destroyers and PT boats supporting the sea supply route to Baybay or just looking for trouble in Ormoc Bay had had several encounters with Japanese convoys, warships, and aircraft in the area. American forces had given a fine account of themselves, but the extent of Japanese activity boded no good for the Ormoc assault force.

Rear Admiral Arthur D. Struble's Ormoc Attack Group—Task Group 78.3, to use its more official designation—sailed south through Leyte Gulf with the 77th Division, passed unmolested through Surigao Strait, and turned north along the west coast of Leyte. At twilight of the 6th, a group of eighteen Japanese bombers passed overhead in the direction of the Leyte airfields: Tominaga's paratroopers flying to their death. Down below, the twelve screening destroyers of the assault convoy encountered nothing to disturb them. Nor did PT boats and other destroyers patrolling Ormoc Bay that night. Finally, as the convoy slipped past the Camotes Islands to enter Ormoc Bay just before dawn, a Japanese naval lookout on one of the islands flashed the belated news of Struble's arrival to Ormoc.

Now the Attack Group was off the landing beaches, a narrow strip of hard sand just south of the tiny barrio of Deposito, itself

barely three miles below Ormoc. A shore battery opened fire on
the destroyers, fired two, three uncomfortably close salvos, then
was quickly silenced by the American gunners. For twenty minutes the destroyers and two rocket-firing landing craft pounded
the beach area while the troops climbed down into their assault
boats and assembled along the line of departure. Promptly at
seven o'clock fighter planes from Tacloban and Dulag appeared
overhead and the 77th Division assault wave started in. The line
of landing craft touched down practically simultaneously at seven
minutes after seven on December 7. The timing was almost too
good to be true.

On the basis of aerial reconnaissance and guerrilla reports,
General Bruce had chosen a landing beach that he believed
would be lightly defended. He was right. "New York's Own"
walked ashore unopposed and all troops and supplies were
landed within two hours. Bruce himself, with his entire headquarters, had gone ashore only thirty-five minutes after H hour.
Not until 9:30, with its initial objectives secured, did the division
encounter any resistance at all, scattered opposition by a handful
of Japanese service troops, which Bruce's men quickly and easily
overcame.

At about 8:15, meanwhile, a message had informed Admiral
Struble that a Japanese convoy was approaching the northwest
coast of Leyte, several hours' sailing distance away. On board
were about 5,000 troops of the 68th Independent Brigade. Scheduled to reach Ormoc on the 6th, the convoy had been delayed to
allow the use of its assigned air cover in the *Wa* Operation. The
one day's postponement proved fatal, for now, coincidentally,
the brigade was supposed to land at almost the same time and
place as the 77th Division. Struble felt it unwise to send any of
his destroyers to intercept, so he called on Kenney's air units to do
the job.

Even as Struble's request went out, Fifth Air Force planes hit
the convoy and sent it scurrying for shelter in San Isidro harbor,
on Leyte's wild and mountainous northwest tip. For most of the
day, army and Marine fighters and bombers were over the Japanese ships. Only a few Japanese aircraft put in an appearance,
and then did little damage. The 68th Brigade suffered well over
300 casualties and lost about half its artillery and signal equip-

ment and a substantial amount of ammunition and other supplies. More important, it was out of touch with Thirty-fifth Army headquarters and too far from Ormoc to participate in its defense. Yamashita ordered Suzuki to send barges from Ormoc for the brigade, but those vessels, if there were any still afloat, would have been sitting ducks for Kenney's flyers. In any event, none ever left Ormoc. The 68th Brigade, meanwhile, set out to join the 1st Division in the northern Ormoc Valley, but took two weeks to traverse the rugged mountainous route. It never really had any effect on the campaign.

Back on December 7, while the 68th Brigade convoy had been taking its lumps, the Japanese were throwing their own airpower against the 77th Division assault shipping and transports. Beginning at about 9:30 A.M. and continuing until nearly nightfall, first navy and then, with the cancellation of the *Wa* Operation, Fourth Air Army planes struck again and again at American shipping in Ormoc Bay.

The initial assault was delivered by twelve navy bombers and four fighters from nearby Cebu. Ignoring heavy antiaircraft fire and attacks by American fighters, they dove on two picket ships. Three of the Japanese fighters fell into the sea and several of the bombers were hit. But the bombers along with the other, undamaged planes came directly at the two vessels in a massive kamikaze attack. Some of the Japanese dove straight down out of the sky, some came skimming over the water as if to drop torpedoes. Good shooting knocked down several of the planes, able ship handling kept others from hitting their targets. But the odds were too great, the suicide tactics too overwhelming. First the destroyer *Mahan* was hit by three planes that struck her bridge, waterline, and side, setting off huge explosions and fires. Try as they might, the crew could not save her. Within a dozen minutes of the attack the skipper ordered abandon ship, and an hour later a sister destroyer put her under with gunfire and torpedoes. The destroyer-transport *Ward* also was mortally wounded by a kamikaze. This vessel had fired the first shot of the Pacific war almost exactly three years earlier when she destroyed a Japanese midget submarine at the entrance to Pearl Harbor. But now her war was over. Within a few minutes of being hit, the *Ward* had to be abandoned and later was sunk by gunfire.

The attacks continued during the day, both on the anchorage and on Struble's ships as they retired south from Ormoc Bay. By afternoon Tominaga's planes had turned up in large numbers. They sank a landing ship and heavily damaged a destroyer and a destroyer escort before the task group made good its escape into the dark and stormy night. They also made some ineffective strafing runs on the beach.

But the Japanese had paid dearly. Of nearly 100 planes, the majority from the Fourth Air Army, that were over Ormoc Bay on the 7th, two thirds fell victim to antiaircraft fire or the attacks of army and Marine fighters. Almost all the Japanese army bombers left in the Philippines were lost this day. And the attacks had failed to prevent or even hinder the 77th Division landing. In the words of Bruce's intelligence officer, Lieutenant Colonel F. Clay Bridgewater, the Japanese air reaction had been "too little and too sporadic."

On land, meanwhile, the initial advance of the 77th Division had gone so well that General Bruce abandoned his original plan to consolidate on the beachhead line before pushing on. Just before ten o'clock he ordered his troops to attack north, toward Ormoc. Not until just after noon did any real Japanese resistance develop, when a small detachment of 26th Division rear-echelon troops opened fire with machine guns from positions underneath a group of native huts. Bruce's men were forced into a temporary house-by-house advance, but since the Japanese were few in number, the attackers soon wiped out most of them. The survivors, retreating from the area, set a building full of ammunition aflame and the resulting fireworks slowed the American advance again. By evening, nevertheless, "New York's Own" had seized the town of Ipil, a mile north of Deposito, and dug in on a beachhead two miles wide and a mile deep. Patrols were probing south toward the 7th Division, but most of the men were looking north, toward Ormoc.

Where, now, was the enemy? Until mid-November the Japanese had counted on their air and naval strength in the central Visayas to deter or prevent the passage of any American amphibious force through the narrow passages leading to Leyte's west coast. But just as they had misjudged American ability to penetrate San Juanico Strait to Carigara Bay, so they erred in assuming that other waters around Leyte were closed. As Kinkaid's PT boats and destroyers became active in the Ormoc Bay area in late November, Suzuki warned Yamashita that these operations might well presage an amphibious assault. Yamashita agreed to send troops to defend the Camotes Islands and Suzuki himself began planning coastal defenses, although, with few men to spare, not many fieldworks were ever built.

Nor could Suzuki make up in troop strength what he lacked in fortifications. Initial Japanese optimism about Ormoc's security combined with the later need to commit almost all Thirty-fifth Army troops to tactical operations left few units available for the immediate defense of Ormoc. On the morning of December 7 this task was the responsibility of the Ormoc Defense Headquarters, a miscellaneous collection consisting primarily of service units under a Colonel Mitsui and somewhat reinforced by a few 26th Division and Thirty-fifth Army rear-echelon troops. Additional strength was provided fortuitously that morning by the landing of two companies of the 30th Division which arrived from Mindanao in small boats and came ashore at Ipil, apparently right under Admiral Struble's nose. But none of these forces was in position to oppose the 77th Division's landing.

Many American accounts of this landing state that the attack by the 7th Division a few days earlier had drawn Japanese troops south from Ormoc, thus clearing the way for General Bruce's men to go ashore unopposed. This is not so. Not only were there few troops around Ormoc to begin with, but the only major unit that might have defended the area, the 26th Division, was committed to the abortive *Wa* Operation, indeed had withdrawn troops from the 7th Division front solely for this purpose. The 68th Brigade, its journey to Leyte delayed, never reached Ormoc, but, if it had, was in any event scheduled to reinforce the 1st Division in the northern Ormoc Valley. The Japanese had simply left their back door wide open.

At Ormoc, on December 7, General Tomochika was doing his best to close it. As soon as he learned of the American landing, he had ordered Colonel Mitsui's forces to occupy defensive positions on high ground just below Ormoc. He also directed a unit called the Imabori Detachment, which he had just ordered to the 1st Division area, to rush south instead through Ormoc and attack the beachhead. The detachment, a two-battalion force under Colonel Tessaku Imabori, had landed some time before the arrival of its parent unit, the 26th Division, and had been operating separately in the mountains northeast of Ormoc. It was still deep in the mountains, but immediately began the move south. General Suzuki, meanwhile, at his forward command post halfway to Burauen, had yet to receive word of the cancellation of the *Wa* Operation. By the time he did, it was too late to extricate his advance forces and move them to Ormoc.

Back in Manila, General Tominaga had decided to resume his portion of the *Wa* Operation and drop his remaining paratroopers on the Burauen airstrips. But Yamashita's cancellation of the ground offensive against the airstrips meant that the paratroopers would be isolated and unsupported, and the drop would amount to no more than a raid. Reluctantly, then, he gave up the idea and asked Yamashita where the paratroopers would do the most good. Obviously, they were needed at Ormoc. One of Yamashita's senior staff officers argued that they should still be dropped on the Burauen fields, an obviously impractical notion. Not surprisingly, his suggestion was ignored and Yamashita asked Tominaga to land the paratroopers at the Valencia airfield, on the Ormoc Road about eight miles north of that city and well within Japanese lines. After the war the staff officer in question claimed that Marshal Terauchi had sent a message from Saigon ordering the drop to be made at Burauen instead of Valencia. According to this story, an "enraged" General Muto had dispatched a reply to Terauchi within minutes, "utterly refusing to entertain the idea." The account seems a dubious one. In any case, reinforcement of Ormoc was clearly far more important—indeed necessary—than attempting another raid on the airstrips.

With few transports or other large aircraft left to him, Tominaga could not advance all his remaining paratroopers to Valencia in one movement. Even if he could, that much activity on the Valencia airfield would be certain to invite the attention of American long-range artillery, now capable of hitting the field from the mountains to the east and north. Beginning at first light on December 8, then, and continuing for four or five successive days, some 500 men of Lieutenant Colonel Jisaku Saida's 4th Parachute Regiment jumped in small groups on Valencia airfield. They trav-

eled in flights of about ten planes, which did not dare to land but
simply dropped the paratroopers at dawn or dusk in order to min-
imize American observation of their arrival. Once on the ground,
the men assembled and moved off immediately to join the fight.

Other reinforcements also were on the way. Late on the 8th
the troops promised by Yamashita for the Camotes Islands, about
two companies of infantry, finally sailed from Manila. The next
day a reinforced battalion of the 30th Division, which had sailed
from Mindanao in small boats, came ashore at Palompon, a port
on Leyte's west coast that gave access via a winding mountain
road to the Ormoc Valley. It would be a while before this battalion could reach the combat zone, but it was obviously no longer
safe to attempt a landing at Ormoc. At the same time, a relatively
large convoy left Manila for Palompon. Four transports, escorted
by three destroyers and two subchasers, the ships were carrying
the only force Yamashita could scrape together on short notice:
the 5th Infantry Regiment of the 8th Division and about 400
naval troops provided by Admiral Mikawa's Southwest Area
Fleet headquarters in Manila.

As the convoy threaded its way through the Visayan sea toward dusk on the 10th, an American search plane spotted the
ships and quickly reported them. It was too late for an immediate
attack, but early the next morning more than two dozen bomb-
carrying Marine fighter planes from Tacloban struck the convoy.
Diving on their prey in the face of extremely heavy antiaircraft
fire, they scored direct hits on a big transport, set it aflame, and
tore a huge hole in its side. The ship went down, carrying with it
almost an entire battalion of the 5th Infantry. As the Marines
were turning to other targets, about twenty Japanese navy fighters arrived on the scene from nearby Cebu. They managed to
break up the attack and shot down one Marine, who was later
picked from the water by Filipinos. But at least half a dozen Japanese fell victim to the American pilots.

That afternoon the Marines were back, accompanied by
nearly a score of army fighters. They came on the convoy about
thirty miles from Palompon. First the army planes attacked, diving out of a broken cloud cover and releasing small bombs on the
remaining transports. But, in the words of one of the Marine
pilots, "they accomplished nothing except to make interesting

splashes . . . and wake up the Japs." The awakened Japanese then proceeded to throw up as much antiaircraft ammunition as they could muster, which amounted to quite a bit. Through this intense fire dove the Marines. Several took hits as they came in, but they sank one more transport and set fire to another, forcing it aground on the Palompon shore. The rest of the convoy scattered under the attack, losing a destroyer in the process. Overhead Americans and Japanese mixed it up in a wild dogfight in which both sides destroyed several planes.

Marine Lieutenant M. A. Gudor was one of those shot down. He had just sent a Japanese plane into the sea when two Japanese navy fighters, nicknamed "Zekes" by the Americans, spotted him. They "turned toward me," he recalled later, "so I turned into them, for the book says: 'In a head on run a Jap plane will either turn aside or blow up.'" But the Japanese pilot had apparently failed to read the book. "We were closing fast, prop to prop. All my six 50-caliber guns were going and pieces were flying off the Zeke's cowling." Finally, "at the last possible instant," Gudor nosed his plane violently down. The Zeke passed over his head and exploded, but not before it had sheared off half of Gudor's rudder and his left stabilizer. The plane began to vibrate heavily, oil pressure vanished, "and the propeller froze stock still." Gudor leveled off at 800 feet and bailed out. He floated down to the sea where, early the next morning, a "beautiful" navy flying boat sat down and picked him up.

On the same day, December 11, a portion of the 5th Infantry managed to get ashore at Palompon. Also, the ships carrying the troops for the Camotes Islands had got mixed up with the Palompon convoy and these troops now went ashore alongside the 5th Infantry. The remnants of the convoy, the transport carrying the naval troops and two destroyers, had meanwhile fled south and turned into Ormoc Bay. As Lieutenant Commander Ito, the troop commander, explained later somewhat ingenuously, "We thought Ormoc was in our hands and that we could land there under the protection of our forces, but on landing discovered it was quite the opposite."

Quite the opposite indeed! The Japanese ships had the misfortune to blunder into an American resupply convoy for the 77th Division. The American ships had been undergoing kamikaze

strikes of the same intensity as the attacks on the Japanese convoy, had lost a destroyer, and had suffered considerable other
damage. But they were still combat-ready. Just before 2 A.M. on
December 12, radar on the destroyer *Coghlan* pierced the night
to pick out the Japanese transport and destroyers. *Coghlan* immediately opened fire. She sank one of the destroyers, but the
other ships escaped. Some of the naval troops landed on the
northwest shore of Ormoc Bay. Others, coming in near the city
itself, were all but wiped out by men of the 77th Division, which
by now had captured the city.

The arrival of Commander Ito's men in the predawn hours
of December 12 marked the last Japanese effort to bring ground
reinforcements into Leyte. Since A-day they had attempted to
land nine major convoys as well as many lesser collections of
barges and small boats in their endeavor to reinforce the Leyte
garrison. So long as the Americans were unable to base many
planes on the island, the Japanese enjoyed a considerable amount
of success. But as soon as American air strength began to build up
on Leyte, and American engineer troops were able to put in airstrips to accommodate this strength, Japanese reinforcement and
supply convoys ran into trouble. Not only did these convoys
themselves take greater losses, but Japanese air strength also
dwindled, reducing further the chances of maintaining the supply
line to Leyte. Significantly, the attempts to provide air cover for
the Palompon convoy represented the last major employment of
massed Japanese airpower in the Leyte campaign. Individual or
small groups of kamikaze planes continued to nip at American
shipping around the island, but there were no more large air
offensives. And no more reinforcements.

Meanwhile, on December 8, the 77th Division had attacked
north from Ipil. Correctly reasoning that the Japanese had been
caught off guard, General Bruce was determined to move as fast
and as far as possible before Ormoc's defenders could get organized. About half his force was needed to defend the flanks of the
beachhead, but the remainder pushed on toward Ormoc. For a
while resistance was light—a few squads of 26th Division troops
perhaps—but the opposition stiffened around noon and the Americans began receiving artillery fire from Colonel Mitsui's positions
below Ormoc. Japanese infantry, dug in along the wooded ridges

that crossed the main coastal road, showered an increasingly heavy rain of rifle and machine-gun fire on the advancing troops. In the afternoon, about two companies of the Imabori Detachment reached the area and immediately attacked. Twice they threw themselves at Bruce's men and twice they were hurled back by heavy mortars firing high-explosive and white phosphorus projectiles. When they sought cover, the searing, choking white phosphorus forced them out into the open again, to be blown apart by the high-explosive shells. By evening Colonel Imabori's advance troops had been all but wiped out and the 77th Division was a mile closer to Ormoc. From his command post, near the forward positions, Bruce could clearly see the town.

During the night the first resupply convoy reached Ormoc Bay, bringing badly needed supplies as well as elements of the 77th Division that had not been able to accompany the assault force. Thus strengthened, General Bruce attacked early on the 9th—only to discover that the Japanese also had been considerably reinforced. The remainder of the Imabori Detachment, the first group of paratroopers, the two companies of the 30th Division that had landed at Ipil, and other miscellaneous elements had joined with Colonel Mitsui's force—making a grand total of perhaps 1,750 Japanese troops below Ormoc. General Tomochika had apparently placed everything under the command of Colonel Imabori, for whose abilities he had the greatest respect. Now Imabori's forces were well entrenched on a series of ridges blocking the road. From these positions they threw mortar, machine-gun, and small-arms fire at the Americans, who had to advance over ground that was open and almost devoid of cover. Bruce's troops took increasing casualties. But his supporting artillery, plus the overwhelming infantry strength he was able to bring to bear, pushed the Japanese back again.

During the attack a platoon led by First Lieutenant Albert J. Golia was cleaning out a Japanese pocket, with Golia and three riflemen scouting ahead. Suddenly a lone Japanese, concealed in the tall cogon grass barely 100 yards away, stood up and fired at the platoon leader. Golia shot back and killed the man with one round. As if on signal, some fifty Japanese rose from the bushes and dense grass to charge the four Americans. Their fixed bayonets glinting in the sun, they ran forward shouting *"Banzai! Banzai!"* and firing raggedly. Golia and his men instinctively returned the fire, halting the charge. As the Japanese began crawling through the grass, Golia ordered the others to fall back under his own covering fire. Two of the three enlisted men succeeded in reaching a low terrace where the rest of the platoon was dug in. The other man, Private First Class Dennis Fortenberry, halted halfway back and opened fire to cover Golia's retreat. Golia had just reached him and started shooting again when a Japanese bullet creased the officer's scalp, sending his helmet flying through the air and knocking him to the ground. Fortenberry tried to apply a compress to Golia's bleeding scalp, but Golia waved him away and began firing again. As the Japanese pressed closer, Golia hurled two grenades at them, and he and Fortenberry dashed back to the platoon position.

From here, standing only partially protected behind a coconut tree, Golia directed the fire of his men at the oncoming Japanese. Blood flowed from his wound and ran down across his forehead and into his eyes. Japanese bullets chipped away at the tree. Yet Golia, seemingly unperturbed, continued to shoot and to call out orders to his men. They, in turn, shouted to the officer to get down, since he was obviously a primary target. He replied that if he took cover he wouldn't be able to "see a damn thing"—and remained where he was. Then a burst of machinegun fire struck a bandoleer of ammunition draped across his chest, tossed Golia head over heels, and knocked the wind out of him.

Stunned but miraculously uninjured, Golia refused the help of an aidman, and, according to witnesses, simply shook his head, threw a grenade at the nearest Japanese, and rose once more to his feet. Without a helmet, his head and face covered with blood, he continued to shoot and to direct and encourage his platoon. He moved back and forth through the position, sometimes crawling, sometimes running, sometimes standing erect to point out targets. By his efforts he finally succeeded in knocking out two machine guns that had been covering the Japanese assault. Slowly the Japanese fire diminished and then, suddenly, stopped. The attack had been beaten off. Golia directed mortar fire on the retreating Japanese and then, finally satisfied that the danger was over, allowed someone to dress his wounds. Thirty-five Japanese lay dead in front of the platoon. Golia himself had killed nearly half of them.

By late afternoon the 77th Division had advanced another mile. Ormoc lay just ahead. Bruce called in his senior commanders and gave them his orders for the final assault. At almost the same time General Tomochika sent instructions to Colonel Imabori to "make every possible effort to prevent the enemy from invading Ormoc."

The attack began on the morning of December 10 with a brief but furious bombardment. Every gun and mortar in the 77th Division opened fire on the Japanese defenses. Howitzers on the amphibian tanks joined the barrage, dropping explosives and smoke shells into the heart of the city. From offshore, rocket-firing landing craft sent terrifying showers of missiles darting into the center of town, while the crews aboard the small vessels traded machine-gun and rifle fire with the Japanese along the waterfront. In less than fifteen minutes Ormoc had turned into a fiery hell of exploding white phosphorus and high explosives, flaming houses, and bursting ammunition dumps. A thick curtain of black smoke hung over the city, mixed with a gray choking dust that rose from the blasted mortar and concrete.

Into this inferno, Bruce sent the 307th Infantry Regiment, while the 306th Infantry swung right to envelop the town from the east and northeast. The frontal attack of the 307th was slowed temporarily by a deep ravine just at the edge of Ormoc, where Imabori's men had dug in on both sides and along the top. Mortars, rifles, grenades, and then finally bayonets had to be used before the defenders were dug out or destroyed in place. Then the regiment advanced into the burning city. The Japanese lay in wait under each house, it seemed, keeping up a steady fire with rifles and machine guns. The Americans, in turn, maintained a continuous barrage with mortars, mobile artillery, and machine guns to cover their advance. Four Marine flyers, out looking for another target but unable to find it, dropped their bombs in the center of things, adding to the general noise and destruction.

By early afternoon the 307th Infantry had been able to seize only a portion of the town, but then the flanking movement of the 306th began to take effect. Sweeping wide around Imabori's flank, the regiment brushed aside light resistance and pressed in against Ormoc from the northeast. The Japanese were now trapped between the two wings of Bruce's attack and the sea. As American artillery and small-arms fire increased, Imabori's vulnerability became evident. Caught in an untenable position, the defenders withdrew north through the city under a crescendo of fire. Thirty-fifth Army headquarters had already gone. By evening Ormoc was in American hands. Pockets of Japanese still remained to be rooted out, but Bruce's front lines were now on the northern outskirts of the town. Surprisingly, American casualties for the day totaled only thirteen.

Earlier in the Leyte campaign General Whitehead, the Fifth Air Force commander, had offered a case of Scotch for the capture of Ormoc. Now Bruce claimed his reward. "Where is the case of Scotch . . . ?" he radioed. "I don't drink but I have an assistant division commander and regimental commanders who do." It was evident that the 77th Division leader needed no artificial stimulants to celebrate. "Have rolled two sevens in Ormoc," he informed Hodge and Krueger. And then, in an obvious but excusable reference to the 7th and 11th Airborne Divisions driving toward Ormoc from the south and east, he added, "Come seven, come eleven."

Bruce's jubilation was not unnatural. The capture of Ormoc had rendered the situation of the Thirty-fifth Army virtually hopeless. Suzuki had now lost his main supply port, along with the better part of his reserve supplies. The retreat of those Japanese troops still operating east or south of Ormoc had been effectively cut off. Only Palompon remained for the landing of reinforcements, but by now this offered slim hope. Outnumbered and trapped within the narrow Ormoc Valley corridor, the Thirty-fifth Army was all but helpless. Troop areas, supply dumps, and equipment offered concentrated and almost unresisting targets for American artillery and aircraft. Courage and tenacity, which the Japanese had displayed abundantly for nearly two months, were now all they had left.

xxi Closing the Vise

THE END of the battle for Leyte was now in sight. While the 77th Division consolidated its positions around Ormoc, the 7th Division drove north from Damulaan, one battalion linking up with Bruce's troops. The 11th Airborne continued to press east across the mountains against the remnants of the ill-fated 26th Division. Concerted attacks by the 7th and 11th Airborne Divisions would soon crush General Yamagata's force between them. Farther north, 96th Division troops patrolled the central mountain range, combining aggressive reconnaissance with a slow advance against the scattered but still dangerous remnants of the Japanese forces that occupied this wild area. Beyond the 96th Division, the 1st Cavalry made progress in its push southeast through the central mountains. And the 32nd Division maintained steady pressure against General Kataoka's troops holding the entrance to the Ormoc Valley. Farther west were elements of the 24th Division, probing the trackless northwest peninsula in a difficult and almost fruitless attempt to hunt down the men of the 68th Brigade who had come ashore at San Isidro. Krueger thus held the Thirty-fifth Army in a slowly tightening vise.

On December 13 General Suzuki finally made his way out of the mountains and reached the small town of Huaton, four miles above Ormoc, where Tomochika had re-established Thirty-fifth Army headquarters. In accordance with Yamashita's orders—and unwilling, in any event, to concede defeat—Suzuki set about organizing an attack to recapture Ormoc. But before he could even complete preparations his plans were roughly shattered by the 77th Division.

Attacking north from Ormoc on the 13th, Bruce's men fought their way through extremely well-prepared defensive positions manned by troops of the Imabori Detachment. Colonel Imabori's soldiers were obviously skilled in the military uses of the shovel. They had worked frantically to dig foxholes, caves, spiderholes, and other entrenchments, so cleverly concealed in the underbrush and tall grass that many were invisible at distances greater than ten feet. Overlooking these defenses was a two-story reinforced stone building, from which the defenders could pour covering fire on the entire area. Neither mortars nor artillery seemed to be able to knock out these positions, so, as usual, it fell to the infantry to do the job. A coordinated attack by two regiments finally captured the stone building and overran the area by nightfall of the 14th. The men used flamethrowers, grenades, and armored bulldozers to destroy the Japanese in their holes. Many of Colonel Imabori's best troops were buried where they stood.

Bruce continued to maintain the pressure. One regiment pushed north along the Ormoc Road against steady and tenacious Japanese resistance, while patrols swung west of the road and then probed north again into relatively unoccupied territory. On the 15th Bruce sent his other two regiments into this open area. They moved in a wide sweep aimed at Valencia, smashing, in the process, those elements of the 30th Division that were moving east from Palompon to participate in Suzuki's projected attack. The Thirty-fifth Army commander himself was almost captured by advance units of the 77th Division, which entered Huaton on the 17th. He had some sort of revenge that evening when Imabori Detachment troops, attempting unsuccessfully to envelop Ormoc from the east, sent several rounds of artillery crashing into Bruce's command post. One shell even hit the general's latrine.

Suzuki retreated above Valencia to establish new headquarters and threw in his last troops, elements of the 5th Infantry Regiment that had just arrived from Palompon. But by now he was only going through the motions. His defenses in the southern Ormoc Valley had all but collapsed. To the north, X Corps pressure had finally shattered the stubborn resistance so long maintained by what was left of the 1st, 30th, and 102nd Divisions. These units were still holding out, but they had lost their strongest positions and were reduced to a few thousand men. It was just a matter of time before they would be annihilated.

In Manila, meanwhile, General Yamashita had lost all hopes of retrieving the situation on Leyte after the landing of the 77th Division. Whatever his earlier pessimistic views, the Ormoc invasion had completely convinced him of the futility of trying to hold the island, much less of making it the scene of a great victory. Still, he had his orders. So, against his better judgment, he had sent some reinforcements and then planned one last effort. On December 10 a regiment of the 10th Division reached Luzon aboard two fast transports. Fourteenth Area Army staff officers immediately pulled out an old plan for a counterlanding at Carigara. Neither Yamashita nor Muto cared for it now. Better, they said, to forget about Leyte, hold the newly arrived regiment for the defense of Luzon, and use the transports to build up supplies for further delaying actions in the Visayas. "An unstudied and unprepared counterlanding" in the face of the enemy, to use Muto's words, "would most certainly fail." Yet Imperial General Headquarters liaison officers in Manila supported the idea of a counterlanding, and Yamashita finally gave in, "sacrificing himself," said Muto, "to the will of Imperial General Headquarters." The landing would take place just after midnight of December 16. Appropriately, it was given the code name of *Ketsu*, meaning "decision."

But *Ketsu* was not to be. On the morning of the 13th Japanese aircraft spotted an American convoy in the Mindanao Sea. They trailed it that day and the next as it sailed north through the Sulu Sea, striking at it with punishing kamikaze attacks but unable to halt its progress. To the Japanese the convoy appeared to be headed for the western Visayas. Late on the 14th Muto radioed Southern Army headquarters that the need to throw all available air and naval strength against this new invasion left the *Ketsu* Operation without escort forces. The Carigara landing, therefore, "ought to be suspended." Moreover, said Muto, the Fourteenth Area Army feared "an early invasion of Luzon." So it was preparing for an all-out battle there and would order forces in the rest of the Philippines, including the Thirty-fifth Army, "to conduct a flexible delaying action on their own." "I should like to have your opinion on these matters," he concluded. Field Marshal Terauchi dispatched his chief of staff to Manila to find out what was going on.

But even before General Iimura left Saigon, the American convoy began putting troops ashore at Mindoro early on December 15. Luzon was now practically isolated from the rest of the Philippines and *Ketsu,* in Muto's words, was "out of the question." The initial postponement of the Mindoro invasion had permitted an American landing that ensured victory on Leyte. Now the launching of the Mindoro assault prevented a Japanese landing and, as Muto said later, "thus ended the Leyte campaign." The Fourteenth Area Army chief of staff dictated a message to Suzuki. The Americans had landed on Mindoro, he informed him, *Ketsu* was off, and the Thirty-fifth Army could expect no further reinforcements. The message reached Suzuki on the 17th. Sadly he ordered his staff to draw up plans for the Thirty-fifth Army to fall back for a last-ditch defense in the Palompon area.

Iimura arrived in Manila late the same day. Once he understood the situation, he wasted no time. In a message to Terauchi he recommended immediate approval of the Fourteenth Area Army plan. Terauchi agreed, but transmission difficulties slowed the exchange, and it was the 19th before the field marshal's approval reached Yamashita. Yamashita at once sent a formal order to Suzuki. The Thirty-fifth Army would continue to hold out unsupported in the central and southern Philippines, denying the air bases there to the enemy, and be prepared to support any future Japanese counteroffensives. The decisive battle for Leyte was ended.

This change in strategy was confirmed almost simultaneously in Tokyo—although not without considerably upsetting Premier Koiso. The previous August, as we have seen, the Japanese high command had promised Koiso that the "decisive battle" called for in the *Sho* plans would be an all-out effort for victory and not simply another indecisive exchange of blows. In October, after the American landing, Koiso had again raised the subject with Japan's military leaders, recalling their earlier promise and asking if they intended to keep this pledge on Leyte. Again he was told categorically that the high command would meet the challenge at Leyte "with the firm conviction of victory." Thus encouraged, the premier addressed a huge rally in Tokyo, declaring that the Japanese, in the "decisive battles that are to come," would fight "until the enemy licks the dust."

During the weeks that followed, Koiso maintained this position, constantly reassured by optimistic statements emanating from Imperial General Headquarters. On November 8, for example, in a radio broadcast, he again stressed the decisive nature of Leyte, comparing it with the sixteenth-century battle of Tennozan, which had settled for many years the issue of who was to rule Japan. To the tradition-conscious Japanese people, the meaning of this historical precedent was clear and forceful. Leyte would be decisive and Japan would win.

On December 14 Admiral Koshiro Oikawa, chief of the navy general staff, reported to the Emperor that the army and navy had agreed and were determined to press ahead with a decisive battle on Leyte. "The Leyte operations," he said firmly, "will continue according to plan." That evening Imperial General Headquarters received an information copy of Muto's radio to Saigon announcing Yamashita's plan to shift his attention from Leyte to Luzon. The Tokyo staff immediately began to reconsider Japanese strategy in the Philippines. Since the army planners had initially favored Luzon as the site of the decisive battle, it took them little time to accept Yamashita's position. By the 18th they had drafted a new policy statement for the *Sho*-1 Operation and persuaded their navy counterparts to agree to it. This completely reflected the Fourteenth Area Army concept: a delaying action in the central Philippines to deny air bases to the Americans while all troops and supplies scheduled to go to the Philippines, including three additional divisions already on their way, would "be poured into Luzon Island in an all-out effort to strengthen operational preparations."

Two days later Premier Koiso went to the Imperial Palace for a routine report to the Emperor. There he encountered War Minister General Sugiyama, who informed him briefly that Imperial General Headquarters had "abandoned plans for a decisive battle on Leyte in favor of a decisive battle on Luzon." Koiso, as he put it later, was "stunned." This was the first inkling he had received of the change in strategy and it completely upset him. Pulling himself together, however, he hurried on to his audience with the Emperor. Imagine his consternation when the Emperor immediately raised the question of the Philippines and asked how Koiso intended to explain to the public his earlier remarks about

Tennozan and the decisive battle of Leyte. Poor Koiso! He could only shake his head, explain that he had just heard about the shift in plans himself, and stammer something about thinking "of a way to make the best of the situation." Then he executed a hasty retreat.

He regained his tongue at a meeting of the Supreme Council for the Direction of the War that followed almost immediately. As a former general himself, Koiso did not have the usual civilian fear of the military members of the Council. In no uncertain terms he accused the army and navy heads of breaking their promise to him and of placing him in an untenable position. Leyte had been "designated in the basic war policy as the theater to decide the fate of the war." The high command should stick to this policy "and do its very best"—or at least it should have warned him in advance of the change. Probably, said Koiso later, he should have resigned at this point. But again the military leaders reassured him. Luzon would positively be the scene of a decisive battle to win an overwhelming victory. Reluctantly, but with little choice, the premier accepted this reply.

The next day, December 21, Lieutenant General Shuichi Miyazaki, operations officer in the Army Section of Imperial General Headquarters, arrived in Manila bearing a copy of the new policy statement. Conferring with Muto, Iimura, and other top staff officers, Miyazaki announced, in effect, that henceforth Yamashita could run things as he pleased in the Philippines. Strategy decisions, Muto quoted him as saying, would "be left to the discretion of the commander of the area army."

Communications between Manila and Leyte were anything but good. A constant stream of Japanese and American radio traffic jammed the airways and bad weather affected transmission and receipt. Not only did messages have to go by cable via Cebu to ensure their arrival at Leyte, but with Ormoc lost and Thirty-fifth Army headquarters now almost constantly on the move there was no guarantee that the dispatches would reach Suzuki at all. Since Yamashita's staff was unsure whether or not Suzuki had received the messages sent on the 14th and 19th, two further ones went out on the 25th and 26th. These in effect repeated the earlier instructions and directed Suzuki to evacuate his headquarters and major units from Leyte in order to carry on delaying operations elsewhere in the central and southern Philippines. Apparently only one of these reached Suzuki, and its contents were somewhat garbled. But he could make out enough of it to understand what he had to do, and the collapse of the Thirty-fifth Army left him little choice.

Yamashita sent Suzuki one other message. He apparently wrote it himself, for it was a personal one and it reflected the compassionate nature of the Fourteenth Area Army commander. He dispatched the message on Christmas Day—although, not being a Christian, the full significance of this timing may have been lost on him.

Two months had elapsed since the invasion of Leyte, Yamashita began, during which time the Thirty-fifth Army, "under the forceful leadership of its commander," had "waged many a heroic battle against superior enemy forces and in the face of numerous difficulties." The Thirty-fifth Army had given "a great blow" to the enemy, "deprived him of freedom of action," and delayed him. The enemy, nevertheless, had "increased his material power and war potential" and, "solely on the strength of his material superiority," now threatened Luzon. This being the case, "we shall seek and destroy our enemy on Luzon Island, thereby doing our part in the heroic struggle of the Army and avenging many a valiant warrior who fell. . . ."

> I cannot keep back tears of remorse [Yamashita concluded] for tens of thousands of our officers and men fighting on Leyte Island. Nevertheless, I must impose a still harder task on you. Please try to understand my intentions. They say it is harder to live than die. You, officers and men, be patient enough to endure the hardships of life, and help guard and maintain the prosperity of the Imperial Throne through eternal resistance to the enemy, and be ready to meet your death calmly for our beloved country. I sincerely instruct you as above.

This was one message that reached Suzuki. Whether Yamashita ever received an acknowledgment is not clear.

By now the Americans too were making some shifts. Ever since he had begun detailed planning for the Philippine campaign, MacArthur had intended for Krueger to command the invasion of Luzon. The tough old veteran was MacArthur's top soldier. For what had originally promised to be the roughest battle of them all—and for what still seemed a hard nut to crack—MacArthur wanted the best. On December 15, then, MacArthur ordered Lieutenant General Robert L. Eichelberger and his recently organized Eighth Army headquarters to prepare to assume control of all combat units on Leyte and take over final operations there. Krueger and Sixth Army headquarters would then be free to command at Luzon. The exchange of command would take place on Christmas Night.

In the ten days left to him to direct operations on Leyte, Krueger pressed ahead against diminishing but still stubborn Japanese resistance. By the 18th General Bruce's troops controlled the Ormoc Valley as far up as Valencia and three days later made contact with X Corps units pushing down from the north. Soldiers of the 7th and 11th Airborne Divisions linked up at the same time in the mountains east of Ormoc. Scattered, isolated, and disorganized groups of Japanese soldiers still remained at large in the central mountain area east of the Ormoc Valley. They would be hard to track down and destroy, but they presented no major threat to the Sixth Army.

Krueger's main problem was resupply of his troops around Ormoc, primarily the 77th Division. This was not due to any interference on the part of the Japanese, for the invasion of Mindoro had drawn off what few Japanese aircraft were left to attack Leyte supply convoys. The fact was, rather, that the demands of the Mindoro operation and the preparation of the Luzon assault convoys left very little shipping for the supply run to Ormoc. Pressed for supply vessels, Admiral Kinkaid suggested that Krueger try moving what he needed overland. But this was clearly an inadequate solution, given the sorry state and limited capacity of the Abuyog-Baybay road. The 77th Division, moreover, badly needed supplies. Bruce's men were already short of artillery and mortar ammunition. They had never, in fact, even received the division's extremely useful medium tanks.

At Krueger's earnest request, finally, Kinkaid scraped together enough shipping to send a large resupply convoy to Ormoc. It arrived on December 22, greatly easing what was beginning to look like a critical situation. The next day, with Sixth Army troops in control of the Ormoc Road from Ormoc all the way to Carigara Bay, Krueger wheeled his two corps west and began the drive to the sea.

Suzuki, all this while, was engaged in that most difficult military maneuver: withdrawal in the face of a strong enemy attack. Holding his ground where he could, counterattacking when this was possible, exhorting his men to do their utmost, he sought to gain time to pull his battered forces back and regroup them for the retreat to Palompon. But still, as he put it in one order, the "powerful enemy" was "gradually pressing on toward the west." As the Americans drove ahead, more and more Japanese were dying in a valiant but futile attempt to stop them. Suzuki had no reserves. Every unit was committed. And every unit was taking increasingly heavy losses. Even in Thirty-fifth Army headquarters, now almost constantly on the move, many officers and men were killed and wounded by the rapidly advancing 77th Division.

Yamashita's order of December 19, changing the mission of the Thirty-fifth Army, had apparently reached Suzuki that same day. He immediately issued detailed orders for a gradual withdrawal to the west coast. Before the full text of these orders could be dispatched, however, a 77th Division attack struck Suzuki's command post, forcing him and his entire headquarters to flee for their lives. Not all of the men survived. Suzuki and the others retreated westward along the road to Palompon. As they traveled they passed large quantities of equipment and supplies dropped by Japanese units that had preceded them. General Tomochika, who had fled with Suzuki with nothing but the clothes on his back, was fortunate enough to pick up a new uniform that fit him reasonably well. By the 21st Suzuki had established a new command post a few miles northeast of Palompon. From here he sent liaison officers to each subordinate Thirty-fifth Army unit that could be located. They carried orders directing an immediate withdrawal to the western coastal area.

But even the Palompon sector soon proved unsafe. The 77th Division, driving east from the Ormoc Valley along the Palompon road, found itself slowed by rugged terrain, weakened or destroyed bridges, and an impossible roadbed. Bruce suggested to Hodge, who passed it on to Krueger, that a small force traveling in amphibious tractors and landing craft, might well be able to take Palompon from the sea. Krueger readily approved the plan and asked Kinkaid for a destroyer escort. But Kinkaid had no destroyers to spare, so assigned the mission to several PT boats—which proved to be more than enough.

General Kenney's flyers hit Palompon on December 23, dropping napalm and setting large fires. Marine pilots dive-bombed the town the next day. And a battery of XXIV Corps artillery moved into position just west of the Valencia airfield to support the landing with long-range fire. On Christmas Eve a reinforced battalion of the 77th Division sailed from Ormoc on a tedious and almost uneventful trip. Three of the amphibious tractors swamped in choppy waters, but their passengers were easily rescued. An artillery barrage on Palompon greeted Christmas morning, and shortly after seven, mortar-firing landing craft leading the way, the troops went ashore unopposed. Pushing rapidly through the battered, empty town, they pressed inland. The last port of any practical value to the Japanese on Leyte was now in American hands. And Thirty-fifth Army headquarters was again in danger of capture. Once more Suzuki had to leave in a hurry, this time moving north some fifteen miles to a steep, heavily wooded plateau overlooking the sea above Villaba, "a natural fortress," in Tomochika's words, well suited for defense. Suzuki ordered Thirty-fifth Army units to fall back on this area.

General Bruce had witnessed the entire Palompon landing from a cub plane overhead. When he saw how well it was going he "obeyed a rather boyish impulse," as he put it later, and had the pilot swoop low over the assault troops. Leaning from the plane, Bruce clasped both hands over his head in the traditional boxer's sign of victory. Then he flew back to his headquarters and sent this message to Hodge, Krueger, and MacArthur: "The 77th Infantry Division's Christmas contribution to the Leyte Campaign is the capture of Palompon, the last main port of the enemy. We are all grateful to the Almighty on this birthday of the Son and on the Season of the Feast of Lights."

At one minute after midnight General Eichelberger took command on Leyte. A few hours later MacArthur declared the Leyte campaign to be officially over "except for minor mopping-up operations." This expression later proved a source of considerable irritation to Eichelberger, who felt, with some justification, that there were still enough Japanese on the island to make his task a hard, bitter, and extremely dangerous one.

Of the more than 65,000 Japanese troops who served on Leyte, the Sixth Army claimed to have killed over 56,000 and captured several hundred more. This claim is undoubtedly somewhat high, but Eichelberger was told there were at most 8,000 Japanese left when he took over—so the totals, at any rate, are approximately correct. Japanese records indicate that there were between 11,000 and 16,000 troops on Leyte at the end of December. Tomochika put the figure at 15,000, and the Eighth Army claimed to have killed, found dead, or captured nearly 25,000 Japanese after Christmas. Obviously the Eighth Army figure, like the Sixth Army claim, was too high—especially when we add to it about 1,200 Japanese who succeeded in escaping to other islands early in 1945. But exaggerated notions of enemy casualties are not unusual, particularly if the nature of the fighting makes it necessary for many of these claims to be based on estimates rather than an actual body-count.

A reasonable course would seem to be to take Tomochika's figure of 15,000. This can be supported by other Japanese sources. It appears large enough to cover all contingencies. And it is not out of line with apparent Japanese losses from October through December. When compared with the size of the Eighth Army, 15,000 Japanese were not a great number. But they were certainly enough to make the Leyte "mop-up" a difficult and costly experience.

Mopping up is at best a grim business. It is usually accomplished by small groups of soldiers, sometimes supported by tanks but not often by artillery, who set out to look for trouble and are only successful when they find it and wipe it out. Against an enemy who refuses to surrender and has to be, literally, dug out or buried alive, it is one of the most dangerous forms of warfare. The enemy knows he will die in the end, is prepared to die rather than give up, and is determined to take as many of his attackers with him as he can.

This was the situation on Leyte. By New Year's Day, 1945, the Eighth Army controlled every important area of Leyte, but many pockets of Japanese continued to hold out or to remain hidden in the deep forests and rugged mountains. Suzuki's troops—sick, wounded, low on ammunition, practically out of food and medicine, without hope—were still resolute, still brave, still able fighters. "Hundreds of pale soldiers of Japan are awaiting our glorious end and nothing else," wrote one Japanese in his diary. And until that end came most of them gave a good account of themselves.

For the Americans it was rough, exhausting, painful going. Small groups of Japanese might be cleaned out or sealed off with flamethrowers, grenades, and other infantry weapons. But larger forces had to be attacked in full strength, with artillery and air support. In such cases an action might be as hard-fought and bitter as the battles of Breakneck or Shoestring Ridge. Unit after unit reported that it was having a more difficult time than it did in the two months after A-day. Casualties continued.

And all the while Suzuki tried to gather his scattered, broken army onto the high plateau near Villaba where he now made his headquarters. In a long order issued in early January, the Thirty-fifth Army commander outlined his policies for "independent operations to the end." Apologizing "that the situation should have come to such an unfavorable condition," he expressed his sympathetic understanding for "the bitter feelings of the officers and soldiers," his "deep gratitude" to the units which had "fought so well amid hardships," and his "regret before the noble spirits of the countless heroes who fell in the field." Now, however, the army must strive "to contain as many enemy troops as possible and facilitate the decisive battle of Luzon." "Exceptional circumstances require exceptional resolution. . . . The operation shall be continued to the last man in our determination to guard and maintain the prosperity of our Imperial Throne, which is eternal as heaven and earth."

At the Villaba assembly area the natural protection of the heavy woods and surrounding rocky heights barred searching American eyes. But American artillery occasionally shelled the area, killing or wounding many men. Without medical supplies, there was little to be done for these victims. Their screams, said Tomochika, were "pitiful." Still, there was a bright side. A few cultivated fields nearby, captured stocks of newly harvested crops, and even a wandering carabao or two provided food for the Japanese. No one grew fat, but no one at Villaba died of starvation.

Not so those men who roamed the muddy, rain-soaked forests inland. They straggled aimlessly in small groups, searching for food or for a way to escape the pursuing Americans. Many were badly wounded, sick, covered with festering jungle ulcers, or driven out of their minds by the combination of their difficulties. When commanders could hold their men together, they traveled and sometimes even fought as units. But often the sick and wounded lagged behind and formed their own groups, or others deserted to find food or to flee American artillery fire. Sometimes officers asked their seriously wounded men to kill themselves, to relieve the burden on those who were still relatively healthy. Many committed suicide. "Only Japanese could have done a thing like this," noted Tomochika later, "and yet I could not bear to see the sight." The living struggled on, exhausted, filthy, emaciated, until they too fell to the ground, their sodden uniforms their only shroud. "Mixed with the sour, vegetable smell of the rain-soaked grass," recalled one who lived, "that pungent odor which I knew so well began to hover over the greenery."

For those who made it to the Villaba area there was still a chance of escape. In accordance with Yamashita's orders, Suzuki hoped to evacuate most of his troops, sending the best ones first to secure areas on other islands. At the beginning of January, Yamashita dispatched some barges to Leyte, and Suzuki ordered the 1st Division to embark for nearby Cebu. General Kataoka demurred, however. Too many of his officers and men had died on Leyte, he said, for him to desert them now. Why not send the larger 68th Brigade, with its relatively fresh units, for such an important mission? But Suzuki wanted the 1st Division to go, so Kataoka and about 800 of his best troops left the island in three groups during January.

Only a few hundred other men were able to get away before American aircraft and PT boats sealed the route of escape. And some of these, to Suzuki's disgust, left in disobedience to orders to remain. A few were later court-martialed and executed. One who was not was Lieutenant General Shimpei Fukue, commander of the 102nd Division, who left Leyte, despite a direct order from Suzuki to stay behind. Administrative foul-ups and poor communications saved Fukue from punishment, however, and he ended up with a command on Mindanao.

Suzuki meanwhile had sent General Wachi to Manila to report on the situation to Yamashita. He also dispatched several other staff officers to Cebu to set up an alternate Thirty-fifth Army headquarters there. Tomochika, still fuming over the Fukue incident, was scheduled to leave at the end of January and again a month later but each time, he recalled, "I waited on the beach for several days for a boat that never arrived." Finally, in early March, Suzuki decided to move his headquarters to Cebu, where an American invasion was expected soon. On St. Patrick's Day two large boats arrived, and Tomochika and over 100 others departed for Cebu. Suzuki followed on the 23rd.

Left in charge of Japanese forces on Leyte was the 16th Division commander, Lieutenant General Makino. He was the only one left of the senior commanders. Kataoka and Fukue had long since departed. Yamagata had been fatally wounded in the retreat to the west. Makino himself was too ill to even say good-by to Suzuki. Neither he nor any but a handful of the men he now commanded survived the final Leyte mop-up.

In early April Suzuki decided to transfer his headquarters to Mindanao, which held the largest concentration of Japanese troops in the Philippines south of Luzon. Despite the fact that American aircraft and naval vessels dominated the waters between Cebu and Mindanao and that Suzuki's staff tried to dissuade him from the journey, the general was determined to go. On April 10 Suzuki, Tomochika, and some forty others left Cebu in five boats, sailing on different routes. Six days later the boat carrying Suzuki was attacked by an American plane and the Thirty-fifth Army commander was killed.

Just before leaving Cebu he had written two short poems. One, entitled "A Farewell," spoke of a soldier's "duty" to "sacrifice his life in war." The other, "Memory for Departure," also considered death and ended with the lines,

> *For I am the commander, and*
> *Fortunately I am still able to serve.*
> *Give me many glories.*

xxii Leyte: The Decisive Battle

FOR Douglas MacArthur, the American victory on Leyte was the dramatic fulfillment of his pledge to return. Nearly three years earlier, at the small airfield at Alice Springs, Australia, he had given his word. At that time a large and formidable barrier of Japanese-held territory stood between him and the redemption of his promise. As late as a year before the assault on Leyte, MacArthur's troops were still fighting in the humid swamps and sweltering jungles of New Guinea, almost 1,500 miles from his target. But now he stood at the very center of the Philippines, within easy striking distance of every island, his forces, as he said, "in a position to become masters of the archipelago." Barely two weeks after he had announced the end of organized resistance on Leyte, American soldiers poured ashore on Luzon. And in another seven weeks MacArthur strode proudly into the state reception room at Malacañan Palace in Manila to formally return the capital city to President Osmeña and the Philippine government.

In recapturing Leyte, MacArthur claimed to have inflicted on Yamashita "perhaps the greatest defeat in the military annals of the Japanese Army." He might have added that Japanese naval and air forces also had suffered crushing blows, and that it was the combined air, sea, and land victory over the Japanese that really guaranteed the American triumph in the Philippines and, ultimately, sealed the fate of the Japanese Empire.

Yet the cost was relatively light for what was accomplished at Leyte. Total American army casualties were approximately 12,000 wounded and 3,500 killed, with most of these losses coming during the Sixth Army phase of the battle. Naval casualties, both sailors and airmen, totaled about 2,500, divided roughly equally between killed and wounded. Army and Marine air losses, both killed and wounded, amounted to only a few hundred. The cost in warships, assault shipping, and aircraft was just as disproportionately light, considering the Japanese losses.

But if Leyte was a great victory achieved at little cost, it was also something of a disappointment. Bad weather and unsuitable soil conditions prevented the island from becoming the major air and supply base that American planners had hoped to make of it. Not only was it impossible to support the invasion of Luzon from Leyte, as originally planned, but the Leyte campaign itself was prolonged by the difficulties of airfield construction on the soft and rain-soaked ground. Unable to bring his air strength forward, MacArthur could not prevent the heavy flow of Japanese reinforcements into the island nor even, until the land campaign was almost ended, wrest for himself air supremacy over the area. The struggle for Leyte thus lasted far longer than it would have if General Makino's outnumbered 16th Division had constituted the sum of Japanese resistance on the island. And the delay on Leyte held up the invasion of Luzon.

Could the delay have been avoided or in any way lessened? Probably not. Sixth Army planners as well as those at MacArthur's headquarters had studied Leyte's weather and terrain and were aware of the difficulties ahead. Practically everyone expected considerable rainfall, although there was apparently less understanding of the soil and drainage problems. And no one was rash enough to ignore the probability that rain and mud would impede construction. Some even admitted that there was a fair element of chance involved.

But the risk had to be taken—or else delay the return to the Philippines at least six months. And had this occurred, the Japanese there would have become powerful enough to meet and perhaps bloodily repulse an invasion anywhere in the islands. A delay even until mid-November—the time originally set for the Mindanao landing that was shelved in favor of Leyte—would have allowed the Combined Fleet to assemble at a single point, with plenty of fuel and a full complement of planes and newly trained flyers for Admiral Ozawa's carriers. It would have permitted a buildup of army and navy land-based air strength in the Philippines. It would have given Yamashita another month to ready his defenses, and considerably more troops with which to

man them. MacArthur and his staff could not know this, of
course, but they sensed it. And in proceeding with the Leyte invasion despite the obvious difficulties ahead, they made the right
decision.

But if the American choice was correct, what of the Japanese?
The Japanese decision, while perhaps supportable, was under-
mined by the inflexible nature of the *Sho* plan, the mistakes of
Admirals Toyoda and Kurita in implementing it, and the problems of divided command. Divided command, to be sure, nearly
proved tragic for the Americans at Leyte Gulf, but it was nowhere near so damaging for Halsey and Kinkaid as it was for the
Japanese. And in the end the poor timing and indecision that
brought catastrophe to Japanese naval and air power were easily
matched by the stubborn sacrifice of Japanese ground forces in a
hopeless cause.

For Yamashita, the Leyte campaign was a tragic nightmare.
Sent to the Philippines barely two weeks before A-day, saddled
with a last-minute change of plan—an impossible plan, at that—
and inadequate means to carry it out, he did his best. With the
loyal and indefatigable Muto at his side, he did everything in his
power to prevent the tragedy on Leyte, while at the same time
conscientiously carrying out his orders to make that island the
scene of decisive victory. In the latter effort, he sent many of his
best troops and sorely needed supplies to Leyte, weakening himself critically on Luzon. When events at last proved Yamashita
correct and he was finally allowed to concentrate on the defense
of Luzon, he was too weak and it was too late. He lost the battle
of Luzon on Leyte, where he had never wanted to fight. "I believe . . . I did the best possible job I could have done," he said
after the end of the war. "However . . . my plans and my
strength were not sufficient to the situation."

But the Japanese defeat at Leyte did more than simply ensure
the loss of Luzon. In their rash attempt to win a decisive victory
at Leyte, the Japanese committed the major portion of their air
forces, the bulk of their fleet, and an important part of their army.

After Leyte, Japan had no air force. All that remained was a
strange and terrible new weapon called kamikaze—dangerous,
frightening, and under the right conditions very effective. But it
was hardly a decisive weapon, and it was certainly not airpower.

After Leyte, Japan had no fleet. She had only a skeleton force of ships and men, without fuel, without striking power, incapable of major offensive action.

After Leyte, Japan had no army. There were millions of men under arms. But the best Japanese troops—65,000 of them dead on Leyte, a third of a million more doomed throughout the rest of the Philippines—were already committed, cut off, isolated, and equally unable to mount a major offensive.

After Leyte, Japan no longer had access to the resources of the Indies. The supply line to the south had been severed, the Empire was split, the home islands denied the raw materials necessary for the nation's survival.

Admiral Mitsumasa Yonai, the Japanese navy minister, summed it up neatly. "Our defeat at Leyte," he said later, "was tantamount to the loss of the Philippines. When you took the Philippines, that was the end of our resources." Japan no longer possessed the means to wage effective warfare. She might delay the inevitable. But she was unmistakably, inexorably defeated.

Index

The Author

STANLEY FALK is Associate Professor of National Security Affairs at the Industrial College of the Armed Forces, Washington, D. C., where senior officers and government career officials are trained for key policy-making roles in the national security structure. He is also the author of *Bataan, The March of Death*, the complete story of this incident in the Philippine campaign.